SOVIET *BLITZKRIE*

SOVIET
BLITZKRIEG
THEORY

P. H. Vigor

St. Martin's Press   New York

Printed in the United States of America

First published in the United States of America in 1983

ISBN 0-312-74755-1
ISBN 0-312-74756-X (pbk.)

Library of Congress Cataloging in Publication Data

Vigor, P. H. (Peter Hast)
  Soviet blitzkrieg theory.

  Includes index.
  1. Lightning war. 2. Soviet Union—Military policy.
3. North Atlantic Treaty Organization. 4. Europe—
Defenses. 5. World War III. I. Title.
U167.5.L5V53 1983   355.4′3′0947   82-10421
ISBN 0-312-74755-1
ISBN 0-312-74756-X (pbk.)

Contents

Acknowledgements

My thanks are due to my friend and colleague, Mr C. N. Donnelly, of the Soviet Studies Research Centre, for having read through the whole of my typescript and for making a number of valuable suggestions. They are also due to Mr M. J. Orr of the War Studies Department, Royal Military Academy Sandhurst, for his help with the chapter dealing with Moltke's campaigns.

As always, I am deeply indebted to the staff of the Central Library, Royal Military Academy Sandhurst, to St Antony's College, Oxford, and to Chatham House. Without their unfailing patience, kindness and helpfulness this book could never have been written.

P.H.V.

Prologue
Key quotations from senior Soviet officers

'The essence of [his] theory of "lightning" war consisted of using such things as surprise attack ... to inflict a decisive defeat on the enemy's first strategic echelon [which in modern terms would be those NATO forces which on any given day in peacetime are actually in position – P.H.V.]; and then, by continuing with a speedy offensive into the depths of his territory, to complete his total defeat before he was able to mobilise and make use of his military and economic potential.'

General S. P. Ivanov, *Nachal'nyi Period Voiny*
(Voenizdat, 1974)

'Those States which failed to concentrate and deploy their main forces in peacetime found themselves in a very serious position. They proved unable to oppose the enemy in the first days of the war on the main axes of his advance with sufficiently powerful forces, nor could they beat off his massed surprise attacks from the air delivered at the war's outset, nor could they prevent the deep penetration of his ground forces into their own territory. This made it extraordinarily difficult for them to complete the strategic deployment of their own armed forces, because this had to be done simultaneously with the waging of difficult defensive battles.'

Ibid.

'Of decisive significance in a future war will be its initial period. . . . The more effectively a country uses at the outset the troops and the equipment it has accumulated before the war, the greater the results it can achieve at the very beginning of a war, and the more quickly victory is achieved.'

Marshal Sokolovsky, *Voennaya Strategiya*
(Voenizdat, 1968)

Author's note

Throughout this book the expressions 'initial period of a war' and 'opening phase of a war' are used synonymously. I define them as meaning 'that period of time which elapses between the start of a war and the completion by the combatants of their mobilization, concentration and strategic deployment'. Because the aggressor in modern times has usually completed his own mobilization, concentration and deployment *before* the war begins, it is only his victims to whom the concept of the 'initial period' is generally applicable nowadays.

1 The Soviet need to defeat NATO quickly

Everyone knows that the tactics of the Soviet ground forces are designed for the fighting of a mobile, fast-moving battle. Speed is of the essence. If by any chance there is anyone who is still unaware of the fact, he is advised to cough up his $2.50, or whatever the price is nowadays, and buy a copy of the Soviet textbook *The Offensive*, by Colonel A. A. Sidorenko, which has been translated into English by the US Air Force and is freely available in the West.

But though everyone, or at any rate *almost* everyone, is aware of the Soviet urge for speed in the waging of a battle, by no means so many appreciate that the Russian defence planners feel the same need for speed in the waging of a war. That is to say that, in the Soviet view, the war has got to be short.

This Western absorption with the nature of the *battle*, and the virtually total Western neglect of the nature of the actual *war*, is very curious, especially in the case of the British. The British are extremely fond of saying that they lose every battle except the last; and by that phrase they betray their realization that it is what happens to the *war* that is important; and that, compared to this, the winning or losing of battles is a secondary affair. This is surely true. And yet the British are as bad as anybody at trying to assess the nature of a war that the USSR might feel impelled to start.

Of course, in one sense that statement is plainly wrong. All the Western nations, including the British, spend a lot of time in trying to determine whether such a war would be nuclear or conventional or some sort of 'mix' of the two. But although it is clearly very important to try to find an answer to this question, it is not necessarily the most important question to be asked about the nature of a war in Europe that the Soviet Union might start. This, surely, is particularly true in view of the number of comments emanating from NATO, concerning the recent build-up of Soviet ground forces in Central and Eastern Europe. And what is especially relevant to this present chapter is NATO's assertion that, as a result of these improvements in the Soviet ground forces, the amount of warning time likely to be available to NATO regarding an impending Soviet attack must now be reckoned at about 48 hours, instead of the couple of weeks or so that used to be thought to be likely.

In my own humble judgement, the reason for the reduction in warning time is intimately linked with the Soviet requirement that a war with the West must be short. And this in turn is linked with their military concept of 'the opening phase of a war'. But since the latter is merely the *means* that will help the Russians attain their *end* (which is a short war), a discussion of why they set such store by a short war must obviously be undertaken first.

The first and most obvious reason is that, according to the Russian way of thinking, if it came to a long war the Soviet Union would almost certainly *lose*. As Marx, Engels, Lenin and all their successors have continually hammered in to the Soviet consciousness, war is essentially a function of economics; and victory in war generally accrues to him who has the greater economic potential. Obviously, the human factor also plays a considerable part in the matter; and if the war were started at a time when the soldiers in NATO had lost all willingness to fight the Russians, no amount of superior Western economics would preserve NATO from defeat. It follows from this that the state of morale of the ordinary NATO soldier must constantly occupy the attention of the Russians; and that, if they want to start a war, they will take his morale into careful consideration when deciding the *date* of the attack. That is to say that, all other things being equal, they will try to launch their attack when morale in NATO is low.

Assuming, however, that the worst has not yet happened, and that SHAPE has succeeded in preserving the morale of NATO at a tolerable level, we are then left with the Soviet viewpoint that war is essentially a function of economics, and that the victor in war will be he who possesses the greater economic potential, *provided, of course, that the war continues long enough for that greater potential to be realized.* This is important. Western nations should continually remind themselves that in the First World War it took the ultimate victors some 2½ years to replace the initial losses caused by their unhappy experiences in the opening phase of the war, and to realize their full industrial and military potential; nor that in the Second World War it took them nearly 4 years (or, to be accurate, it took the British very nearly 4 years; the Americans, 3; and the Russians about 2½ years) to do the same.

Such a time-lag obviously provides an opportunity for an economically *inferior* aggressor to win the war before his enemy's superior military potential has had the time to be realized. But in order to be able to do this he has got to be quick.

Furthermore, it is absolutely essential for him within the given time-lag to win the war as a whole; the winning of a battle is not enough. The winning of a battle, or twenty or thirty or forty battles, will avail him nothing in the long run, if the war drags on. Japan's performance in the Second World War is an obvious example of the truth of this. The economic potential of Imperial Japan was a great deal less than the combined potential of the countries she attacked; so although she won brilliant victories during the opening period of her war, and seized and occupied enormous tracts of territory, yet in the end, as we all know, she went down in defeat. She could not get at the vital economic centres which nourished her enemies' war effort; therefore the latter were able to mobilize that effort; and therefore, when they had done so, they defeated her.[1]

The next advantage to be derived from a short war is that it furnishes fewer opportunities than a long war for various things to go wrong. The human brain's capacity to foresee the future, and to make provision for the happenings of the future, is very limited. The opening stage of a battle can be planned with care; but unless the battle can be won within that stage, within the time-frame when all has been provided for, the local commanders and the troops subordinated to them will have to react to the enemy's reactions, not all of which may have been properly foreseen when the High Command drew up its plans for the battle. And in this instance at least, what is true of battles is true also of wars.

That this is so is clearly demonstrated by a number of wars of this century. The German advance into France and Belgium in 1914, Hitler's attack on Russia in 1941, the Egyptian attack on Israel in 1973 were all designed to win the whole war in the opening phase; and as everyone knows they all began with brilliant initial successes, and then they all went wrong.

It cannot, however, be inferred from the above that it is simply impossible for any war to be won in its initial period. All that can be asserted, and asserted without fear of contradiction, is that no war in modern times has, in fact, been won during that period (and by 'modern' is meant here any war that has taken place between major developed countries since the end of the wars against Napoleon).

There have, of course, been attempts to assert the contrary, particularly on the part of the Russians. General Ivanov, for example, in the book that has been mentioned above, regards Hitler's campaign in Poland in 1939 as a 'war' in its own right.[2] Few would agree with him. Subsequently in that same book he goes on to declare that the Soviet campaign in Manchuria in 1945 was also a war in its own right; and, certainly until very recently, the standard description for that campaign in Soviet military writing has been 'The Soviet–Japanese *War* of 1945'.[3] Again, few Western commentators would agree with this description. In the Western view, although the campaign in Manchuria was a new theatre of war for the USSR, it was only one part of a war against Japan which America, Britain, Australia, New Zealand, China, Holland and other countries had been actively prosecuting for years. It cannot, therefore, be called a 'war'; it must be termed a 'campaign'.

In the Western view, therefore, it is unquestioned fact that no modern war has been won in its initial period; while it is the Soviet view that, on the contrary, there has been one single war in modern times which has indeed been won in its initial period; that this war was the Soviet–Japanese War in Manchuria of 1945; and that it was the USSR which won it.

It is, of course, the Soviet view of such matters with which this book is chiefly concerned; and the Soviet view expressed above cannot therefore be simply dismissed. In any case, having established that in the Soviet view history has shown it to be possible, though admittedly extremely difficult, to win a war in its initial period, it must be common ground between East and West that, if such a thing is indeed feasible, the advantages of succeeding in doing so are many and very great. For one thing, as has been indicated earlier in this discussion, you are much more likely to win the war if you can win it in its opening phase. This is because, in a war won quickly, you are far less likely to be confronted with unexpected, and therefore potentially critical, situations. On top of that, your total casualties are likely to be far less, so that you will not be reduced to fighting your war with reserve officers and inferior, inexperienced conscripts. Furthermore the strain on your domestic economy is bound to be significantly reduced.

In addition to all this there is, from the Soviet viewpoint, another consideration of very great importance. War, they have learnt from Marx and Engels and the rest of them, exerts a profoundly revolutionizing effect upon those societies which engage in it. This is because the prosecution of a war of other than purely Lilliputian dimensions is bound to entail a drastic upheaval in the lives of the citizens of the country concerned and a major re-deployment of its economy. The stresses and strains that ensue from this, and even the actual deaths that result from the fighting, will be borne with fortitude by the inhabitants of the country, provided that they believe in the justice of their cause, and that they can also see a reasonable chance of winning. Admittedly, countries have fought like lions in the face of the virtual certainty of defeat; but they have never done so under such circumstances in anything but a short war, and usually then only in those conflicts when the issue has been of truly momentous importance to them personally.

In the contrary case – where the war has been long, the chance of victory by no means certain, and the issues at stake of no great personal importance to the inhabitants of the combatant country – there the stresses and strains have been born unwillingly, at least in the later stages of the conflict; and significant changes have then been produced in the social structure of the country. The Vietnam War is an obvious case in point.

But what great personal import would the issue at stake, in the case of a war in Central Europe, possess for the ordinary citizen of the USSR? The answer to that question would naturally depend on the particular purpose for which the Russians had begun the war in the first place. Nevertheless, it is hard to imagine a purpose underlying a war of aggression against the Western Alliance that could be presented to the Soviet general public in any way that could inspire them with enthusiasm.

Of course it could be done quite easily if the war were short. No people, and especially no old-fashioned people (and the Russian people in many ways are really extremely old-fashioned), objects to waging a short, victorious war, where the war in question is not so much a conflict as a triumphal march through the streets of the enemy's capital. If a Soviet attack in Europe could achieve the winning of the war within a fortnight, the man-in-the-street in Moscow would support his Government's action without question.

But we are here supposing a long war, a war which would entail great suffering for the Russian people, a war in which the ultimate victory could only be had at the cost of tremendous sacrifice, a war in which it was not even certain that it could ever be had at all. What would be the issues of such a war (we are speaking always of a Soviet attack upon NATO) that could inspire the Soviet public to endure these miseries?

It really is extremely difficult to think of any. The Russian people have a great pride in their country, and would fight like tigers to defend it, if we invaded. But they appear to have no particular urge to go and conquer other peoples; though if this can be done without any trouble they are happy to acquiesce in it. What cannot be shown, however, is that they have so great a longing to see the Hammer and Sickle floating triumphantly over Bonn or London or Paris or Rome or Dublin or The Hague (or all of them together) that they will willingly embrace the calamities of war in order to see this happening.

Nor does their Party propaganda encourage them to embark on wars of conquest nor has it tried to encourage them to do so for a great many years past. During by far the greater number of the years that have elapsed since the October Revolution, the Communist Party of the Soviet Union has proclaimed incessantly that the Soviet armed forces will *not* be used for the waging of wars of conquest. Certainly, it has said that they *may* be used to wage wars of national liberation; but these are wars in the Third World, not in Europe. It is also true that it has not denied that the Soviet armed forces may be used to support their fellow proletarians in another country, if the latter were engaged in a civil war; so that, if a civil war were to erupt in Central Europe (or in Central Northern, or Central Southern, Europe), the Soviet armed forces might conceivably intervene, with the full backing of Soviet propaganda and a good deal of support from the people of Russia as well.

But we are talking here about a Soviet attack on NATO at a time at which there is no civil war in Europe. Such an attack would be the kind of war that Soviet propaganda with its brazen lungs and the Soviet Communist Party with its immense authority have for 40 or 50 years now been assuring the Soviet people would be an immoral war, an unjust war, and one which the Soviet Union would never contemplate. So supposing it did contemplate it? Supposing the Soviet leadership coolly and cold-bloodedly decided that they would deliberately start that kind of a war which they have told the Soviet people for half a lifetime that they would never have to fight?

Provided the war were short, it would make no odds. Provided the war were over in a week or two, the Soviet people would gladly find acceptable whatever excuse for the starting of it might suit the Kremlin best. People, as I have said, like victory parades. But if the war were protracted then all the cracks and fisssures in the structure of Soviet society, which even now are discernible to the diligent observer, would be exposed to the titanic strains that the waging of war entails. As Marx wrote presciently long ago, 'War puts nations to the test, Just as mummies fall to pieces, the moment that they are exposed to the air, so war pronounces its sentence of death on those social institutions which have become ossified.' He was speaking of capitalist Britain, of course; but he could easily have been speaking of Soviet Russia today; naturally, the Kremlin knows this. Not only do the Soviet leaders know their Marx a great deal better than I know mine, but they belong to a people which during this century has twice been tested in a major war. In the Second World War they passed that test, but in the First World War they failed it.

So, once again, on this account the war has got to be short. And on top of this there is yet another reason pointing in the same direction, and every bit as compelling. This has to do with the morale of the Soviet Army.

The conscripts who form the bulk of the Soviet Army are continually told that the soldiers of NATO are useless; that the Western armies may well have competent equipment, but that the men who are to use it will not fight properly.

If the war is over quickly this will not matter. Either the NATO soldiers will have behaved in the way in which Soviet propaganda habitually depicts them as behaving, or else they will have fought bravely, but will have been defeated. In either case there will have been a Soviet victory.

Soldiers like short, victorious wars as much as any civilian; and the soldiers of the Soviet Army, if they get one, will undoubtedly be perfectly happy. But supposing they do not? Supposing, instead, they become embroiled in a long, extremely hazardous war in which the chance of victory, if they see it at all, will be seen at the end of a protracted and fearful corridor of blood and mud and pain? What will their morale be like then? What will they think of their officers (and especially their political officers), whom they will know by then to have been telling them lies for more than half a century? What motive, what compelling war aim, will induce them to continue the struggle?

If we turn to history to suggest an answer, it is likely to be a dusty one, so far as concerns the prospects for the Russians. In the Second World War, the ordinary Soviet soldier fought stoutly enough; but then, in the Second World War the ordinary Soviet soldier had plenty of motive. He was trying to get the infamous hordes of Nazism out of his country, and prevent his friends and his womenfolk from being taken for slaves or hanged. But the ordinary Soviet soldier in the *First* World War had little personal motive to continue the struggle: the marvel is that he continued to fight as long as he actually did. Even so, it was clear by the autumn of 1916 that he was not prepared to go on fighting longer, even in order to preserve the territorial integrity of the Russian Empire, still less in order to fight his way to Berlin.[4] Two years earlier, however, in August 1914, when he thought that the war would be short, he marched out to fight the Germans and Austrians with plenty of enthusiasm. So, if the answers suggested by history are in any way relevant to a war begun by the Soviet Union against NATO (and I think they are), then once again the war has got to be short. And once again the Soviet leaders will realize it.

There are yet other reasons, unconnected with the lessons of history, which will make the Kremlin eager to win its wars in the initial period. The first of these is the danger of a war that is *not* short, a war that drags on with no victory clearly impending, but attracting other combatants into its orbit, so that it then becomes for the attacker a war on two fronts. Every intending aggressor has always feared this possibility which, in the case of Russia attacking NATO, might entail an attack on Russia by Communist China. Western experts, for the most part, tend to discount this possibility; for the Russians, however, it is one which is very real. The second reason impelling the Kremlin to win its wars in their opening phase is the danger of escalation. It is generally agreed by Western experts that the USSR does *not* want nuclear war, if she can help it. The reasons for this are obvious: in a non-nuclear contest between NATO and the Warsaw Pact, the chances of a meaningful victory for the latter are very significantly higher than they would be if nuclear weapons were used; furthermore, in such a war it is quite impossible for the NATO forces to do any significant damage to the territory of the USSR. In addition to this there is ample evidence from Soviet emigrés who have served in the Soviet armed forces that the Soviet soldier is really frightened of the prospect of fighting a battle with NATO in which the West uses nuclear weapons. Finally, in a nuclear war the casualties are bound to be far more heavy than they would be in one in which only non-nuclear weapons were employed; and this is true whether we are referring solely to the military in the context of a war in which only tactical nuclear weapons were employed, or whether we are referring to an all-out war in which strategic nuclears killed the civilian populations in their tens or scores of millions. The strains of accepting casualties of this sort, whether among the Soviet armed forces or the Soviet civilian population, and the risk of the breakdown of morale among them if these casualty rates are to be deemed acceptable, are far too great to be viewed with equanimity by any Party leader or Soviet general. It therefore follows that, if the rulers of the Soviet Union were to decide to fight a war against the West, it is a non-nuclear war that they would seek to fight.

We have now examined nine important reasons why the senior Soviet policy-makers, if they plan a war against NATO, will be bound to conclude that they have got to have a short war. So how do they set about getting it? An attempt to suggest the methods by which they will do so will therefore form the next part of this book.

NOTES AND REFERENCES

1. This is the essence of the Soviet view of the subject. See General S. P. Ivanov, *Nachal'nyi Period Voiny* (Voenizdat, 1974) p. 10.
2. Ibid., p. 219.
3. See, for instance, *Bol'shaya Sovietskaya Entsiklopediya*, 3rd edn, 1971, vol. 5, p. 490.
4. See the comments on the morale of the Russian people by the Chief of Police, Vassiliev, in October 1916; *Istoricheskii Arkhiv* (Moscow, 1960).

2   Attempts to win wars quickly, 1848–1914

One obvious way in which a war can be won more quickly is to move faster. Indeed, the quest for a short war and the need for speed in the waging of it are two concepts so closely linked as to be virtually synonymous. But so long as mechanical transport had not been invented, the maximum speed attainable by an army was that of a man on foot.

Sometimes this speed could be surprisingly high. Thus Napoleon in 1812, in his advance from the Niemen to Moscow, covered approximately 1200 kilometres in 82 days, an average speed of about 15 kilometres a day. Suvorov, as the Russians love to tell us, did 33 km a day for 12 days during the campaign in Italy in 1779.[1] The trouble with these speeds, however, is that they were not sufficiently high, nor could they usually be maintained for long enough, to allow of a war being won in its initial period. They were quite sufficient to win battles quickly, and sometimes to win campaigns; but they were not sufficient to win whole wars in the sort of time-scale we are envisaging. That was scarcely possible without machinery.

The invention of the railway and its widespread application provided the means for a General Staff to speed up things considerably. Furthermore, as engines improved, bigger trains could be run than was formerly possible, and at speeds higher than those attained by their less efficient predecessors. Bigger armies could therefore be mobilized and, what is more, could be mobilized much more rapidly. If in the horse-and-cart era it took Napoleon 4 months to raise and equip an army in Southern France and move it into Italy, then in 1866, at the start of the Austro-Prussian War, Moltke was able to mobilize 280,000 men, concentrate them, and deploy them in the frontier area in less than 6 weeks; while in 1870 it took him only 11 days to get 400,000 men into their allotted positions. Moreover, if the mobilization, concentration and deployment of the German army in 1870 was done more quickly than that of the Prussians in 1866, in 1914 that same process was done more quickly still. Full-scale mobilization began in Germany on 1 August of that year and was completed by 5 August, while the concentration of the mobilized forces was successfully accomplished by 17 August.[2] Since the total number of Germans that were mobilized at this period and deployed on the Western frontier was approximately 1,485,000, it is clear that better railways had engendered better results.

Nevertheless, all that the railways did in these three wars was to speed up the mobilization and deployment process. Once that process was complete and the attacking army started its offensive, the army in question had to get out of its magnificently speedy railway carriages and make its advance on foot. This was because the railway engine, viewed as a military instrument, suffered from serious defects.

Firstly, so long as the war in question was one between two industrialized countries, what railways could do for the one side they could also do for the other. Moltke was in advance of his time in his recognition of the military value of railways; but other generals in other countries soon came round to his view. Indeed, in 1870 it was not the defects of the French railways, but those of the French mobilization plan, which were responsible for the debacle; while after 1870 the French General Staff paid fully as much attention to their country's railway network as did Moltke's successors to theirs; and the efficiency of the best French locomotives was not noticeably inferior to the German. As a result, in 1914 the French mobilization was completed on the same day as the German, while the strategic deployment of the French forces lagged only 2 days behind.[3]

The second defect of the railways in relation to our present subject is that trains, in order to move at all, need specially prepared tracks. In other words they can only go where there are railway lines to take them. The disadvantages of this were clearly obvious in the Austro-Prussian War. In 1866 the railways leading in the direction of Austria from Germany were not particularly numerous; neither were they, from the point of view of warfare, particularly well placed. Since, however, in this war speed was of the essence for the Prussian Government, and since, moreover, greater speed was attainable by making use of railways trains than by despatching men on foot, Moltke accordingly used the railways for the deployment of the Prussian army. This, however, resulted in a very wide dispersion of the Prussian forces, since the trains went to the places where the rail tracks went to, and not where Moltke wanted them. Between the westernmost railhead at Zeitz and the easternmost at Neisse was a distance of some 450 km. This over-extension of the Prussian forces might easily have been dangerous, had the Austrian army been more enterprising and more offensively minded.

Admittedly, in 1870 things went a great deal better. There was then a much greater peace-time traffic between Germany and France, and consequently a much better railway network, than there had been between Germany and Austria in 1866. In 1870 there were nine lines available for the German deployment against France, as compared with the miserable three and a half that were available for use against Austria. Furthermore, within Germany in Moltke's time the building of new railways and the improvement of existing ones was always done with at least one eye on their potential military usefulness. In the event of a war against France, therefore, there was obviously a much greater likelihood that the German railways would take the German armies to the places where they were wanted by their commanders.

Nevertheless, even if all this had been perfect (which the event showed that it was not),[4] the German railways stopped at the German frontiers. From there the traffic had to be carried on French railways. And though the French railways might perhaps go where the French generals wanted them to go, it still remained true that the lines would be built to suit French, not German, purposes. When the actual invasion began, therefore, German generals could not rely on the enemy's tracks being laid in the particular directions they wanted. Some were, and some were not; and this obviously greatly affected the German ability to supply and to reinforce.

The third defect of railways as an instrument of war was that their tracks were always liable to destruction by the enemy; and that, when this happened, the trains were unable to run. Once this occurred, the army whose units the railway had been serving was obliged to revert to feet and horse in order to maintain its advance.

The fourth defect of railways, as a means of winning a war quickly, was that troops in trains were unable to fight a battle. In order to be able to fight one, they had got to get out of the train;

and while they were getting out of it, and still more while they were in it, they were very vulnerable. Since in all the great wars of the nineteenth century the invading forces were going to have to do a considerable amount of fighting, it was quite impossible to use the railways to continue to transport them, once they had got so near to the enemy that active operations were to be expected. And once they were out of their trains, their speed of movement was back to that of the foot soldier.

Consequently, when we talk about the railway in the nineteenth century having increased the speed of military operations, it is important to remember that, for the most part, this is true only of the initial period; that is to say, the period of the mobilization, concentration and deployment of the combatant armies. That trains could hasten this process enormously in respect of armies belonging to countries with developed railway networks has already been shown by the examples that have been given above. Once that process was complete, however, things were very different.

In 1866, after the successful and (by the standards of those days) rapid completion of the initial period, the Prussian army began its serious operations in the main theatre of war on 22 June; it got to the outskirts of Vienna, having defeated the Austrians at Königgrätz on 22 July, and an armistice was concluded on that day. The Prussians therefore took 31 days to cover approximately 400 km, which gives an average rate of advance of 13 km per day.

The first fighting of the Franco-Prussian War took place on 2 August, when the French assaulted Saarbrucken; and the war may be said to have reached its climax when the investment of Paris was complete. This, according to Moltke, took place on 19 September.[5] The distance from Saarbrucken to Paris is about 380 km, which gives as average speed of advance of a little under 8 km per day.

The First World War is the last of the wars that may properly be called the 'railway wars'. True, the motor-car was used in it, but not on a very large scale. In the early stages, at any rate, things were done in much the same way as they had been in 1870; the armies were mobilized and deployed by train, and then they set off on foot. The German Army crossed into Belgium on 4 August 1914; it arrived at the outskirts of Paris, as it wheeled south to the Marne, on 31 August. The distance from Liège to that point near Paris which was the nearest that they got to the city, is approximately 370 km, and it took the Germans 28 days to do it. That gives an average rate of advance of 13.2 km per day. These figures do not pretend to be absolutely accurate; but they do show clearly that, once operations had started, the German army of 1914 advanced no faster than the Prussian Army of 1866.

Nor did the advent of the internal combustion engine, in the shape of the motor-car and the motor-lorry, do much to speed up the fighting, because, in respect of actual combat, both these vehicles share the same defect as the railway-train: it is impossible for men to fight from them.

Of course by 1916 it became possible for men to do so, because by then the internal combustion engine had appeared in the guise of the tank. That, however, did not take place until more than 2 years after the beginning of hostilities, when the notion of a short war was obviously no longer applicable.

There was, however, a third way of getting out of the difficulty; and one which began to be experimented with in the course of the nineteenth century. If one's speed of advance on the battlefield was necessarily that of the foot-soldier, if one's speed of mobilization, though fast, was inevitably matched by the enemy, there remained throughout the nineteenth century only one means of speeding up the war. That was by trying to snatch an advantage as a result of completing one's mobilization, concentration and deployment before ever the war started. In other words, according to this notion, all this preparatory business should be done in peace-time; and one could then fall like a thunderbolt upon an unprepared enemy.

Unfortunately, however, this proved impossible in practice. In 1866, for instance, Austria began as early as the middle of that March to take preliminary steps for preparing for the war which would not be declared till June. The fortresses were prepared for defence; the troops in Bohemia were reinforced; the quarters of many regiments of the Austrian army were changed, so as to bring the battalions into the vicinity of their recruiting depots. All in all, by the end of March (i.e. 3 months before the start of the war), about twenty battalions of infantry and a number of regiments of cavalry were added to the strength of the Austrian forces in Bohemia.[6]

Despite all attempts at secrecy with regard to these measures, however, the Prussian Government was very soon informed of them, and at once began to start its own mobilization. During the last days of March its five divisions stationed along the frontier were placed on the highest peacetime footing; and, in addition to this, five brigades of field artillery were brought up to full establishment, while work was begun on the refurbishing of a whole string of fortresses.[7] Further measures by Austria to augment her war preparedness were naturally answered by further Prussian counter-measures. The fact of the matter was that the invention of the electric telegraph had made it impossible to gain an advantage over the enemy by the use of the sort of methods we have been describing; because news could be flashed from one place to another far faster than trains could run. Nor was it possible to gain this advantage by censoring every telegram: the imposition of censorship would at once sound the alarm.

We thus have a situation where, throughout the nineteenth century, any attempt to gain an advantage of this nature was at once cancelled out by the counter-m asures that were taken by the other side. In the early twentieth century it was much the same. In the First World War, for instance, each of the belligerents had prepared for the war by doing some of its mobilization and concentration before ever war was declared; but since all the combatants did it, none gained any advantage.

It might be thought, as we look back on it, that the 2 days' gap between the German and French completion of their respective deployments would have been long enough to have given the Germans a very substantial advantage, if only they had had the requisite technology to have allowed them to exploit it properly. However, the requisite technology, the armoured fighting vehicle, had not yet been invented; and since at the beginning of the First World War no new methods of mobilization and no new means of fighting the battle were introduced by any of the combatants, we must rank that war with those of the nineteenth century, so far as concerns the subject of this book. In other words, in 1914 the technology necessary for winning the First World War in its initial period simply did not exist.

Another method of winning a war quickly is to fight a decisive battle as soon as possible. Assuming that in that battle the main forces of the enemy are completely smashed, it only remains to march across his territory, occupy such areas as will prevent him raising a new army, and dictate the terms of peace. There are two means by which this can be accomplished – the military means and the diplomatic means; and the two should be complementary. In other words it should be the task of one's diplomacy to weaken the potential strength of the enemy's forces by depriving him of allies, while at the same time to increase the strength of one's own forces by securing allies for oneself. Once this has been done it should then be the task of one's army to deal with what remains of the opposition.

Thus, before the outbreak of hostilities in 1866, Bismarck secured from Napoleon III a promise of French neutrality, and thereby prevented Austria from acquiring a valuable ally. This obviously considerably reduced the strength of the anti-Prussian forces which might otherwise have been raised against him. Furthermore, by inducing Italy to ally herself with Prussia, the strength of the anti-Austrian forces was considerably augmented. As a result of this latter step, Austria was obliged to keep in the south a large army of 240,000; and the task of the Prussian generals, as they advanced from the north, was thereby rendered much easier.

Once diplomacy had done its work the rest was up to the soldiers. It was the generals' job to create a first-class army, provide it with the best equipment available, and train the army to use the equipment properly. That done, it only remained to get the troops to the battlefield and win the ensuing battle.

This may appear to be asking a lot of generals and statesmen alike; but the history of the nineteenth century bears ample witness that, in those instances where both diplomats and soldiers played their parts successfully, and furthermore (and even more important) co-operated fully with each other, the wars were very short. Thus, the war waged by Prussia against Denmark in 1864 lasted for only 6½ months, of which 2 months in the middle of that period were taken up by an armistice. Actual hostilities in this war therefore lasted for only about 4 months.

The war waged by Prussia against Austria was also extremely short. The 'general engagement' of classic military doctrine (in this case, the Battle of Königgrätz) took place within 12 days of the outbreak of hostilities in that particular theatre of war. Three weeks later the whole war was over and Prussia was victorious.

As for the war against France in 1870, that took the Prussians a little longer than those against Denmark or Austria; but still, by the standards of most wars, that war too was short. The first actual fighting took place on 2 August, while the decisive battle took place at Sedan a mere matter of 5 weeks later; and 6 months after that the war was over.

At first sight, therefore, it might appear that there had now been found a foolproof method of winning a war quickly. The trouble was that it, too, was found to have serious disadvantages.

In the first place, it might be impossible for the diplomats to prevent their country having to fight a war on two fronts at once, and hence being unable to bring to bear their maximum military strength for the decisive battle. In 1914, for instance, not even a Bismarck could have secured for Germany the neutrality of Russia. All he could have done would have been to have thrown the immense weight of his authority against allowing the war to occur at all.

By 1914, however, there were strong military reasons why Germany should think that it *ought* to have its war at that juncture rather than postpone it. France was spoiling for revenge; she was openly preparing to fight a war that should wipe out the shame of 1870 and, at the same time, recover Alsace-Lorraine. Russia was in alliance with her; and although in 1914 Tsarist Russia was far from being technologically the equal of the more advanced European countries, she was none the less catching up fast. In particular, she was rapidly improving and expanding her railway network; and she was also devoting herself to learning the lessons of the Russo-Japanese War. The Russian General Staff, indeed, was by then of the opinion that their armed forces would reach a level of efficiency not far below that of Germany or France by 1917.

Seen from Berlin, therefore, it seemed to be very probable that France would force a war on Germany as soon as it was convenient for her. Consequently, war was believed by Berlin to be inevitable. If the inevitable war were delayed for a year or two longer, Germany would still have to fight it on two fronts, and would have to fight it, moreover, under far less favourable circumstances than those prevailing in 1914. There were therefore genuine and cogent military reasons why Germany should be willing to go to war in the year that she did, rather than attempt to avoid it because Russia was no longer neutral. Furthermore, these reasons were sufficiently compelling to ensure that not even a Bismarck could have ignored them; though he might, perhaps, have failed to be persuaded by them.

It is, of course, possible that, had Bismarck been at the helm, he would never have allowed the Russo-French alliance to be formed against him in the first place; he might perhaps have seen this as leading almost inevitably to the downfall of Imperial Germany and, by making appropriate concessions to Russia, have stopped the alliance forming. On the other hand, France was implacably hostile, and was likely to remain so for many generations; furthermore, not even Bismarcks live for ever, and not every successor to his post of Imperial Chancellor could possibly be a man of Bismarck's calibre.

There is a similar tale of lack of diplomatic success in the case of the war between Prussia and Denmark in 1848. Not that Prussia was constrained to fight that war on two fronts at once: she never had at that time more than the one enemy, and that enemy was Denmark. On the other hand she had no friends and several potential enemies; and when the Prussian generals (for reasons we shall come to later) proved themselves incapable of winning a decisive victory speedily, the war simply dragged on. This made it possible in 1850 for Austria and Russia to put pressure on Prussia to abandon the war, under the none too covert threat that, unless she did so, she might find herself faced with a second, and possibly even a third, enemy. Prussia therefore was obliged to make peace without having attained the politcal objective for which she started the war.

If we now turn from the doings of the politicians and study the military commanders, we shall find that they were as liable to error in their own field as were their political masters in theirs. The mistakes committed by Moltke The Younger are a classic example of this. Germany could win the First World War only provided she won it quickly; and whatever chance she had of winning it quickly was lost by Moltke The Younger's incompetence and indecision. It cannot be said that it was due to Moltke that she failed to win Battle of the Marne; but it can be said that it was Moltke's fault that she ever had to fight the Battle of the Marne, when she ought either to have been fighting the Battle of Amiens or the Battle of the Channel Ports, or else refraining from war-making altogether.

A second disadvantage of relying on fighting a major, and decisive, battle as soon as possible is that the enemy might avoid battle. This is what happened in Denmark in 1848, for instance, where the Prussian army was quite unable to bring about a 'general engagement', for the simple reason that the Danish army refused to accept battle. The Danes deliberately avoided a 'general engagement'; and, profiting by the clear superiority of the Danish Navy over the wretched assemblage of sloops and corvettes which was all that Prussia could boast of, they removed to the islands, on to which, as a result of the Prussian naval weakness, the Prussian army was unable to effect a landing. Nor could the Prussians win the war by adopting that other prescription for victory, the seizure of the 'key to the country'. In so far as, in 1848, a key to the country of Denmark existed at all, it was undoubtedly Copenhagen. This, at any rate, was the view of Moltke The Elder in his memorandum of 1862. But Copenhagen is not built on that section of Denmark which forms part of the European mainland; it is built on one of the islands; and in 1848 the Prussian navy was no more capable of assisting the Prussian army to land on that island and capture Copenhagen that it had been to land it on other islands and bring the Danish army to battle.

A similar example can be found in the history of the Russo-Japanese War of 1904–05. Here, the success of Kuropatkin in postponing the decisive battle, the Battle of Liao-Yang, nearly succeeded in preventing Japan from winning the war at all. It was the outbreak of the attempted revolution in Russia, the armed clashes in the streets of the big Russian cities, which were far more influential than the successes of the Japanese armed forces in compelling the Tsarist Government to sue for peace. Nor, in any event, was the Russo-Japanese War a short war; and it was most certainly not won in its initial period. It does show very clearly, however, that it is quite unsafe to rely upon the bringing about of a decisive battle in the early stages of a war or campaign as a foolproof method of achieving victory quickly. From this it follows plainly enough that there is a further risk involved in this particular method. This is that the commander, having brought about his longed-for battle, may yet end up by losing it. The disastrous Battle of Königgrätz was not forced upon an unwilling Austria by superior Prussian generalship: the Austrian commander, Benedick, himself selected the battleground, chose it as being suitable for his expected 'general engagement', and then sat back and waited for his enemies. He acted as he did because he judged it expedient to do so. He was proved wrong. Other generals in history have equally been proved wrong.

Even the cases of those generals who succeeded in winning their battles do not inspire the attentive observer with too much confidence in the infallibility of this particular method of keeping the war short. In 1864, in 1866, and again in 1870 it was rather a matter of the enemy losing the battles than of the Prussians winning them. For the Danish war of 1864 and the Austrian war of 1866 were both won by a happy combination of superior Prussian numbers and better weapons. The Danes, for instance, had no reply at all to the Prussian artillery; while in 1866 the Austrian musket was immeasurably less efficient than the enemy's needle-gun. As for 1870, the French commanders' incredible mistakes, their lunatic strategy, the muddle and mess of their plan of mobilization did far more to bring about a Prussian victory than anything that Moltke ever accomplished.

We thus see that not even the famous partnership between Bismarck and Moltke The Elder could devise a recipe for winning a war quickly which might justly be called infallible. The term can scarcely be applied to a prescription wherein, however successful the preliminary diplomacy, success in the actual fighting appeared to depend as much on the enemy's military errors, or his inferior numbers, or his archaic weapons, or his muddled administration as on any special merit of the conquerors. One cannot always rely on one's opponents being so kind as to make mistakes of strategy and tactics, or to go to war with inferior numbers or outdated military technology. Furthermore, as history has shown, it was possible for even German generals to commit serious military blunders. Moltke The Elder may not have done so, but Moltke The Younger unquestionably did. Not only this, but Moltke The Younger's political superior, Bismarck's successor, Chancellor Bethmann-Hollweg, also committed blunders in his diplomacy. The fact of the matter seems to be that failure cannot be deemed impossible even when a Bismarck and a Moltke are in overall charge of a war; and it also seems that failure is not merely possible, but is actually very probable, when the Bismarck/Moltke recipe is concocted by an inferior cook. Bismarck and Moltke themselves, of course, were cooks of the highest class; but Bethmann-Hollweg and Moltke The Younger were little more than scullions. That being so, it is obvious that, even as late as the First World War, the search for a method of winning a war quickly was far from being over.

NOTES AND REFERENCES

1. General S. P. Ivanov, *Nachal'nyi Period Voiny* (Voenizdat, 1974) p. 26.
2. These and subsequent figures are taken from Soviet sources, because it is Soviet thought-processes which are the subject of this book.
3. Ivanov, op. cit., p. 40.
4. For the muddles and delays on the German side in the Franco-Prussian War, see Lt Col F. E. Whitton, *Moltke* (Constable & Co., 1921) pp. 193–4.
5. Field Marshal Count Helmuth von Moltke, *The Franco-German War of 1870–71* (Harper Bros, 1907; trans. by Archibald Forbes) p. 128.
6. For details of these and other measures, see Col Sir H. M. Hozier's *The Seven Weeks' War* (Macmillan, 1905) pp. 18–29.
7. Ibid.

3 Later attempts: Nazi Germany and Imperial Japan

By 1939, however, military technology had developed sufficiently extensively to make it perfectly possible for wars to be won quickly. The improvements to the tank and to the aeroplane now enabled an invading army not merely to advance rapidly but to advance rapidly while at the same time fighting the enemy. Mechanization of the infantry and the logistics units to the extent to which it was actually undertaken, was a further step in the same direction, and a very valuable one too.

As a result, Hitler had no difficulty whatever in defeating Poland in 18 days in 1939, nor in getting his armoured units to the Channel coast in 10 days in 1940, nor in forcing France to surrender in another 38. Similarly, the Japanese made quite astonishing conquests in the opening weeks of the fighting in the Pacific. On the other hand, the basic principle enunciated above remained, and remains, valid. This asserts that what one side can do, the other can do also. The truth of this assertion has been demonstrated on innumerable occasions since the end of the First World War. The Nazi tanks in Russia, for instance, were met, and ultimately defeated, by Soviet tanks. The initial successes arising out of the Allied landings in Normandy in 1944 were unable to develop in the way, and at the tempo, that had been envisaged (and British armour, in particular, got badly hammered) largely as the result of the vigorous counter-action that was taken by the Nazi panzers. The armoured thrusts that were developed by the Egyptians and the Syrians in 1973, by means of which the Egyptian and the Syrian Governments had hoped to win the war, were rendered ineffective by the Israeli armour.

Naturally, the other arms of the forces of the various defenders (their infantry, their artillery, their engineers, and so on) all played their parts in the repulse of their respective assailants; and it is also true, as Goodwood demonstrated, that guns alone can defeat tanks; but the point that is relevant to the purpose of this present study is that the fighting qualities embodied in the tanks of the attacker are all too liable to be cancelled out by those embodied in the tanks of the defender. A similar point might be made, *mutatis mutandis*, about the attacker's and the defender's aeroplanes.

We thus come to the conclusion that the invention of the tank and of the aeroplane, though an essential prerequisite for the winning of a war in its initial period, was not of itself sufficient to ensure that it would in fact be won. Nor, indeed, does there exist any historical example to prove that the winning of it is possible. Hitler's and Hirohito's presumptive examples to the contrary were all of them *campaigns*; they were not *wars*. When it comes to the respective *wars* of which these various campaigns were part, then the important thing to note is that the aggressors lost them. The possession of tanks and planes, and the ability to handle them, thus represents no more than an additional step forward towards the solution of the problem which is the subject of this present book; but to say that, of course, is merely to say that yet other steps must be devised and taken before the problem can be considered solved. What those other steps are, must therefore be the next thing for us to consider.

Japan's attack on Port Arthur had already pointed the way. To start a war without warning in an age when such a warning, in the shape of a formal declaration of war, was the accepted mode of procedure, was clearly to gain for the attacker a tremendous advantage. In 1904, however, as we have already noted, this advantage was unable to be properly exploited because in 1904 there were no tanks or aeroplanes to make proper exploitation possible. All that Japan got, therefore, out of what was then generally regarded as her barbaric and outrageous behaviour, was a valuable reduction in the battleworthiness of the Tsarist fleet at Port Arthur, but little else. These gains were simply not sufficient to allow Japan to win her war in its opening phase.

When the First World War broke out in 1914, the Japanese formula was not employed by any of that war's participants. It is therefore worth remarking that the First World War was another war which failed to be won in its initial period. In 1939, however, and again in 1940 Hitler used the formula with great effect; and since Hitler's war was fought at a period when the technology needed for the proper exploitation of the advantage gained from the initial surprise had already been invented and successfully developed, circumstances seemingly were exceedingly propitious for the winning of this war in its opening phase. However although, as we all know, Hitler won the Polish campaign, he lost the Second World War.

Nevertheless, the seeds of ultimate triumph had already been sown. The importance of diplomacy as a weapon for winning a war quickly was already widely recognized. It was seen that, if it was handled effectively, it could enable the would-be attacker to gain allies, to deny them to his opponent, and in particular to ensure that his own generals and admirals would not be faced with the appalling task of fighting a war on two fronts. In other words, a successful use of diplomacy would allow the maximum number of men and the maximum amount of equipment to be deployed for the purpose of crushing the enemy, and thus delivering the maximum weight of blow at the start of the war. This, as will appear subsequently, is a highly important consideration.

Secondly, the actual technical means of winning wars in their opening phase had been invented and developed. Tanks and aeroplanes were available, and merely required to be used. By 1939, moreover, ideas for their proper use were already current; though it is true to say that Germany, usually regarded as the *Blitzkrieg*'s real progenitor, did not possess, even as late as 1941, a universally accepted doctrine for a *Blitzkrieg*, by which I mean that not all the German generals understood it or believed in it; and that furthermore the bulk of the Nazi forces, in terms of weapons and equipment, were kitted out and trained much more for conventional warfare than they were for any *Blitzkrieg*.

The third seed of potential ultimate triumph in the lengthy quest for a formula for speedy and decisive victory was found to lie in surprise. The idea of launching the initial attack without going through the ceremony of declaring war was the first step in the right direction, that of attaining total strategic surprise. It was, indeed, the attainment of total strategic, as well as operational and tactical, surprise that was to prove to be the key to the whole problem.

On the other hand, owing to the complexities of the lock, the key that was needed to open it was exceedingly hard to make. Modern wars demand for their successful prosecution very large numbers of troops; and if a war is to be won in its initial period these troops have presumably got to be mobilized and deployed in their forming-up positions before ever the war begins. If, in addition, the intended victim is going to have to be surprised strategically, the troops of the attacker have got to be amassed without the defender finding out about it. Or, as an alternative, if he *does* find out, he has got to be persuaded that the scores of divisions and supporting arms deployed along his frontier are not being deployed for an attack on him, but for some quite different purpose.

Impossible as such a task might seem, the fact remains that it has been solved successfully on more than one occasion. It was successfully solved by Japan, for instance, at the time of her attack on the Russians in February 1904: it was solved by Nazi Germany in 1941; it was also solved by the Japanese in December of the same year, and solved again by the Egyptians in 1973. In all these instances a fully mobilized country, which the intended victim knew to be fully mobilized, achieved nevertheless a surprise which was total at the tactical, the operational and the strategic levels. The Japanese failure to declare war in 1904 and 1941, and the German and Egyptian failures to do so in 1939, 1941 and 1973 respectively, unquestionably helped to achieve this surprise; but it is important to stress that it is the surprise which is the essential, and that the omission of a preliminary declaration of war is no more than one means of attaining it. As we shall see, there are a number of other means, all of which must be used together, and used in conjunction with this one. Obviously, surprise will *not* be achieved by ceremoniously clinging to the old usage, and courteously informing the intended victim that a state of war is about to exist; for all this does is to tell him bluntly that one intends to attack him shortly. On the other hand, merely to omit this declaration will not of itself be sufficient to achieve surprise.

The measures needed to achieve surprise will clearly have to be studied in considerable detail. Before we go on to study them, however, we must first remark that, despite the big step forward towards winning a war in its opening phase that was represented by achieving surprise, this in itself was still not nearly sufficient to attain the goal. In other words, despite the fact that on five occasions since 1904 the attacker has succeeded in surprising his enemy at the strategic, operational and tactical levels, this success has never enabled the attacker to win his war. Usually, the attacker has won the campaign which opened it, but no attacker has ever succeeded in winning the war as a whole. It is therefore clear that, even in 1945, the search for an infallible method of winning wars in their initial period had by no means been successful. By that date, however, the world had gained a considerable amount of experience in this direction; and we shall have to proceed to analyse that experience. Before embarking on that analysis, however, we must first determine what is meant by the expressions 'war' and 'campaign'; and what exactly needs to be done in order to win either of them.

4   What is a war, anyway?

The Western view of this question is much the same as the Russian. Communist and 'bourgeois' writers alike agree that a battle is part of a campaign; and a campaign is part of a war. East and West are also in agreement in saying that it is by no means impossible for a war to be won in just one single campaign; and that when this happens, the campaign and the war are to be regarded as co-terminous.

But this tells us really very little about what we mean by a 'war'. Given that we say that a particular campaign is co-terminous with a particular war, how do we know that what we say is true? Of course we can tell that the campaign itself is over, for the very simple reason that the fighting has stopped; but a cessation of fighting does not necessarily indicate that the war as a whole has been concluded. There was a cessation of fighting in Europe in 1939 after Hitler had conquered Poland; but it would be wrong to deduce that the Second World War had therefore ended with it. On the contrary, the Second World War had only just begun.

We often assume that a war is over because the combatants have signed a peace treaty. If, having done so, they subsequently renew hostilities, we generally regard the new outburst of fighting as constituting a new war. Thus, we talk of the Napoleonic Wars (plural) instead of the (singular) *War* Against Napoleon; because that particular bout of hostilities was punctuated by a peace treaty, the Treaty of Vienna. For similar reasons, we speak of 'the Dutch Wars'.

This is all very fine, so far as it goes; but numerous wars have unquestionably been ended without any signing of any peace treaty. The Second World War is a case in point: Germany, which was defeated by the anti-Hitler coalition, has not yet signed any treaty of peace with the members of that coalition. If the mark of the ending of a war is to be taken as the signing of a peace treaty, we must presumably conclude that the Second World War is still going on today.

It will probably be objected that the Second World War must unquestionably be regarded as over, because Nazi Germany and her attendant allies surrendered unconditionally. The objection is clearly valid. We must therefore add unconditional surrender to the list of reliable indicators showing that a particular war is ended; and accordingly we now have two such indicators: the signing of a peace treaty and unconditional surrender.

Unfortunately, however, the English language refuses to be neat and tidy. When referring to the fighting in the Middle East between the Arabs and the Israelis we use such phrases as the Six-Day *War* and the Yom Kippur *War*; though neither of these outbursts of fighting was terminated with either a peace treaty or a surrender. We use similar language with respect to the Thirty Years War, the Hundred Years War and many others. French and German usage agrees with ours; so that we may say that the West is remarkably vague about what it means by a 'war'. But if you do not know what a war is, how can you plan to win it?

This is not so silly a comment as it sounds. If the Germans in 1871 had *really* known what a 'war' is, they might not ultimately have lost it in 1945. If the British and French in 1914 had really known what a 'war' is, they might not have had to have fought it again in 1939.

But this book is concerned with *Soviet* strategy and with *Soviet* plans for winning wars. In which case, perhaps the Russian language is better organized than Western languages, so that the Soviet military planner knows a very great deal more accurately than a Western planner what it is that he is required to win?

To a large extent the answer to that question is 'no'. That is to say that Russians term the hostilities of 1870–71 the Franco-Prussian *War*, just as we do; and furthermore they speak of the Napoleonic Wars and the Wars of the French Revolution, just as we do.[1] They also refer to the Six-Day War and the Yom Kippur War, and so forth and so on. Nor can it be said that in these instances they follow 'bourgeois' usage, as a result of the fact that in these instances it is 'bourgeois' wars they are talking about; they apply similar terminology to wars in which communist countries have been engaged. Thus, the conflict of 1939–40 between the USSR and Finland is called in Russian the Soviet–Finnish *War*;[2] while the fighting in Manchuria in 1945 is often, though not invariably, termed the Soviet-Japanese *War*.[3] So far, at least, communist usage and capitalist usage are virtually identical.

On the other hand, the USSR has a view of war which was developed by Lenin from Clausewitz, and which is largely lacking in the West. The English-speaking West, in particular, has practically no conception of it. This view of war is founded upon Clausewitz's dictum that 'war is a continuation of policy by other means'. In other words, 'policy begat the war'. But although a particular government may have coolly decided to employ war as a means of pursuing its policy, no fighting will in fact ensue unless the other side cares to resist. That is to say that (according, at least, to the Leninist view) what really causes wars is a conflict between two policies.

If this is so, it is an obvious and logical deduction that no war can really be regarded as ended until the policy conflict that gave it birth has itself been finally settled. On this view, therefore, we are clearly wrong to talk about the Franco-Prussian *War*; because the policy conflict between France and Germany was very definitely *not* settled by the Treaty of Frankfurt of 1871. Similar remarks apply to the Six-Day War of 1967 and the Yom Kippur War of 1973.

In other words, we ought perhaps to regard the Franco-Prussian War, the First World War and the Second World War as being merely episodes in one single protracted war between France and Germany, which began in 1870 and continued until 1945, but which was punctuated by two temporary cessations of hostilities, one of them running from 1871 to 1914, the other from 1918 to 1939. In any case, even if we regard this view as somewhat too extravagant, we are surely bound to accept that the so-called Six-Day War of 1967 and the Yom Kippur War of 1973 were definitely neither of them wars at all, but merely campaigns of that war between the Arabs and the Israelis which first began in 1948 and has continued to the present day. And the reason why it is still not finished (as it is not) is that the policy conflict which brought on the war (the Israeli policy of preserving an independent State of Israel versus the Arab policy of wiping out that State) is a conflict which has still not yet been finally settled, despite the various attempts at settlement that have been made on several occasions.

But though we are clearly incorrect in speaking of the 1967

hostilities and those of 1973 as being 'wars' instead of 'campaigns', we must surely be right in talking about the 'Vietnam *War*'. This is because the policy conflict which begat the war was in fact definitely and finally settled (and settled to the United States' disadvantage) by the Paris agreement of 1973. The conflict of policy in question turned upon the issue of whether South Vietnam should go communist or should remain 'bourgeois'. As a result of the 1973 agreement, South Vietnam has gone communist; the policy conflict that begat the war has accordingly been settled; and therefore the war is over.

To sum up, there are two important points to be remembered about the Soviet view of the matter under discussion. The first is that the Russian language, the language which the Soviet military strategist uses to express his views, is just as arbitrary and capricious concerning the use of the word 'war' as are the English, French and German languages. The second point is that, nevertheless, the Soviet planner has a view of war which is an *addition* to our own, because whenever he comes to think about it he is naturally of the opinion that a war can only really be ended by completely resolving the policy clash that engendered it.

But in order completely to end the war, he has got to end the policy clash permanently. It is no use winning a war and making an advantageous peace treaty, if a new war is soon to erupt and cancel the gains of the first. Yet the history of warfare shows very plainly that such a thing is extremely likely to happen.

Indeed, it was this phenomenon which provoked Lenin into uttering the *dictum* that 'peace is a temporary, unstable armistice between two wars'. His reasoning was that, unless you are dealing with a war which has been ended by a *complete* resolution of the initiatory conflict of policy, a second war will inevitably follow the first. This was why the first of the Napoleonic Wars was quickly succeeded by the second. Napoleon's policy was to dominate Europe; Britain's, to prevent him. The Treaty of Vienna in no way provided for either Napoleon or Britain to abjure their policies; so the old policies continued to be pursued, and a new war resulted.

A second war will also follow the first war, and every bit as inevitably, *if the victor permits the vanquished to retain sufficient political and economic potential to allow him to dream of a war of revenge at some time in the future.* In classical times a common solution to this problem was to wipe the beaten nation from the face of the earth. *Delenda est Carthago*. The Punic wars, as we all know, were only finally terminated when the Roman armies had not merely captured Carthage, but had destroyed the city and enslaved and removed its people, and had thereby put an end to the city's existence. With the existence of Carthage ended, the potential of Carthage to wage wars was also ended for ever.

Sophisticated modern political techniques have made it possible to avoid employing such starkly barbaric methods. The imposition of State Socialism upon the defeated country's economy, and of a Leninist-type Communist Party upon that country's government, are just as effective in preventing that country's resurgence as the sowing of the ruins of the defeated city with salt; consequently that brutal Roman gesture once employed against Carthage has now ceased to be necessary. The imposition of State Socialism and control by the local Communist Party upon, for instance, the countries of Eastern Europe has made those countries, which in times gone by were extremely troublesome to the erstwhile rulers of Russia, now no longer capable of creating trouble on any scale sufficiently serious to disturb the men in the Kremlin.

We have arrived, therefore, at the conclusion that in order to win a war you have got to resolve the policy conflict that caused it to erupt. In addition, you have got to take sufficiently thorough measures to make it impossible for the beaten country to aspire to a war of revenge. Once these two aims have been achieved, the war may be regarded as 'won'. It is worth remarking that in almost all of the wars which have been won by the Soviet Union during the 60-odd years of its existence (and irrespective of whether these wars were, or were not, begun by the Russians), the Soviet leaders have always seen to it that, having achieved their victory, they also achieved the two objectives that have been expounded at the start of this paragraph. This is true of the war against Georgia in 1921; it is true of the Russo-Finnish War of 1939–40; it is true of the wars against Latvia, Lithuania and Estonia that took place in 1940; it is true of the war against Germany of 1941–45; it is also true of the war against Czechoslovakia in 1968. In the case of this last, for instance, not only did the Soviet Union, by dismissing the existing Czech Government and preventing its reinstatement, resolve the conflict of policy between the Czech Government and the Soviet Government (the former, it will be remembered, had been aiming to introduce more political freedom into Czechoslovakia, while the latter had been aiming to prevent this), but at the same time the USSR, by means of military and political controls, made a war of revenge for the Czech people a quite unrealizable dream. In the case of Nazi Germany (a far more important example) the original intention of the Soviet leaders had been to have the whole of Germany demilitarized, and then administered as an entity by a *demokraticheskii* (i.e. Communist) government. The actual events of the post-war years rendered this plan impossible of achievement; so the Kremlin settled for a method almost as effective: that of accepting as permanent and *de jure* the *de facto* division of Germany, and of locking the Soviet-held portion of Germany into a Communist system of controls. So long as these arrangements continue, and so long as the German Federal Republic is denied any nuclear weapons, there can be no Germany militarily and economically strong enough to embark on a war of revenge. On the other hand, in the case of the one exception, the Russo-Finnish War of 1939–40, where no such programme of 'bolshevization' was embarked upon by the victorious Russians, the Finns began their war of revenge (in conjunction with the Nazis) only 18 months after their previous war had ended.

It is, however, important to make clear that, even according to Soviet philosophy, the need for recourse to 'bolshevization' or drastic measures of a similar nature only arises when the war and the foe are important. In other words, the Russians follow Clausewitz in asserting that there are indeed such things as 'limited wars', where the aim of the war is, by definition, limited, and the means employed to wage it are therefore themselves limited. Nor is it true that these are wars which are only fought by 'bourgeois' nations: the Soviet war against Finland of 1939–40 is a clear example to the contrary.

In this war the aim of Soviet policy was to acquire certain portions of Finnish territory which the Russians considered to be essential for an effective defence of Leningrad. The defence of Leningrad was not a vital, though it was an important, element in the defence of the Soviet Union as a whole. The area of territory demanded by the Russians constituted approximately 11 per cent of the then total area of the Finnish State. Consequently, what was at stake was something very considerably less than the total surrender of Finland. In other words, according to Clausewitz's definition, it was a war fought for limited aims on both sides. As a result although the Russians, having been victorious, took the territory they wanted, they neither totally devastated the rest of Finland nor forced upon the Finnish people a Soviet-style political and economic system.

The reason for this, by Soviet reckoning, was that the war was limited. The policy conflict which had engendered the war had definitely been settled by the subsequent peace treaty; and all that remained to be accomplished was to prevent a war of revenge. This was difficult. In the circumstances of 1940 it was not possible to do this by the standard Soviet methods, because the Second World War was engulfing Europe and threatening to engulf Russia. Despite the fact that at least one member of the Politburo was in favour of a Soviet-style solution,[4] Stalin decided that the dispersion of resources that would be necessary (large numbers of NKVD troops, Communist Party 'activists', and so forth and so on) could not be spared at that moment. Their not being spared made it perfectly possible for Finland to wage a war of revenge, whenever circumstances should prove to be favourable; Hitler's invasion of Russia provided the necessary favourable circumstances; and accordingly in 1941 the Finnish Government embarked on its war of revenge.

However, what was not possible for the Kremlin in the circumstances of 1940 proved not to be necessary in those of 1945. The re-drawing of the map of Europe that followed upon the defeat of Hitler rendered Finland's geo-strategic position a very great deal less favourable than it had been in 1939. The nearest 'bourgeois' countries, which in 1939 were to be found quite close to Finnish territory (Latvia, Lithuania, Estonia, Poland and Germany), in 1945, as a result of the Red Army's victories, were now no nearer than the westward end of the Baltic. Sweden, the one 'bourgeois' country in close proximity to Finnish territory whose political complexion had not changed, had failed to help the Finns in 1940, and was therefore extremely unlikely to help them now. Provided Finland agreed that she would accept, and, what was more important, would abide by the Treaty of Mutual Assistance of 1948, this in the new circumstances appeared to the Soviet leaders to be sufficient guarantee that the Finnish Government would never again embark on a war of revenge. Their inclination to adopt this view was further strengthened by the realization that to adopt a Soviet-style solution to the problem would be to antagonize the Western Powers, and this at a time when the latter were strong and Russia was extremely weak.

We have now examined the Soviet view of what a war consists of. It is a tool for settling a particular issue, and settling that issue permanently. Those fourteen words, however, lay bare with a brutal starkness an important difference between the Soviet and the Western conceptions of what the word 'war' means. For the Western view has evolved in common with the history of Western warfare; and Western warfare (certainly European warfare) has seldom aimed at settling an issue *permanently*. In order to settle an issue permanently, the vanquished have got to be destroyed; or, if for some reason it is not desired to exterminate the vanquished, they have got to be rendered impotent, and permanently impotent.

Western warfare, however, has almost never envisaged the vanquished's extermination, nor even measures to keep him permanently impotent. To the extent that measures to keep him impotent have indeed been intended by the victor, the inefficient technology of all save the present century has rendered his intention useless. Moreover in a world in which there were many States not far removed from one's territory, and each possessed of a considerable military potential, it would have been sheer madness for the winner of a war to blot his foe from the face of the earth, when in 3, 4, 5 or 6 years' time he would need that foe as an ally against some new enemy that had arisen. Thus in 1854, in the Crimean War, Britain allied herself with France and Turkey against Russia; by 1914 Russia was our ally, and Turkey was one of our enemies.

This was the consideration that was always in the mind of the victor when pondering over the conditions of peace he would offer to the vanquished; and those conditions were therefore never made so onerous as to be totally unacceptable. It was an effective *modus operandi*, and one which was always much in the minds of British diplomats in particular. As a result this was the view of war and peace that was held by most British strategists. Liddell Hart, for instance, was so imbued with this view of things that he refused even to contemplate that 'total war' was a viable military concept.[5] Yet if there is one phrase which might best be held to describe the Soviet view of our subject, it is surely 'total war'.

We can put the matter in another way by saying that, in the

Soviet view, a battle is to be regarded as a constituent part of a campaign. If all goes well the sucessive battles will be made to complement each other, so that each one will build on the achievement of its predecessor, and thereby help to improve the chances of victory in the campaign as a whole. In any case, it seldom happens that the fate of a whole campaign depends upon the issue of a single battle: an army can lose a battle, indeed quite a number of battles, and still end up by winning the campaign as a whole. Moreover, it is actually possible for an invading force to win its campaign without fighting a single battle: the campaigns by Nazi Germany in 1938 and 1939 against Austria and Czechoslovakia, those of 1940 waged by the Soviet Union against Latvia, Estonia and Lithuania, and its subsequent campaign against Czechoslovakia in 1968 resulted in no battles. Nonetheless, they were successful: the Nazis and the Russians both got what they wanted.

As for the difference between a campaign and a war – that, in the Soviet view, is very simple. A campaign is something in which victory does not resolve the policy clashes that brought about the war. A war, however, can really only be considered to be ended when the policy conflict that gave it birth has itself been finally settled. But the policy conflict can only be settled by the peace treaty, or by the way the conqueror profits by the unconditional surrender. But there will not be either peace treaty or unconditional surrender until the war has been won; so the next question to exercise us is: 'How exactly do you win a war?' or 'What do you mean by "victory"?'.

NOTES AND REFERENCES

1. See, for instance, A. A. Strokov, *Istoriya Voennogo Iskusstva* (Voenizdat, 1965) pp. 16 and 43.
2. See, for instance, the appropriate entries in *Sovietskaya Voennaya Entsiklopediya* (Voenizdat, 1976).
3. *Bol'shaya Sovietskaya Entsiklopediya*, 3rd end, 1971, vol. 5, p. 490. Another name for this bout of hostilities is 'The Manchurian Campaign of 1945'. When the Soviet Government is trying to improve relations with the Japanese Government, the latter expression tends to come into vogue with Soviet writers.
4. Djilas, *Conversations with Stalin* (Rupert Hart-Davis, 1962) p. 140.
5. *The Memoirs of Captain Liddell Hart* (Cassell, 1965) vol. 1, p. 138.

5 The new notion of victory

Discussion, whether of strategy or of tactics, has often been bedevilled by a lack of precision about what is meant by 'victory'. To begin with there is (or there very easily can be) a confusion between the victory in a given battle and the victory in the war as a whole. Reference to this has been made in preceding chapters; but it may be as well to remind the reader at this point that the winning of a battle, though useful, is useful only in so far as it permits the winner to go on and win the war. Certainly from the viewpoint of this present book it is victory in the war as a whole that really matters; and the winning of a battle is no more than a minor component in the chain of events that lead up to that culminating victory.

In the eighteenth century, however, the winning of wars was not nearly so prime a consideration as it was to become in the succeeding centuries. At that time the prime consideration was to win battles, as a result of which one might hope to win a campaign. In the eighteenth century, therefore, the winning of a major battle (combined, in the more fortunate instances, with the winning of a campaign as a whole) was what was likely to be the major concern of governments and commanders-in-chief. When these battles had been won, the position of the victor at the peace conference was thereby greatly strengthened; and the town he had stormed or the province he had seized could then be used as a bargaining-chip to secure a more favourable peace treaty.

Since, therefore, in the eighteenth century it was the winning of *battles* that mattered, victory was assumed to depend on those factors that allowed the battles to be won. At that time victory in battle was thought to be produced chiefly by seizing some vital piece of territory (the so-called 'key to the country'), the loss of which, it was believed, would inevitably compel the enemy to acknowledge defeat. But since the defeat in question usually

36

comprised just the losing of a single battle, the resultant victory was only a tactical victory. In other words it was not nearly serious or important enough to compel the defeated enemy to sue for peace. Moreover, even in those instances where the successful commander was victorious in a plurality of battles or won the whole campaign, the consequences of this were seldom sufficiently serious to make it inevitable for the opposing side to regard the *war* as lost.

In the nineteenth century, however, victory was held to depend on smashing the enemy's army in a pitched battle. Napoleon used this method, and so did Moltke. Once again, the victory that it envisaged was largely tactical: it was designed to further the civilized negotiations that would be pursued at leisure at the peace conference, rather than to produce a situation where, the war having been won by means of a total victory and all means of resistance having been totally crushed, the beaten nation would be curtly informed by its conqueror of the fate that he intended for it.

Given that all that was envisaged was this limited result, the method described above was very effective. When Napoleon annihilated the Allied armies at Austerlitz he was able to cash his victory for a profitable peace. When Moltke destroyed the Austrians at Königgrätz he produced the conditions that allowed Bismarck to obtain for Prussia the limited political benefits for which she had fought the war.

The trouble with this method, as we have seen earlier, was that, although it deprived the enemy of his army, it did not of itself do anything whatever to stop him from raising a new one. Only in those few instances where the enemy State was so minute, geographically speaking, that the area of the battlefield of the fateful 'general engagement' was almost the size of the country as a whole, could the Napoleon/Moltke recipe for winning victories be expected to deal with the problem mentioned above. Such countries were few, at any rate in Europe: San Marino, Liechtenstein, Andorra, possibly Luxembourg were probably the sum total. In the case of bigger countries, additional measures were needed; and the Franco-Prussian War provides an admirable example of how, in the case of a really rather large country, the enemy's resistance could be prolonged for a considerable time after his original armies had been defeated in the 'general engagement' and virtually ceased to exist. So

conscious indeed was Moltke of the difficulties and dangers of a
'People's War' that he wrote pessimistically after the Battle of
Coulmiers:

> Now when the whole French army has migrated, as prisoners to
> Germany, there are more men under arms in France than at
> the beginning of the war. Belgium, England and America
> supply them with arms in abundance, and if a million were
> brought in today, within a few days we should have a million
> more to deal with.[1]

The experience of the First World War demonstrated very
plainly how valid were Moltke's fears. The German advance into
Luxembourg, France and Belgium in August 1914 was in many
respects a highly successful military operation. Not only did the
German armies make great headway – such great headway,
indeed, that many doubted whether it would ever be possible to
stop them – but they also managed, in the course of their
advance, to inflict on the French, the Belgians and the British a
number of serious defeats. Mons and Le Cateau are remembered
with pride in Britain as notable feats of arms by the British
Army, as are Nancy, the Ardennes and Charleroi in France as
memorials to the French Army, and the defence of Namur in
Belgium as a tribute to Belgian valour. Nevertheless, the fact
remains that, however legitimate the pride that is felt by these
three countries at what their armies achieved in them, the battles
in question were German victories, and in no sense German
defeats.

On the other hand, however impressive this string of initial
successes of the German Army, and however far that army
managed to penetrate into the depths of the territory of its
enemies, it never managed to penetrate sufficiently far to make it
impossible for the Belgians, the French and the British to carry
on with the war.

This state of affairs should be contrasted with that obtaining in
the summer of 1940, when Hitler's armies achieved a degree of
penetration of Holland, Belgium, Luxembourg and France that
was so deep, so broad, and in general so extensive that all these
countries were forced to surrender to the Germans, and the
British forces were compelled to leave the Continent and return
across the seas to their native islands.

By the end of the First World War, therefore, it should have been clear to every strategist that, in order to win a war – as distinct from winning a battle – it was not sufficient to destroy the enemy's original armed forces, nor was it sufficient merely to seize and occupy the so-called 'key' to his country. What was required in modern war in order to achieve victory was the successful accomplishment of both these things: the enemy's army had got to be completely smashed and, in addition, a big enough tract of his territory had got to be occupied in order to stop him finding further resources with which to continue the struggle. Where both these things were successfully accomplished, as they were in France in 1871 and again in Poland in 1939, the hostilities were brought to a successful conclusion in the sense that both those countries were forced to capitulate and accept whatever terms, however rigorous, their conqueror chose to impose upon them. Where, however, they were not, as in France in 1914, there was then no outright victory; and as an inescapable consequence the war went on.

It will be seen, therefore, that even by 1870 the whole concept of the 'general engagement' (that modish term for the crucial opening battle between the principal forces of both sides), that whole concept was falling into desuetude. What had originated at the start of the Napoleonic era as a view of war whereby defeat or victory depended wholly upon the one main clash of arms between the assembled mass of the forces of the respective combatants, had become by 1870 a strategic concept which was simply no longer tenable. Whereas in 1866 it could still be said that the issue of defeat or victory in the Austro-Prussian War depended upon the outcome of the one big battle, Königgrätz; and that this battle, therefore, could still be thought of as a 'general engagement' in the classic mould, no such 'general engagement' is really discernible by the time that we get to the Franco-Prussian War.

Of course it might be said that Sedan was the 'general engagement' of the war in question; but the more one looks at it the less this seems to be true. In the first place, Moltke was never attempting deliberately to bring on a 'general engagement' when he planned his strategy and directed his forces as he did. Nor was Napoleon III attempting to do so, either. Napoleon's plan of campaign was to invade Germany; and the reason he got himself caught in Sedan was mere administrative muddle.

Furthermore, closer inspection of the Franco-Prussian War reveals that there was not, in fact, just the one big battle, Sedan, which is what is required by the theory of the 'general engagement'; but that, although Sedan was certainly the biggest, other big and important battles preceded it, and others took place subsequently; so that what brought about the loss of the war by France was not defeat in just one battle, but a string of defeats in a string of battles.

The history of the First and the Second World Wars was to make it clear that in this respect the Franco-Prussian War was no aberration. Important battles were fought in both world wars; but the outcome of the war as a whole did not depend on the outcome of any one of them. The Battle of the Marne, for instance, was clearly an important, even a decisive, battle; but it was decisive only in the sense that, having lost it, Germany was no longer capable of winning the war *quickly*. The Battle of the Marne was not of itself decisive in determining whether Germany could win the whole war at all.

Of course, even before the First World War there were many who perceived this, and who also perceived that, in modern war, not merely had the enemy's armed forces to be defeated, whether in a 'general engagement' or otherwise, but also that the greater part of his territory had got to be occupied if the war was going to be won. Schlieffen, for instance, in the final discussion of his last operational war-game in 1905, went out of his way to impress upon his audience that the winning of the 'general engagement' in a war could no longer be considered sufficient. 'After the battle', he told them, 'comes the pursuit, you can read that in any basic manual, and this takes a long time';[2] and he went on to make it clear that in the Franco-Prussian War the 'pursuit' was as much an essential element of the final Prussian victory as was the Battle of Sedan itself.[3] Furthermore, like the battle, the pursuit had got to be total: it had got to extend so far across France that the Germans would not merely win the war, but win the war decisively. However, this view of the pursuit, as held by Schlieffen, is very different from that of the elder Moltke. The latter's opinion is made very clear in a memorandum dating from 1877 which dealt with the possibility of a new war against France. Moltke in this memorandum certainly expected a 'great, decisive battle'; but he went on to say that, even if the Germans won it, they could not extend the pursuit as far as Paris. They would have to call it off long before they had got to the French capital; and then it would have to be 'left to diplomacy to see if it can achieve a peace settlement on this front, even if only on the basis of the *status quo ante*'.[4]

The change in what was meant by victory in war therefore dates from the retirement of Moltke The Elder and the new views on strategy that came to be pressed by Schlieffen. Gerhard Ritter, indeed, in that penetrating study of the Schlieffen Plan from which extracts have just been quoted, dates the beginning of the concept of total victory, which is the real subject of this present chapter, to Schlieffen's memorandum of August 1892, which calls not just for the defeat of a particular enemy, but for his '*decisive*' defeat. This was in the context of a war on two fronts, a war in which, if Schlieffen were successful, first of all France would be knocked out of the war, and then Germany would concentrate all her forces to deal with the Russian armies.[5] This was a very different thing from the strategy of Moltke The Elder, who 'had never aimed at inflicting a quick, total defeat on a numerically superior coalition'.[6]

By the time that the First World War had ended Schlieffen himself was dead; but from the ruins of his beloved Germany and from those of Tsarist Russia there were to arise two powerful, totalitarian ideologies, each of which would need, for its own purposes, that concept of total victory that Schlieffen had fostered.

The German form of totalitarianism, National Socialism, enshrined its notion of victory in a well-known Nazi journal, *Die deutsche Volkskraft*; and this notion has been summarized as follows by Soviet commentators:

The war of the future will be total not only in respect of the harnessing to it of all the resources of the State, both material and psychological, but also in respect of its consequences. Total victory is postulated by the inner logic of total war; and total victory involves the complete extermination of the conquered people, and their utter and final elimination from the historical scene.[7]

In other words, everything about a war of the future would be total: the total resources of a people, both material and spiritual, would be harnessed to the waging of it; the victory envisaged would be total victory, in which no power of resistance would be left to the beaten enemy; while the consequences of the victory would themselves be total, since the beaten enemy's country, together with its population, would be wiped off the face of the earth.

The Soviet Union's notion of the meaning of victory is not quite so easy to document. The Russian word for victory is *pobieda*; but it is hard to find an official definition of what *pobieda* means. Of course the many and various Soviet dictionaries carry entries for *pobieda*; but they are not such as to leave one with much enlightenment, even after a careful perusal of them. Thus the seventeen-volume dictionary of the Russian language published under the auspices of the Soviet Academy of Sciences tells us that *pobieda* signifies 'success in battle, the complete defeat of the enemy's forces';[8] while the tenth edition of Ozhegov's famous dictionary does little more than repeat this definition, though perhaps with additional emphasis on the completeness of the defeat. Certainly the Russians have a great liking for the term '*polnaya pobieda*' ('total victory'); and the Soviet conscript swears on oath that he will fight till 'total victory' over the enemy has been attained. There are therefore clear indications that in any war it is not just victory, but total victory, for which the USSR will strive.

Furthermore, if one approaches the matter differently, and comes to the subject via a preliminary study of the Soviet view of war, it is clear that the Bolsheviks regarded war, other than minor skirmishes, as something which by its very nature was virtually bound to be total. Believing, as they did, that a war of any consequence could not help but be an all-out conflict between two mutually hostile and irreconcilable antagonists, the capitalist countries and the socialist countries, victory in such a war was bound to entail either the liquidation of the capitalists as a class, together with the expropriation of their material assets, or else the re-shackling on the limbs of the workers of the fetters of their ancient servitude.

Naturally, it was part of the communist belief that the forces of righteousness would work for the victory of the 'exploited'; but it was nonetheless acknowledged that it was quite conceivable that a victory of the 'exploiters' might occur. In this case a similar holocaust of workers' institutions and a similar slaughter of individual workers was obviously to be expected. In other words, whichever side won it would immediately destroy the social and economic structure of its beaten enemies, and would immediately seize and execute the leaders of the enemy society.

The above was the Soviet view of war as it evolved in the 1920s and 1930s; and it remains the Soviet view of one sort of war even to the present day.

On the other hand the USSR recognizes the concept of 'limited war', and therefore she necessarily recognizes the concept of 'limited victory'. We have already considered one example of a 'limited war' fought by the Soviet Union: the war against Finland of 1939–40. The victory it won, as we also saw, was itself naturally limited. Such a victory will seldom prove sufficient to prevent a war of revenge; but a victory sufficiently crushing to prevent a war of revenge could only be a total victory, and hence the product of total war, as we have said.

If it should be asked, 'But why, then, does not the conqueror invariably proceed to fight his war until his victory is total?', the answer is quite simple: it may not be worth his while to make the effort, because it is much more difficult to compel an enemy to surrender unconditionally than to make him come to terms; or it may not even be possible for him, because the extra effort may prove beyond his power. Hence it is true that there do exist both limited victories and total victories; and that both these categories are recognized by the Soviet Union.

As for total victories, it appears to be the Soviet view that now, in the 1980s, a world-wide war between the 'exploiting' and the 'exploited' classes, a world-wide war between capitalism and communism, is no longer considered probable, but only possible.[9]

It is clear that in wars of this kind the results of losing are bound to be disastrous. Each side, therefore, will do all that it can to avoid ending up the loser. In those cases where the war consists of one people trying to subdue another people, as the Nazi doctrine envisaged, each will fight to the utmost to avert this appalling fate. Admittedly, among the population of the defeated country there are bound to be some who will profit by the change, and who are therefore likely to welcome it; but, taken as a whole, the bulk of the people must be expected to dread a defeat of this nature, and hence to be ready to fight to the end in an effort to avoid it.

Consequently, the winning of a war of this kind demands far greater efforts on the part of the intending conqueror than ever were necessary in the 'limited wars' of the eighteenth and nineteenth centuries. He has now not just an army to defeat, but a whole population in arms. As a result it is essential for him to be able to do three things: he must be able to defeat the enemy's forces in battle; he must be able to advance into the enemy's territory and seize those areas that allow the latter to continue with the war; and thirdly, having seized those areas, he must be able to occupy them permanently, so that there is then no hope of the vanquished staging a come-back and reversing his earlier defeat. Once the victor has successfully accomplished these three essential things the enemy population is completely at his mercy, and he can do whatever he likes with them. In the Nazi case this usually meant that he designated them *Untermenschen*, and sent them off to be slaves, or into the gas-chambers. In the Soviet case it has usually meant that the most prominent leaders of the 'bourgeois' have been liquidated; the houses, land and other assets of the 'bourgeois' have been seized; Communist Party rule has been imposed on the whole country; and some form or other of Leninist socialism has been forced upon its economy.

The above is total victory as it was understood by Hitler and by Stalin. The Communist version is the same as the Nazi in essence, and really only differs from it in the terminology used to express it. In the Communist version the war is said to be one between 'classes', instead of one between 'peoples'. It is therefore either a civil war, in which the 'exploited' class of a given nation takes arms against the 'exploiters' of the same nation; or else it is a war between, on the one hand, the USSR, the representative of the 'exploited' classes anywhere on the whole of this planet, and on the other hand, the 'Imperialist' countries, the representatives of the international 'exploiters'. A third possibility is a war of national liberation, in which the peoples of the countries of the Third World strive to break free from the grip of their 'Imperialist' oppressors.

If the terminology differs, however, the essence of the war does not. Instead of there being among the defeated *population* certain elements who will profit by the change, and who therefore must be expected to welcome it, there will now be discernible similar elements among the defeated *class*. A man can be a traitor to his class just as much as to his country: on the other hand, the war being total, the bulk of each class can be expected to display class loyalty. Once again, therefore, the winning of this war is going to demand far greater efforts on the part of the future victor than ever was thought to be necessary in previous centuries; and once again the fate of the vanquished is likely to be calamitous. In the Civil War in Russia, for instance, the beaten class were stripped of their possessions, and a very large number of the members of that class were summarily executed. At the same time the fabric of the old society was ruthlessly destroyed, and the polity and the economy of the old Russia was forcibly sovietized. A similar radical transformation of their political and economic institutions and a similar relentless purging of their middle and upper classes was the fate meted out to Latvia, Lithuania, Estonia and Poland, when the Red Army marched into these four countries in the early days of the Second World War and once more at its end. Finally, the reader must be reminded that the same policies were applied in South Vietnam by the Vietcong after the American withdrawal; they were applied in Cambodia by the Khmer Rouge; and they were also applied in Laos by the Pathet Lao. In other words, total war gives rise to total victory; and total victory, in turn, gives rise to total and utter suppression of the vanquished.

The real point to be noted is that total victories are the product of total ideologies; and it is therefore no matter for wonder if Marxism–Leninism has the same notion of victory as Hitler's Nazism. Moreover, it should be remembered that previous total ideologies have had similar notions of victory. Nothing could be more total, more all-embracing, more devastating for the vanquished than the Puritan ideology of Cromwell's Ironsides; and the results of the application of their notion of victory to the people and the towns of Ireland are with us yet.

By contrast, it is instructive to look at what happened to Nazi Germany at the end of the Second World War. The Anglo-American insistence on unconditional surrender produced in the western regions of Germany the same conditions of total victory as the mere presence of the Red Army automatically produced in the eastern. Yet the fact that the victors in the western zones are non-totalitarian societies meant that the use that they made of this victory was very different from that which the Russians made of it. The former used the unconditional surrender to put an end to the rule of the Nazis and the spreading of Nazi propaganda; they also made some limited use of it (in the opinion of many, not nearly enough) to winkle out from positions of power a number of prominent Nazis; but they did not try, because they did not desire, to destroy the very foundations of German society as it had existed up to then. Private enterprise continued in western Germany; 'bourgeois' forms of government were encouraged to flourish; and there was little difference between the condition of that part of Germany in the years following the Second World War and the state of things which had obtained there in the days before Hitler.

In the eastern part of Germany, however, matters were very different. Not only was Nazism in all its aspects thoroughly rooted out, but the whole cast of German society was shattered and then remoulded. Private enterprise was forbidden in many sectors of the economy, as a first step towards the full introduction of socialism; 'bourgeois' forms of government, such as free elections, were not merely not encouraged, but were actively suppressed; while an unwelcome form of dictatorship, the dictatorship of the German Communist Party, was thrust upon an unwilling people by the bayonets of the Russian soldiers. Nor should we be surprised that this was so. Just as a non-totalitarian victor in the western regions of Germany had used his power to implement a non-totalitarian victory, so the totalitarian victor in the eastern regions of Germany had used his power to implement total victory. What the nature of that victory is, has just been explained above.

If some of my readers may query whether the Soviet concept of victory has not undergone important changes as a result of the death of Stalin, the answer seems to be 'no'. A third world war is still regarded by the Russians as a war of life and death, in which either the Soviet system or the Imperialist system will be wiped off the face of the earth. The most recent edition of the Great Soviet Encyclopaedia, for instance, is perfectly clear on this point.[10] But a total war necessarily has as its consequence a total victory; and total victory furnishes the opportunity to enforce changes of any kind upon the vanquished people. The Communist Party of the Soviet Union is not merely willing to introduce changes, it is positively longing to introduce changes, in all those countries that still operate a capitalist form of society. It is not to be supposed that, if victory in war were to make it in any way possible to indulge its wishes, it would heaitate to do so. Soviet total victory in a total war with the West would inevitably mean the total destruction of Western liberal democracy.

NOTES AND REFERENCES

1. *Letters of Field Marshal Count Helmuth von Moltke to his Mother and Brothers* (Osgood, 1891) vol. 2, p. 6.
2. Quoted in Gerhard Ritter, *The Schlieffen Plan* (Oswald Wolff, 1958) pp. 67–8.
3. Ibid.
4. Ibid., p. 19.
5. Ibid., p. 23.
6. Ibid., p. 52.
7. *Istoriya Vtoroi Mirovoi Voiny* (Voenizdat, 1973). vol. 1, pp. 153–4.
8. *Slovar' Sovremennogo Russkogo Literaturnogo Yazyka* (Voenizdat, 1976) vol. 10, p. 18. It is interesting to note that the new, magnificent, eight-volumed Soviet military encyclopaedia *Sovietskaya Voennaya Entsiklopediya* (Voenizdat, 1976) contains no entry for 'victory' ('pobieda') at all, though it finds room for 'dialectical materialism' and 'the developing countries'. The omission is significant.
9. For a fuller discussion of these points, see P. H. Vigor, *The Soviet View of War, Peace and Neutrality* (Routledge & Kegan Paul, 1975), especially the sections entitled 'The Suppression of the Vanquished' and 'A Summary of the Soviet Attitude to War as It Stands Today'.
10. *Bol'shaya Sovietskaya Entsiklopediya*, 3rd edn, 1971, vol. 5, p. 284.

6 The first Soviet attempt at a speedy victory: the Russo-Finnish War of 1939–40

We have said little so far of Soviet theory in the matter, and virtually nothing of Soviet practice. We will make partial amends by discussing an early example of Soviet efforts to win wars quickly which dates from the Second World War period. This is the Russo-Finnish War of 1939–40.

Let us start by saying that the USSR made considerable efforts to avoid it. Sceptics may say that this was because the USSR in 1939 was still very weak militarily, and was in no condition to indulge in unnecessary wars. This assessment, however correct in respect of the Russians' own view of their chances at that period when locked in combat with a major Power, does not apply to their view of their capabilities when matched against a small country like Finland. Stalin, for instance, appears to have been perfectly confident that in a war against Finland the Red Army would be victorious within a matter of 5 or 6 weeks. A quick drive on Petsamo, in order to seize the only port through which foreign aid could readily reach the Finns; an advance across the 'waist' of Finland to cut the country in two; these, coupled with the main attack which was to cut through the Mannerheim Line as a hot knife cuts through butter, were together expected to bring about a Finnish surrender in the twinkling of an eye.

Nevertheless, it was not possible for the Kremlin (at least in April 1938, when the first negotiations began with the Finnish Government)[1] to be sure that other, and more powerful, countries would not come to the aid of the Finns. Furthermore, even a year later, even in 1939, when the chances of armed intervention on the Finnish side appeared to get progressively less, the habitual caution of the Russians still induced them to make some effort to avoid war – provided, of course, that they could get what they wanted without it.

That they were quite determined to get what they wanted cannot possibly be questioned; and that they were perfectly right to want it (or at least to want the greater part of what they said they wanted) cannot be questioned either. The proper defence of Leningrad in a war with Germany which the Russians regarded as virtually inevitable, depended upon their getting the bulk of the territory they were asking the Finns to cede them. Admittedly some of the Soviet demands, as finally put forward, can scarcely be held to be vital to Soviet security; but the main items in the negotiations represented assets which it was absolutely essential for Russia to have if the Soviet second capital were to be properly defended.

No real effort to exert pressure on Finland was made by the Russians until 9 October 1939 (that is to say, until after the Second World War had actually started).[2] It scarcely needs saying that, once that war had begun, the most likely allies for Finland were inevitably prevented from giving her more than token military assistance. In addition, Sweden, the sole important neutral in the area, was so frightened of Soviet power that she refused to help the Finns. By October 1939, therefore, Finland was virtually isolated; and since her military potential, as compared with that of the USSR, was puny she had no real alternative but to accede to the Russians' requests. The Russians knew this; and therefore during October and November 1939, they kept on stepping up their demands and also increasing their pressure.

The part played by Soviet diplomacy in helping to ensure that the Soviet demands would somehow or other be granted, was therefore very considerable. If it was the fortuitous outbreak of the Second World War which made France and Britain very unlikely to be able to give the Finns effective assistance, it was the Nazi–Soviet Pact, the fruit of Soviet diplomacy. which made it quite impossible for Germany to do anything whatever to assist the Finns. And Germany was not only a most formidable military power; she was also the Power most closely located geographically to the Finnish border.

Further fruits of pre-war Soviet diplomacy had been the negotiation of treaties with the Baltic States, at that time independent. These treaties, among other things, permitted the

Russians to have air bases on their territories; and the air bases in question were of the very greatest value to the Russians when they came to assault the Mannerheim Line in early 1940.

To sum up, we may therefore say that before the outbreak of hostilities, Soviet diplomacy had isolated its opponent and had thereby ensured that, if war were to come, it would not be a war which the USSR would have to fight on two fronts.

The whole of this present book proceeds upon the assumption that the Soviet Union is very interested in securing strategic surprise when it comes to war. It is therefore very noteworthy that on 28 November 1939 the USSR denounced the non-aggression pact which had been signed between Russia and Finland in 1932; and that on the following day, 29 November, she broke off political and economic relations with Finland;[3] and finally that it was only on the third day, only on 30 November, that Soviet forces crossed the Finnish frontier. So the USSR had engaged in a number of activities which had jeopardized, to say the least, the achievement of strategic surprise. Nor was this all. This flurry of Soviet diplomatic activity had been preceded by a remarkable incident on November 26th, when seven shells were fired by a piece or pieces of artillery in the general area of Mainila, near the Soviet/Finnish frontier. It seems to be reasonably certain that they were fired by Soviet guns; and since their effect could only have been to heighten Finnish vigilance it is plain that a further effect would have been to lessen the chance of surprise.

Yet the strange thing is that surprise was effectively secured. Of course, in one sense this is wrong. Obviously in one very important sense the Finns were in no way surprised. The whole trend of events since 1938 had made the Finnish Government aware that war was a possibility. Accordingly, in the light of this awareness, they had taken measures to meet it. The Mannerheim Line, for instance, was begun in 1938; and, although it was never as strong as legend repeatedly had it, and although it made no pretence to be as sophisticated militarily as the Siegfried or Maginot Lines, the Finns nevertheless put a great deal of effort into its construction; and it served them very well. In addition to building the Mannerheim Line the Finnish Government, as the crisis deepened, called out certain classes of reservists.

Nevertheless, the evidence shows that at the strategic level and, north of Lake Ladoga, at the operational level, the Finns were effectively surprised. The Finnish Government did not actually expect the war to break out when it did; the Russians operating in the sector north of Lake Ladoga were able to mount offensives with a weight of blow and speed of advance that astonished their Finnish counterparts; the routes they chose for their offensives lay along axes which the Finns believed to be incapable of supporting such a weight of troops; and so forth, and so on.

There were, for example, the thrusts that were launched in the sector that stretches from the north of Karelia to the Arctic Ocean. The Finnish General Staff had believed that, on account of the poor communications in the area, it would not be possible for the Soviet forces to attack in that region in strength. As a result the Finnish forces there had been reduced to a mere skeleton, the rest being sent to reinforce the troops who were guarding the Mannerheim Line. The communications were indeed as poor as the Finnish General Staff had postulated; but the Soviet armies nevertheless managed to sustain an offensive of five rifle divisions with supporting armour. As the Finns had little more than a total of nine battalions in this area, because they had reckoned that more would be superfluous, the advantages reaped by the Russians as a result of their choice of route are very evident.

In the same vein, the Soviet 163rd Division surprised the Finns in the area around Suomussalmi, when they took an inferior road to get there, instead of using the better one some 30 miles to the south. The Finns had expected that the Russians would choose the route that offered the better going; therefore it was along the southern route that they concentrated their defensive preparations. The choice of the worse (the northern) road by the Russians enabled the latter to capture Suomussalmi easily.[4]

A third example is to be found in Soviet 8th Army. This army, based on Petrozavodsk, was nicely placed to outflank the Mannerheim Line; but it was the view of the Finns that, because of the scanty roads, it could not mount an offensive of more than three divisions. Consequently the Finns had only kept in this area a couple of divisions and three battalions of covering troops to hold a 60 mile front. However, from the Murmansk railroad the Soviet 8th Army built a spur line, which ran westwards from Petrozavodsk to within a few miles of the Finnish frontier; and it was thereby enabled to employ for its offensive four rifle divisions with supporting armour; while the railway enabled it to replace its casualties as fast as these were incurred. Moreover, by bringing up troops along the Murmansk railroad, it was able to obtain from the interior of the Soviet Union as many reinforcements as it needed.[5]

The geography of Finland·did not permit the Russians to hit their enemy over the whole depth of the latter's positions, as they were to do subsequently in Manchuria. The main centres of the Finnish population lay down in the south, only a few miles north of Leningrad. On the west, Finland is bordered by the waters of the Gulf of Bothnia and by the land frontier with Sweden. Sweden not being an ally of Russia, no Soviet attack on Finland was possible from the west by land; while the USSR at that time was virtually wholly incapable of mounting a large-scale invasion by sea. This fact alone ruled out the Gulf of Bothnia as an approach route; and consequently an attack on Finland from the west could not be launched. Up in the north was the land frontier with Norway, which again was not an ally of the Soviet Union, and a small sea frontier bordering the Arctic Ocean, which was the sea area served by the port of Petsamo. The Soviet Union's Northern Fleet could certainly help to capture Petsamo; and in that sense we may certainly say that the Russians assaulted Finland from the north. Since there is no doubt that they certainly assaulted her from the east and the south as well, it might be said that the same pattern of strategy as was shown later in the Manchurian Campaign was also shown in the Russo-Finnish War.

To say this, however, would be to make an extremely superficial comparison. The circumstances of the war against Finland were very different from those of the war in Manchuria. What happened in Finland was that three major offensives were developed simultaneously; that the purpose of two of these offensives was to deprive Finland of any help from abroad; while that of the third was to smash the capability of the Finnish people for continuing with the war. The three offensives in question, however, were not planned concentrically; two ran more or less east to west, while one ran south to north. Nor was it ever intended that they should meet somewhere in the middle. The resources of the Soviet Union allowed for three quasi-independent operations to be undertaken, of which the one in the south, the biggest, was intended to smash the bulk of the enemy's army and occupy the politically and economically most important part of his territory. The task of the other two operations was to see that nothing interfered with the first one.

That is sound strategic planning; but it is not the same strategic planning that shaped the Manchurian Campaign.

Obviously, an enormous advantage in favour of the USSR was the size of its armed forces. Those enumerated above, for instance, were only the tip of the iceberg. If that tip failed to secure for Stalin his confidently expected victory, the rest of the iceberg could be brought into use to crush the Finnish resistance. This indeed is what happened. The Finnish troops were for the most part so effective that one might even argue that, if the Soviet forces had been confined to those committed to the initial offensive, the Soviet invasion might have been beaten back, and rejection of the Soviet demands continued. As things were, however, every Soviet soldier killed, every Soviet tank destroyed, every Soviet plane shot down was immediately replaced from the inexhaustible reserves in the interior of the USSR.

The ratio of Soviet aircraft to Finnish aircraft must make it obvious that mastery of the air was secured by the Russians from the start. The fact that the Finnish planes were obsolescent models, such as the Fokker D.XXI and the Gloster Gladiator II, while the Soviet planes, though far from being the equivalent of the latest British and German aircraft, were technically much better than those of the Finns, merely increased the ease with which the Russians secured their mastery of the air. The wonder is that the Finnish fighter pilots caused any losses at all to the Soviet air force; not that they did not cause more.

As for mastery of the sea, here too additional factors simplified the Russians' task. Not merely was the size of the Finnish navy Lilliputian when compared to the Russian, but such ships as Finland possessed were not permitted, by the terms of a treaty with the USSR, to sail the waters of the Arctic Ocean, and, as a result they were unable to play any part whatever in the defence of Petsamo.[6] All in all, the Finns were wholly incapable of denying to the Russians the mastery of any relevant sea area; and all that prevented the Red Navy from accomplishing more than it did was the lack of decisive leadership among the commanders of the Soviet warships and also the very cold weather, which froze both the Gulf of Finland and the Gulf of Bothnia, so that naval operations in those waters became a physical impossibility.

If one had to select just one single cause of the Soviet Union's victory, one would undoubtedly choose attrition. Over and over again with the Finnish Army, as subsequently with the Nazi armies, the thing that forced them to yield ground, to suffer tactical and operational defeats, was the attritional effect produced by the Soviet hordes. Each Finnish soldier, before he died, might kill a dozen Russians; but if there were a score more Russians to replace that dozen, and no more than a single Finn to replace that Finn, the Soviet forces were bound to emerge as the masters of the battlefield. No other outcome was possible. Whole Soviet divisions might be destroyed for minuscule losses on the part of the Finnish forces; but within the teeming womb of Mother Russia there were hundreds more divisions available. Those additional divisions could be, and would be, used to whatever extent was necessary to let Stalin win the war: Finland, with a total population of only about 4 million (as compared with the Soviet Union's approximately 171 million), had a paltry nine divisions at the start of the war, and no hope of increasing that number to any meaningful extent.[7] Numerically, therefore, her position was utterly hopeless.

The Russians knew this, and they capitalized on their knowledge; consequently we get the spectacle, repeated over and over again during the Russo-Finnish War (as it was also to be repeated over and over again during the subsequent war against Hitler), of a defending force, which in one sense was outstandingly successful, being wiped off the map by a Soviet force which was militarily much less competent, but which went on trading man for man till no more Finns were left. The inexpertise of the Soviet troops may attract the censure of professional soldiers and military historians; but the fact remains that the survivors upon the battlefield were Soviet, not Finnish, units. Consequently the ultimate victory – the cruel, hard victory of the real world as compared with that of military romance – belonged not to the Finnish Army, but to the armies of the Soviet Union.

As for subversion from within by Finnish communists or by other sections of the Finnish population hostile to the existing Government, there was evidently none whatever. Chew quotes Tuominen, the Secretary General of the Finnish Communist Party, as witness to Stalin's amazement that Finnish communists enrolled by their 'tens of thousands' in the Finnish forces.[8] Finland's defeat owes nothing to any Fifth Column.

Seaborne landings were carried out on several occasions; but they were all on an extremely minor scale. Their purpose was to seize a number of the scores of islands that lie dotted off the coasts of Finland. Some of these islands were small; others considerably bigger; none can be regarded as vital from the military point of view.[9] Such as they were, however, they no doubt contributed somewhat to the Soviet victory; and that is all that can be said about them.

As for airborne landings, I am aware of none that have been reported in Soviet sources. The Finns speak about some effected by Soviet citizens coming from the region of the Inkeri, descendants of a small tribe living west of Leningrad whose speech was indistinguishable from that of the native Finns.[10] But that is all. Since it is not claimed by either side that 'the descendants of the Inkeri' were militarily at all effective (and the USSR would undoubtedly have claimed it, if it were true), we may agree, I feel, that Soviet airborne landings were a wholly negligible factor in the winning of the war.

The last point to be mentioned is that the final Soviet victory was secured by the successful storming of the Mannerheim Line; and that this success was achieved as a result of the traditional Soviet massing of men and materials on the axes of the main advance. The forces allocated for the attack on the Mannerheim Line (that is to say, the successful one, the one that began on 11 February 1940) consisted of the following: 24 rifle divisions, 1 tank corps, 5 independent tank brigades, 21 artillery regiments and 24 air regiments.[11] The 21 artillery regiments and the various tank formations mentioned above were in addition to those organic to the infantry formations. As a result, there was produced for the preliminary artillery barrage and the subsequent artillery support what Soviet sources have described as 'thousands of guns',[12] while the attack itself was launched in conditions of 'an absolute [Soviet] superiority in tanks.'[13] In the light of the condition of the Finnish forces in February, the Soviet order of battle may be described as overwhelming. Nor is this a rhetorical figure of speech. History records that, despite their most obstinate endeavours, the Finnish defenders of the Mannerheim Line were ultimately overwhelmed.

NOTES AND REFERENCES

1. These first negotiations were extremely tentative, but they were nevertheless the first (see, for instance, Tanner, *The Winter War* (Stanford University Press, 1957) p. 3). Had the Finns responded favourably to the Soviet *démarches* a treaty would doubtless have been signed within a matter of weeks. It was the Finns' unfavourable response which caused the negotiations to be so protracted. I am not, of course, arguing that the Finns were wrong to respond unfavourably; but neither am I arguing the contrary. The question of the rightness or the wrongness of the Finnish attitude lies outside the confines of this book.
2. The dates for this section come from Tanner, op. cit., pp. 22–88.
3. Ibid., p. 88.
4. Allen F. Chew, *The White Death* (Michigan State University Press, 1971) pp. 9–10.
5. Ibid., p. 11.
6. The Finnish Navy at that time consisted of 'two monitors, five submarines, and a few minesweepers, minelayers, patrol boats, gunboats and torpedo boats' (Chew, op. cit., p. 130). These were all in the Baltic. The treaty forbidding Finnish ships the navigation of the Arctic Ocean was the Soviet–Finnish Peace Treaty of 1920 (*Dokumenty Vneshnei Politiki SSSR*, Politizdat, 1959) vol. 3. p. 268. The ban was not total: Finland could keep in the Arctic Ocean as many warships as she liked, provided each ship's gross tonnage did not exceed 100. She could also keep 15 warships of up to 400 tons each. She could not, however, have any submarines in the Arctic Ocean nor any military aircraft in the area.
7. The official Soviet figure for the population of the USSR in January 1939, as given in *Narodnoe Khozyaistvo SSSR v 1961 Gody* (Gosstatizdat, 1962).
8. Chew, op. cit., p. 266.
9. The map facing p. 264 of *Istoriya Velikoi Otechestvennoi Voiny Sovietskoyo Soyuza 1941–1945*, vol. 1 (Voenizdat, 1961) shows the islands seized by the Baltic Fleet between 30 November and 3 December 1939.
10. Chew, op. cit., pp. 13–14.
11. Marshal K. A. Meretskov, *Serving The People* (Progress Publishers, Moscow, 1971) p. 107.
12. *Istoriya Vtoroi Mirovoi Voiny; 1939–1945* (Voenizdat, 1974) p. 363.
13. Ibid.

7 The reasons for all these failures

We can now return to the main theme of our argument. We agreed at the end of Chapter 3 that, even as late as 1973, there were many problems still unsolved concerning the winning of wars in their opening phase. The invention of the tank and the aeroplane had brought their solution a great deal nearer, but had not actually solved them, despite some brilliant attempts.

These intriguing failures may be divided into two classes:

(1) those in which the opening campaign was won, but the war was lost – these include Hitler in 1939, Hitler again in 1940, and the Japanese in 1941;
(2) those in which not only was the war as a whole lost, but the opening campaign was, too – the sole example of this second category is Hitler in Russia in 1941.

The obvious first step towards solving our principal problem is to try and discover the causes of these various failures. Why did Hitler lose his campaign against Russia, when he had won his campaigns against Poland and Western Europe? Why did he and the Japanese, despite their impressive initial successes, end by losing their wars? These are two quite separate sets of questions, and we shall have to answer them separately. We will begin with the second one first.

The reason why the Japanese lost the Pacific War is that they did not possess the military capability for attacking the heartlands of their principal enemies and compelling them to surrender. It simply was not possible for Japan to cross the Pacific and attack America; nor cross the Indian Ocean and the Atlantic and attack Britain. Yet unless these things were done, and were done successfully, America and Britain would retain the ability, despite their staggering initial defeats, to continue with the war.

The Japanese were aware of this. They knew that, although with a bit of luck they might destroy significant quantities of their enemies' armed forces, they had no hope whatever of occupying the 'keys' to their countries. Consequently, although they might win battles they could not win the war. There were therefore only two courses of action open to the Japanese Government: they could decide not to start the war at all, and confine their role in the world conflict to that of passive spectator; or they could do as they did, and attack the British and Americans in the hope that, if they attacked them sufficiently successfully and made sufficiently widespread initial gains, the American and British Governments would decide that the task of mounting a military effort that should be strong enough to retrieve their losses was far too great a burden to be acceptable to their frivolous and decadent peoples.

The gamble, as seen through Japanese eyes, was not so desperate as it is likely to appear to my readers. Japan had emerged from her centuries-old isolation only in 1854. Since that time she had fought two wars, one against China in 1894 and one against Russia in 1904–05. In both those wars she had been victorious; yet in both those wars her victory had been gained by precisely the means envisaged in 1941. In other words, in neither war had she totally defeated her enemy. She had neither destroyed the bulk of his armed forces, nor occupied the key to his country. She had, however, achieved considerable successes, but those in areas far removed from what might be termed the 'heartlands' of her enemies. Consequently they were areas which were definitely not vital either to the Chinese or the Russians. They were, however, areas in which Japan herself was interested. Her will to fight to control those areas ultimately proved stronger than her enemies' will to continue the war to recover them. She was greatly helped in this respect because the government of China in 1894 was very weak, and because in 1904–05 there were serious domestic disturbances in the major cities of Russia, which made it extremely difficult for the Tsarist Government to prosecute the war effectively – even supposing, what many doubt, that they could ever have been capable of doing so. Japan's wars against China and Russia were, therefore not 'total wars' for 'total victory': they were 'limited wars' for 'limited victory'; and because in 1894 and in 1904–05 her gamble came off and her enemies acknowledged defeat, she succeeded in winning her 'limited victories' and acquired her 'limited gains'. In 1941 she believed that the same sort of thing would be possible. She was mistaken.

The Nazis lost their war for the same basic reason that lost the Japanese theirs. Hitler's war against Poland in 1939 could not come to an end until Poland's allies, Britain and France, had either agreed to abandon Poland or else had themselves been beaten. They would not abandon Poland, so the war went on. In 1940 France was forced to surrender; but Britain retired into her island fortress and managed to survive. The war, therefore, continued.

Consequently when, in 1941, Hitler decided to attack Russia, he was deliberately embarking upon a second war before he had finished with the first. To crown his folly he quite gratuitously declared war on America a few months later. Admittedly America, having become involved in hostilities with Japan as a result of the attack on Pearl Harbor, would probably have decided to fight Germany; but such a decision was not certain until Hitler made it so. Consequently, by the end of 1941 Nazi Germany had acquired three enemies, the 'keys' to whose countries were beyond her reach and whose armed forces continued to remain in being.

We thus see that Japan and Nazi Germany lost their wars, despite their original successes, because they had broken that military commandment which surely ought to be mandatory on any intending aggressor: you must not bite off more than you can chew.

History shows that many of the most illustrious military commanders have failed through defying this rule. Napoleon, had he obeyed it, would surely have remained to the end of his life the Emperor of France; Hannibal's contribution to the safety of his beloved country would certainly have been immeasurably greater, if he had not ignored this principle; while the decision of Athens in the fifth century B.C. to attempt the conquest of Sicily was not so much an ignoring of this principle as a flat and contemptuous flouting of it, a flouting whose inevitable consequence was the city's subsequent defeat.

However, despite the number of examples testifying to the validity of this prime commandment, few countries in the world's history have learnt the lesson properly: most indeed, and certainly when in an expansive phase, have proceeded to ignore it. The Soviet Union, on the other hand, has scrupulously observed the rule during the 60-odd years of its existence; though this might be thought too short a time to have any historical validity. In any case, it is also a period when the Soviet Union was militarily weak for by far the greater part of it, and was thus compelled, by the dictates of the merest prudence, to be extremely cautious in its approach to the use of force. That said, it is nevertheless worth remarking that, on those occasions when the USSR has decided to start a war against another country, it has always been against one whose military capacity was far below its own, and whose territory, in addition, was Lilliputian. In other words, it has so far refrained from the classic error of attempting to bite off more than it can chew.

We now turn from wars to consider campaigns. After all, if the Wehrmacht had won its campaign in Russia in 1941, it must be reckoned not improbable that it would have won the war as a whole. We are therefore faced with the question of why it failed to win the campaign.

We may begin our enquiry by remarking that Hitler employed in the Russian campaign the same *Blitzkrieg* strategy and tactics that he had employed in 1939 and 1940. It was not, therefore, some fateful alteration in his battle procedures that caused his campaign, which he code-named 'Barbarossa', to fail. Consequently it must have been some other reason, or reasons.

One of these, undoubtedly, was that he did not provide his generals with sufficient forces. He probably failed to give them sufficient men; he certainly failed to give them sufficient equipment.

The failure with regard to equipment shows up particularly clearly in respect of the air force. The German Air Force the Luftwaffe, had for the invasion of Russia only 3800 aircraft, a figure which contrasts interestingly with the 4200 aircraft that it had for the invasion of France.[1] These are Soviet figures, but then it is the Soviet view of things with which we are concerned in this book. Whereas the 4200 aircraft proved amply sufficient in the relatively small airspace of the West European battlefield, the 3800, when employed in the vastness of Russia, were certainly far too few. In the 1940 campaign the Luftwaffe had to operate over a battlefield which, all in all, amounted to 193,800 sq. km;[2] and this gives a density of aircraft of one 'plane per 51 sq. km. On the Eastern Front the battle area consisted of 1,076,250 sq. km. This gives a ratio of one 'plane to every 245 sq. km.

The same sort of story obtains in respect of tanks. The Nazis in 1940 had 2580 tanks at the start of their campaign; and this works out at approximately one tank per 75 sq. km. In the Soviet Union, by contrast, the Germans' total of 3702 tanks only works out at a density of one per 291 sq. km.[3]

It is therefore clear that for their victory against France, the Nazi Armed Forces the Wehrmacht, employed about five times more 'planes and four times more tanks to each square kilometre of battle area than they did against Russia in 1941, where their *Blitzkrieg* proved a failure. It is not unreasonable to reckon the two phenomena to have some sort of causal connection.

Nor is the picture so very different if we turn from looking at equipment and look at manpower. The number of men in the Nazi forces at the start of the French campaign was 2,800,000.[4] This gives a figure of approximately 14 men per square kilometre of battle area. On the other hand the figure for the campaign in Russia (again employing Soviet figures) in only 4.5 men per square kilometre. This comparative thinness on the ground may well be a reason for the fact that in 'Barbarossa', although large numbers of Soviet formations were either destroyed or captured in the opening battles, nevertheless there were very many others which succeeded in escaping. It had been a prime aim of 'Barbarossa' to liquidate the bulk of the Red Army in the first few weeks of the campaign: the aim failed. Shortage of Nazi troops and equipment was unquestionably a principal cause of this fatal failure.

At the risk of over-labouring the point, it is worth examining in a little detail the deleterious effects on the efficiency of the Nazi ground operations that resulted from their shortage of aircraft. In Poland and in France the activities of the Luftwaffe had been a prime cause of the successes of the Nazi *Blitzkrieg*. Its duties were threefold: it had to obtain mastery of the air, or at least of the local airspace, right from the very start of the campaign; it had to engage in widespread interdiction, so as to prevent, or at any rate hamper, the movement of enemy forces and, in particular, the movement of enemy supplies and reinforcements towards the battle area; and it had to give fire support to the ground forces (to act, in fact, as a kind of mobile artillery). In Poland and France, the Luftwaffe had enough aircraft, of sufficient quality and sufficiently well handled, to allow it to accomplish these tasks. In the Soviet Union, on the other hand, although the quality of the planes and of their handling was as good as it had been on the previous occasions, there simply were not enough of them to allow the three tasks to be properly accomplished across every kilometre of that enormous front at any given moment. This is not to deny that the Luftwaffe, right from the very start of the campaign, secured the *strategic* mastery of the air; but it is to say that it could not effectively employ that mastery over every tactical position. It is also to say that this situation got worse as time went on, for the simple reason that the Luftwaffe incurred unexpected and heavy losses.

With a normal method of waging war these losses might have been acceptable; but with Hitler's method of waging a *Blitzkrieg* they can only be reckoned disastrous. For Hitler's concept of the *Blitzkrieg* was in some ways very peculiar. Contrary to what is generally believed, for instance, it was never Hitler's wish that Nazi Germany should be converted to a 'total war' economy, where everyone and everything would be harnessed to the purposes of the Wehrmacht. In the end, of course, the military situation insisted that this be done; but Hitler postponed the doing of it for as long as he possibly could. So far from his policy being one of 'guns *or* butter', it was rather one of 'guns *and* butter'; because only so, in Hitler's view, could discontent with the conduct of a war be stifled among the civilian population, and the spectre of revolution be exorcised, which he himself had seen in its dreadful panoply only two decades before.

Consequently the German economy was geared to meet the needs of no more than one single *Blitzkrieg* at a time, and only then on the assumption that it would prove a complete success. In other words it was assumed that it would be over quickly, and consequently would entail only very small losses in tanks and guns and 'planes. This allowed the diversion of resources away from the civilian to the military sector to be kept extremely small, which increased the chances of butter being available as well as military victories.

In other words, the whole point of the *Blitzkrieg* was that it should bring a speedy victory at infinitesimal loss. It was therefore clear that a massive switch from peace to war production would not be necessary; since sufficient weapons and equipment would be accumulated before the the war began. So butter as well as guns could be made available; and the civilian population would remain well fed, and therefore content and loyal.

This was splendid, so long as the sizes of the stockpiles were correctly calculated. In the case of France and Poland this proved to be so. In the case of the campaign on the Eastern Front, however, the unexpectedly heavy losses nullified Hitler's arithmetic. By the end of December 1941 the Luftwaffe's losses in aircraft were 2851.[5] Of course the Nazi aircraft factories were continuing to produce war-planes; but their total production for July to December 1941 was only 2487.[6] In other words the rate of new manufacture was insufficient to replace losses; and the strength of the Luftwaffe already too low at the start of 'Barbarossa', was significantly reduced, and dangerously reduced, at the end of the first 6 months of it.

This is the story so far as it concerns aircraft. In respect of tanks and guns and (above all) motor-vehicles, it is depressingly similar.

The USSR, on the other hand, possessed both 'planes and tanks in enormous quantities; and although admittedly they were mostly obsolescent, yet the fact that they existed in such very large numbers was bound to cause a problem for the Nazis. When planning their invasion of Russia the Germans had been of the opinion that the USSR possessed a total of approximately 8000 aircraft and 10,000 tanks.[7] The true figure was something of the order of 20,000 and 25,000 respectively, though only a few of these, it is true, were up-to-date models.[8] Nevertheless, up-to-date or not, they had to be destroyed; and the process of destroying them was expensive for the Wehrmacht. Of course the Germans' rate of kill was extremely cost-effective: nine or ten of the enemy to every one of theirs. On the other hand this ratio, in terms of absolute numbers, was far too low to permit of a German victory. This is because it was imperative for the Luftwaffe to destroy around 10,000 planes of the enemy, if it was to be able to accomplish its essential task of securing mastery of the air. Even at the seemingly highly favourable ratio of 10 : 1 in losses, that still meant that this air mastery was going to cost the Germans about 1000 planes of their own. The Nazi planners had not expected any such state of affairs, and had consequently made no provision for it.

The likelihood of a Nazi success was also reduced, and considerably reduced, by the lack of a generally accepted doctrine of how to conduct a *Blitzkreig*. The concept of the armoured *schwerpunkt*[9] was a relatively new one. Its use in Poland and then in France had been accepted with great misgiving by many senior officers who did not think it would work. Its success in Poland by no means disarmed criticism, because every German had been convinced that the Poles would be defeated, no matter what form of strategy and tactics the Wehrmacht might employ. Its suggested use in 1940 therefore continued to be opposed by many because they did not think it could possibly work against the French and British. When in the event it proved that it could, it was promptly hailed as a miracle-worker that could conjure up victories and win wars just by the mere application of it. Its basic tenets, however, were never properly assimilated by the bulk of the German officer corps, so that even on the eve of the invasion of Russia most of those in the infantry formations had little idea of what a *Blitzkrieg* was, or the way in which it should be implemented.

This defect of understanding spread right to the very top. Had it been otherwise, those responsible for planning 'Barbarossa' could never have accepted as their tool for the waging of it an armed force which was only in part equipped and trained for that purpose.

It is no use having a part of an army motorized if the remaining parts must march, or else ride on horseback. Of the Nazi forces only the actual *Panzer* formations were fully mechanized or motorized: the ordinary conventional infantry divisions had to proceed on foot. As for the artillery, this was chiefly horse-drawn. Incredible as it may seem, and quite at variance with Guderian's wishes, there was very little self-propelled artillery available to the Wehrmacht at the start of the invasion of Russia.

Two things resulted. Firstly, the infantry and artillery lagged behind the *Panzers*, often by a considerable distance. This meant that they often were not available to help maintain the encirclement of this or that pocket of Soviet divisions, nor assist in their liquidation. As a result many Soviet formations escaped the net. Even when, by means of prolonged forced marches, the Nazi infantry arrived on time, as they managed to do at Kiev, they were extremely tired and by no means in top condition for the fighting that lay ahead.

The other unfortunate consequence of this lagging behind of the artillery was that the German striking forces were often woefully short of fire-power. Soviet writers continually stress the importance of this.[10] Where no help could be provided by the Luftwaffe, the *Panzer* formations for most of the time were

forced to rely on their own organic artillery. This consisted of the
guns of the tanks, the very small number of self-propelled (SP)
guns, and the artillery of the motorized infantry. None of these
were of more than medium-calibre. The Pz-3 tanks had 50 mm
guns; the Pz-4, 75 mm; the few SP guns were of 47 mm calibre;
while the artillery of the motorized infantry was of 75 mm. Most
of the time in the early days this lack of sufficient fire-support was
not particularly important. Sometimes, however, it was; and
naturally the lack was most keenly felt when the tanks were
engaged in unsuitable terrain (forests, built-up areas, etc.),
trying to break down a stubborn Soviet resistance that was
holding up their advance.

The mention of stubborn Soviet resistance leads to the question
of faulty German intelligence. The vital work of planning
'Barbarossa' was based upon a number of key assumptions, many
of which proved to be wrong. One, which we have already noted,
concerned the numbers of tanks and aircraft in service with the
Russians. Another concerned the nature of the terrain, especially
as it affected movement. The fact that the majority of Russian
roads were totally unsurfaced, and hence became impassable
when the autumn rains set in, was not appreciated; nor did the
Germans have accurate knowledge of what roads actually existed,
still less of where they ran. The third of the faulty assumptions of
which we need to take note in this present chapter concerns the
degree to which the Soviet forces were likely to be willing to fight.
It was Hitler's declared opinion that, so long as the Wehrmacht
managed to secure resounding initial victories of the sort of size
and scope which they had secured in Poland and in France, then
Soviet resistance would simply collapse and the Bolshevist rule in
Russia would fall to pieces.

It is worth remarking that Hitler's prophecy might well have
been fulfilled, if he had paid much more attention than he did to
the political side of war. He possessed a good understanding of
war's *psychological* aspect, of the degree to which surprise and
speed and terror could be combined to paralyse the enemy's will
to resist; on the other hand, he knew virtually nothing of the
political aspect. He was not aware of the nature of Soviet society
as it had developed under Stalin, and was therefore ignorant of
that society's strengths and weaknesses. In particular the fact that
the Ukrainian people, because of their deep-felt grievances
against Stalin's tyranny, could contribute greatly towards

Germany's chances of victory was not apparent to him. A wise war-lord, planning an attack on a multi-racial society, would surely try to detect the various schisms which must inevitably be present in such a country and seek to profit by them. He would seek to secure the allegiance of this group or of that, by harping upon their grievances and promising reforms. Hitler did not. He aimed to win his wars by the mailed fist and by terror, and by these alone: he thus ensured that he would crush all feelings of sympathy for the Nazi invaders that might be felt, and were felt, by innumerable Soviet citizens at the start of the war. By so doing, Hitler forfeited valuable potential allies, and thereby forfeited a valuable chance of winning his Russian *Blitzkrieg*.

Then there is the final difficulty, the sheer size of Russia. It is one thing to win a war quickly when the distance that has to be covered in order to do so is 200-300 miles; it is quite another, when the required distance is four to five times that figure. If the Germans in 1940 advanced at a speed that averaged about 30 km per day, then in 1941 at the same speed, supposing they could have maintained it continuously for the necessary length of time, it would have taken them fully one hundred days to get to their self-imposed winning-post. This may be a *Krieg*; it is not a *Blitzkrieg*.

But there were additional important consequences resulting from Russia's size. One concerned the fatigue that was felt by men and equipment alike. After a couple of months hard fighting, and after having covered tremendous distances, the tank crews and the tanks themselves were badly in need of a rest. Yet it was virtually impossible to give them any. Nor could the regiments be supplied with the spare parts they needed to keep their vehicles in service after their harrowing wear and tear.

For this there were several causes, of which the most important were the difference in gauge between the Soviet and the German railways, and the enormous number of different types of motor vehicle (over 2000, according to van Creveld).[11] The former inevitably made it extremely difficult to supply the advancing Wehrmacht by rail at all; while the latter meant that the number of spare parts that was actually required by the Nazi forces was many times greater than would have been necessary if their transport had been standardized. Van Creveld states that, in the area of Army Group Centre alone, well over one million spare parts proved to be needed, a truly formidable figure.[12]

But it was not only spare parts which caused the Germans difficulties. Another major consequence resulting from Russia's size, especially when coupled with Russia's backwardness and Stalin's scorched-earth policy, was the sheer difficulty of supplying virtually anything. The further the Germans forged ahead, the greater these difficulties grew. Fuel, for instance, and also ammunition, often ran short in consequence; also in consequence, projected operations had to be postponed. Yet any sort of postponement is a complete negation of *Blitzkrieg*. In other words, victory was once more deferred; and as a result of these numerous deferments of victory there would be no speedy winning of the campaign in Russia.

These are the principal, though by no means the only, causes of the Germans' failure to win their campaign in its opening phase. Seemingly major causes, like the onset of the Russian winter, do not in fact apply; because if the Nazis had succeeded in winning in the initial period of their Eastern Campaign it would all have been over before 'General Winter' ever arrived on the scene. In any case, the causes we have already examined were fully sufficient to explain Hitler's downfall; and we therefore see that the problem that confronts us was never really solved by him. As we have also seen, it was never really solved by the Japanese either.

By the end of 1942, therefore, both the Japanese and the Germans had provided valuable lessons in how *not* to win wars quickly. On the other hand, the campaigns of 1939 and 1940 had provided equally valuable clues as to how to do so. We must now, therefore, try to assimilate those lessons, in the way in which they seem to have been assimilated by Soviet military strategists.

NOTES AND REFERENCES

1. S. P. Ivanov, *Nachal'nyi Period Voiny* (Voenizdat, 1974) p. 222.
2. Ibid. What I have here termed the 'battlefield' is the total area over which Nazi forces operated, according to Ivanov's figures.
3. The figures for German tanks in France and Russia are also taken from Ivanov, op. cit.
4. Ibid.
5. *Istoriya Vtoroi Mirovoi Voiny; 1939–1945* (Voenizdat, 1974) vol. 4, p. 421.
6. Ibid.
7. Barry A. Leach, *German Strategy Against Russia, 1939–41* (Clarendon Press, 1973) p. 172.

8. It is impossible to get an accurate figure for actual Soviet holdings of tanks and aircraft on 21 June 1941. One can arrive at figures for the total production of these items between, say, January 1928, and June 1941; but a certain proportion of those produced must have worn out or been destroyed in accidents before Hitler invaded Russia. The overall production of aircraft for these years appears to have been in excess of 30,000, if we are to accept statements in such works as *50 Let Vooruzhennykh Sil SSSR* (Voenizdat, 1968), Yu. I. Korablev and M. I. Loginov, *KPSS i Stroitel'stvo Sovietskikh Vooruzhennykh Sil* SSSR (Voenizdat, 1959), and I. F. Pobezhimov, *Ustroistvo Sovietskoi Armii* (Voenizdat, 1954); but I would be happy to accept John Erickson's figure, as given in his *The Soviet High Command*, of 20,000 as the actual number of Soviet planes in existence when Hitler struck. Using the same sources we find that the total production of tanks (including armoured cars and tankettes) over the same period was also in excess of 30,000. How many of these were actually in service on 21 June 1941 is extremely difficult to determine. A commonly accepted figure, with which I personally have no quarrel, is approximately 22,000. What is absolutely certain is that the Germans' estimates of Soviet tank and aircraft strengths were a very great deal too low. They themselves admitted this.

9. *'Schwerpunkt'* is the point of concentration in a key area of attack. Traditionally it had been infantry which had been used for the purpose; but the proponents of *Blitzkrieg* of the Guderian school came up with the then novel notion of using massed tanks for smashing through at the decisive place.

10. See, for instance, V. A. Anfilov, *Bessmertnyi Podvig* (Nauka, 1971) p. 68.

11. Martin van Creveld, *Supplying War* (Cambridge University Press, 1977) pp. 150–1.

12. Op. cit., p. 151.

8   Possible recipes for success

Having now mulled over reasons for past failures, it is time to turn to possible keys to success. After all, no matter what critical observations we have made upon previous efforts, some of the generals in wars gone by did very well indeed. Is it not therefore possible to learn from them and from others some useful lessons on how a commander can win? The Russians certainly believe that it is, and have spent much effort in doing so.

We will therefore imagine a Soviet defence planner looking at the lessons of history in order to see what ideas he could glean for winning a war in its initial period. We think it unlikely that our imaginary planner would show much interest in wars that occurred prior to the French Revolution: on the other hand he would, we think, be fascinated by those of the subsequent wars in which Prussia/Germany participated. This is because the Russians regard the Germans as the unquestioned masters of the art of war until the time when the Soviet Armed Forces came to their own maturity; even now, they regard the Germans as being second only to themselves in the matter of soldiering. In this connection, it appears to be a useful confirmation of our thinking that General S. P. Ivanov, in that book which we have mentioned so frequently, accords pride of place to the wars of Prussia/Germany out of all those wars that he has chosen to examine.

Wars which were won by Prussia/Germany were all of them very short wars, while those that lasted a year or more she invariably lost. Since a similar view of the virtue of waging short wars is deeply instilled in the consciousness of the Soviet Union, the desire to study in detail the short wars of Prussia/Germany and discover how always she managed to win them (and also to study the long wars and see why she always lost) must naturally be firmly impressed on the Russians' minds.

The wars that were won by Prussia/Germany between 1815 and 1945 were the Prusso-Danish War of 1864, the Austro-Prussian War of 1866 and the Franco-Prussian War of 1870/71. These lasted 5½ months, 7 weeks, and 6½ months respectively.[1] By contrast, the wars that Prussia/Germany lost were the Prusso-Danish War of 1848, the First World War and the Second World War. These lasted 3½ years, 4 years, and over 6½ years respectively. In this connection it is therefore worth remarking that the very few wars which have been begun by the Soviet Union during the 60-odd years of its existence have all been very short wars, and that each of these very short wars has been won by the USSR. Afghanistan, of course, is now an exception.

If, therefore, it is to be accepted as true that a prime requisite for winning wars is to ensure that they are won quickly, the next essential, clearly, is to see how this may best be done.[2] The whole thing naturally hinges upon the requisites for winning; and we agreed in a previous chapter that, at least in respect of modern wars, these may be regarded as being the total defeat of the enemy's armed forces, together with the occupation of the economically important part or parts of his territory. For good measure, the *strategically* important parts of his territory had better also be occupied. If all these things are accomplished, victory follows.

It is a mere matter of common sense that the attainment of these objectives will be very greatly facilitated if the enemy's armed forces and his territory are small. This does not, of course, mean that if his territory and his forces are both small, victory will inevitably follow: the Prusso-Danish War of 1848 is a clear demonstration to the contrary. On the other hand, in that war there were special factors preventing a Prussian victory (the insular configuration of the Danish kingdom, the lack of a Prussian fleet, etc.,); and we can at least say that, when there are no such factors, the smaller the enemy's forces and the smaller his territory, the easier it must be to defeat him in the opening phase of a war.

It therefore becomes a matter of supreme importance to anyone trying to win a war quickly to ensure that his intended victim should have as small an army and as small a territory as possible. Since, however, it is seldom within his power to cause a reduction in his enemy's armed forces without incurring, as a *quid pro quo*, a similar reduction in his own; and since it is *almost never* within his ability to reduce the actual territory of his opponent during the comparatively restricted time that separates his decision to attack him from the actual moment of the launching of the attack, the ends the would-be attacker seeks must be accomplished by other means.

Really, only two such means exist. One consists of deliberately choosing as one's victim a State whose territory and armed forces are so small by comparison with one's own as virtually to guarantee victory; the other, of at least preventing him from augmenting his forces and increasing his effective territory by concluding alliances with other countries. This can be done either by oneself concluding alliances with those other countries, or else by so intimidating their peoples and governments that they will sit like frightened rabbits and do nothing. Hitler used this latter technique with very great success.

The first method is by no means universally applicable, because it seldom happens with modern governments that their choice of a potential enemy is completely free. That is to say that governments do not ask themselves, 'Whom shall we attack tomorrow?', and then look around and find a suitable victim. What happens is that they find themselves at loggerheads with another State or group of States; and that they then consider, among other things, whether, if it were to come to war, they would be capable of winning. But the size of the armed forces and of the territory of their potential enemies are things that, almost invariably, they are obliged to take as given.

On the other hand it must perhaps be regarded as relevant that, in the various wars which have been begun by the Soviet Union during the 60-odd years of its existence, the enemy chosen for the Soviet aggression has always had such a small army and such a comparatively small territory that failure for the Russians was virtually impossible. In other words, the USSR appears to have absorbed extremely well the concept of 'chewability'.

There is, however, the second method of reducing the strength of the enemy's potential resistance; and that is by preventing him from securing allies. This may be done, we decided, either by the aggressor himself securing as allies those who might, in other circumstances, be allies of the aggressor's victim; or else by rendering impotent the victim's potential allies by a cunning mixture of threats, promises and blackmail.

In the former case the job is largely a matter of good

diplomacy; and the history of Prussia/Germany demonstrates very clearly the degree to which she used diplomacy skilfully and extremely successfully in the case of the wars she won.

Thus in 1864 Bismarck managed so to arrange matters that Denmark got no assistance from other countries in her war against Prussia. His aim had been from the beginning to seize Schleswig-Holstein, and to make it a province of Prussia. He said so himself.[3] The trouble was that Prussia had no claim whatever to Schleswig-Holstein; that she could annex it to the Prussian Crown only by war; and that, although with the help of the Austrian fleet she could certainly conquer Denmark, she would be quite unable to do so if Denmark were to be supported by either of the major Powers on the continent of Europe, Russia or France. The task of securing for Prussia the alliance with Austria, and that of preventing France and Russia from allying themselves with Denmark, therefore fell to Bismarck; and he made sure he accomplished it before he allowed the war to start. Once it had actually started. Denmark was soon defeated; and a prime cause of her defeat was Bismarck's diplomacy.

In 1866 Bismarck's diplomacy again proved very effective. By securing against Austria an alliance with Italy, Bismarck reduced by approximately a quarter of a million men the number of troops that the Austrian Government could put into the field against him, because these men had to be kept in the south to stand guard over Italy. At the same time, by securing for Prussia promises of neutrality from France and Russia, Bismarck prevented a corresponding decrease in the numbers available to the Prussian armies, which otherwise would have had to have been deployed to meet the threat of a French or a Russian attack. Once again, Prussia was quickly victorious; and once again it was Bismarck's diplomacy which had done as much as anything to bring that victory about.

In 1870 a war against France would have been quite impossible for Prussia, if the former had had a promise of help from Russia. No such promise was given, and no help ever materialized. It would be wrong to say that it was Bismarck's diplomacy which alone prevented Russia from assisting France; but it was certainly due to Bismarck's efforts that the inevitable war between France and Prussia did not take place until Russian neutrality was thoroughly assured. In this way Bismarck made his contribution to the ensuing Prussian victory; and Bismarck's contribution was obviously vital. The German armies could beat France if they were fighting a war on one front; they could not hope to beat her if fighting a war on two.

If we now turn to the wars in which Prussia/Germany *failed* to secure the victory, we shall see that not only were they lengthy wars, but they were badly prepared diplomatically. In the Prusso-Danish War of 1848–52, Prussia failed to prevent the major Powers from exerting pressure on her to call off the war. Had she been able to win quickly, the views of the Powers could no doubt have been ignored. In fact, however, the war dragged on; and this made it possible for France and Russia to enforce their will on the Prussian Government and compel it to make peace. The peace, moreover, was not at all a favourable one; and this war therefore must be reckoned a Prussian defeat. It is consequently not without interest to note that at the time of this Prusso-Danish War Bismarck was not yet Chancellor.

In the years preceding the First World War Imperial Germany similarly allowed her General Staff to plan an offensive that took little account of politics. By this time, incidentally, Bismarck was dead. Dead or not, however, the fact remains that the German plan of attack, as laid down by Schlieffen, was virtually bound to add Britain and the British Empire to the number of Germany's enemies, simply because it insisted that the German armies must pass through Belgium on their way towards the seizure of Paris.

This is not to say that, once war with France was decided upon, there was a better way to conquer her than by sending the troops through Belgium; but it *is* to say that if the defeat of France was impossible without the prior invasion of Belgium, then the German Government in the old days, when Bismarck was at the helm, would never have agreed in the first place to have allowed the war to start.

The Second World War saw a comparable denigration by Germany of the importance of politics. Hitler's peacetime diplomacy certainly originally saw to it that the Third Reich embarked upon hostilities against only one enemy at a time; but by the second year of the war this caution had deserted him: by that time Hitler, in defiance of the conventional wisdom, had committed himself to fighting against the Russians in the east before his fight against Western Europe had been properly finished. In other words, as a result of a signal failure of Nazi diplomacy, Germany was embarked on that most desperate of all desperate courses, a war on two fronts at once.

Of course if the Soviet Union had been placed in the same predicament, if Nazi Germany had succeeded in persuading Japan to attack the USSR in the east at the same time as the Wehrmacht attacked her in the West, the resultant disadvantages to the Soviet Union might well have gone far to counter-balance, or perhaps have done more than counter-balance, those disadvantages experienced by Germany as a result of her own imbroglio. If the USSR, as well as Germany, had had to fight a war on two fronts, it might have been Hitler's Reich, not Stalin's Russia, that emerged as the final victor. Whether or not the involvement of Japan in the forthcoming war against the USSR was an important element in Hitler's strategy appears to be uncertain. Barry Leach, in his admirable study *German Strategy Against Russia 1939–1941*, says firmly, during the course of his discussion of the question, that Hitler definitely did *not* want the Japanese to participate (pp. 178-82):[4] Soviet historians, on the other hand, are insistent that he did.[5] However, Western and Soviet historians are unanimous in agreeing that the Japanese were sceptical of the success of 'Barbarossa', and that they had no intention of taking part in the attack on the Soviet Union until German victories had made it clear that Hitler was going to win his war as easily as he had predicted.

The fact remains that, in any case, given the inadequacy of the German forces for the task that lay ahead of them, the participation of Japanese forces, advancing from the east towards the centres of the Soviet munitions industry, was an indispensable precondition for the defeat of the USSR. Even with the participation of Japan the defeat of the Soviet Union might still not have been accomplished; but without that participation there was no hope whatsoever for a German victory.

This point has been fully recognized by the Russians themselves; and it is the chief reason for their invariable clamorous opposition to any attempt nowadays to improve or enlarge the Japanese Defence Forces, or to improve or enlarge the Chinese People's Liberation Army, or to any proposal by Western politicians to 'play the China card'.

To return, however, to the problems of Hitler's Germany in connection with 'Barbarossa', it must be pointed out that not only did Nazi diplomacy fail to make its proper contribution to victory before the campaign started, but that it did not do any better when hostilities had actually begun. Certainly in respect of the war against the Soviet Union, a better appreciation of the political realities and a more skilful approach towards the exploitation of them would have allowed Germany to have derived full benefit from the hatred felt by the Ukrainians for their Bolshevik masters. In fact, however, no such exploitation was ever attempted. The Ukrainian people were lumped by Hitler in the same category as the ethnic Russians, and were classed as verminous *Untermenschen*; and the penalty he paid for disregarding them, and for subsequently maltreating them abominably, was the engendering among the bulk of the Ukrainian population the feeling that Stalin might be hell, but that Hitler was Satan incarnate.

We thus see that, in the six wars we have been studying, an essential requirement for winning was good diplomacy; we also see that it was very largely as a result of that good diplomacy that the three wars which were short wars were kept short in the first place, and that these wars were consequently won. We also see that where the diplomacy of Prussia/Germany, instead of being good, was just downright bad, the wars concerned were long wars, and Prussia/Germany lost.

The actual tasks undertaken by the diplomacy of Prussia/Germany in those wars in which she was victorious may be said to have been the following:

(1) securing for Prussia/Germany the maximum number of allies, and reducing to a minimum those of the intended victim;

(2) ensuring the neutrality in the coming conflict of those States whose active support for the Prussian/German cause it was impossible to procure;

(3) seeing to it at all costs that, whatever else happened, Prussia/Germany should not find herself entangled in a war on two fronts at once.

In view of the demonstrable importance of the value of good diplomacy as a means of winning a war quickly, it should come as no surprise to find that modern Soviet writers attach great importance to it. Thus, Marshal Sokolovsky, in his famous *Military Strategy*, devotes a whole section to it;[6] while a standard textbook of the Soviet Ministry of Defence, *Marxism—Leninism on*

War and the Army, now appearing in its fifth edition, also
stresses the importance of diplomacy in preparing for a war.[7]

So much for diplomacy. But the world of the 1920s and 1930s
was a witness to several highly successful attempts to secure results
much like the above by most undiplomatic methods. Hitler was
the chief practitioner. Hitler saw very clearly that a potential
enemy's will to resist could be weakened by propaganda every bit
as effectively as it could by any diplomacy.

This propaganda was to be beamed at the individual citizens of
the enemy country, and at the individual citizens of any other
country the government of which might betray an unwelcome
readiness to come to the first country's assistance. Since the individual citizens included the individual members of the potential
enemy's government and the individual members of the governments of potential allies, Hitler's propaganda machine could
hope to effect a complete paralysis of the will to resist on the part
of his intended victims. Nor was this merely a matter of hope
alone: it was proved triumphantly in practice. In 1936, when the
Nazis reoccupied the Rhineland, in 1938 when they invaded and
took over Austria, and in 1938 and 1939 when they first isolated
and then seized Czechoslovakia, Hitler showed that his formula
could prove very effective in practice.

Hitler was thus in some ways more effective than Bismarck had
ever been; but then Hitler happened to live at a period when a
number of new and potent tools for international blackmail had
been discovered. First, there was ideology. In Bismarck's day wars
were fought and pre-war diplomacy conducted along strictly
national lines. Germans fought Danes or Austrians or Frenchmen; Frenchmen fought Germans or Russians or Italians;
Russians fought Frenchmen and Turks or Britons; the British
fought Russians. In none of the wars of the Bismarck era did
other than the merest handful of a country's nationals fight on
the side of their country's enemies; and those that did were
regarded by all as traitors. Similarly, in the various diplomatic
negotiations that preceded the outbreak of these respective wars
the French, the British, the Danes, the Germans, the Austrians,
the Turks, the Russians, the Italians, all supported their
respective governments: there was no 'Fifth Column' element.

By the 1930s, however, two important seedbeds of such
elements were germinating their hideous crops. One of these was
political ideology. There were a number of such ideologies; but

the two most important by far were Fascism and Communism; and the aspect of these which concerns us here is that they transcended national boundaries. Fascists, that is to say, were to be found in a number of countries; and the sympathies of, for example, a French Fascist were just as likely to be with the Italians, because Italy was a Fascist country, as they were to be with the attitudes and policies of his own government. The same sort of thing was true of Communism (or Bolshevism). Since, in addition, Fascists abominated Communists, and vice-versa, it was by no means unlikely that a Fascist national would oppose the policies of his own government, where these were seen as likely to benefit Communism or the Soviet Union; or that he would support the policies of another country hostile to his native country where the policies of the foreign country were aimed at Russia's destruction. It was precisely because Hitler was a declared enemy of Communism that so many Englishmen and Frenchmen were his staunch admirers. The same thing was true in reverse. British Communists in 1939–40 did all they could to sabotage the British war effort on the sole ground that the war that Britain was fighting was declared to be undesirable by the *Soviet* Government. It was, by contrast, solely because the *Soviet Union* became involved in the war against Germany in 1941 that this war was from that time onwards officially supported by the British Communists.

To this transcendence of national boundaries must be added quite another. It was the fear of war. The First World War had revealed clearly how horrible a thing was modern war; and it had taken place such a short time previously that very large numbers of men and women in the countries of Europe and the USA had had personal experience of it. They wanted no more of it. They feared it both for themselves and for their families; because the primitive air raids of the recent war had pointed the way to the wars of the future, when the tank and the bomb and the aeroplane, after 12 more years of intensive development, would have reached a point where it was generally supposed that they could blast into instant nothingness whole cities. H. G. Wells' tremendous film, 'The Shape Of Things To Come', was both a potent reflection of these widespread fears and also an awful projection of them; and the effect that it had on British public opinion was very great. Even sober British officials, working at their contingency plans, had no hesitation in basing these plans on an expected total of 10,000 dead per day from air raids alone.[8]

This dread of another war therefore exerted enormous influence on public opinion in the Western democracies and also on their governments. Hitler knew this. He therefore found himself possessed of a weapon which allowed him to cripple the will to resist on the part of his potential enemies.

The manner in which Hitler actually employed this weapon is therefore of enormous importance to us, because it proved so effective a means of hamstringing possible opposition to Nazi policies, and thus of allowing the Nazi leaders to attain their goals with minimal trouble, and without recourse to war, that hazardous undertaking. It was so effective that a modern Soviet defence planner, looking at the lessons of the politico-military history of the 1930s, must surely become attracted to it as a means for ensuring success.

Basically Hitler wielded this tool in three ways. Firstly, he used his propaganda machine to give an inflated impression of the value of the Wehrmacht. The British and French armed forces in 1936 were many times stronger than those of Hitler; and the latter's march into the Rhineland could have been prevented with the greatest of ease. Hitler's propaganda, however, convinced the French and the British public, as well as a very considerable number of their more senior officials and politicians, that the Nazi forces were much more powerful than in fact they actually were; and although the British and the French governments knew perfectly well that they could defeat Hitler, they felt that, in order to be sure of doing so, they would have to mobilize. Mobilization would have been highly unpopular with the French and the British voters, because of this fear of war we have just been mentioning. It was therefore decided to concede the Rhineland to the Germans, rather than resist.

The second method employed by Hitler for wielding this propaganda weapon was to demonstrate from time to time how horrible war could be. Thus, the destruction of Guernica in 1937 doubtless increased considerably the world's dislike of Nazism, and it also increased considerably its fear of the Nazi war machine. People were inclined to draw the inference that this was the sort of thing that happened to those so foolish as to resist Hitler: the wiser course would surely be to capitulate. A year later the British and the French governments capitulated at Munich.

Moreover, the Wehrmacht's methods of waging war contained

an element of deliberate terror which had a profoundly numbing effect on those who were exposed to it. Their very uniforms, the shape of their helmets, the precision and somewhat inhuman movements of their parade-ground drill and their marching, all widely publicized by means of the cinema newsreels, gave to foreigners an instinctive feeling that this was a mighty army and a formidable people whom it would be extremely foolish to seek to provoke, and just as well to conciliate.

When it came to fighting, much of the Nazi success was due to the terror the Wehrmacht deliberately set out to inculcate. The dive-bombers were not particularly effective at actually killing or wounding the enemy troops; on the other hand the noise they made when they dived down on their target (a noise which was deliberately created by means of specially constructed flaps on the aeroplanes' wings) had a horrifying effect upon those exposed to it; and until they had become accustomed to it and learned how to react to it, troops subjected to dive-bombing attacks were always liable either to cower in panic and do nothing, or else to desert their posts and run for their lives.

The six wars we are imagining to be the object of our Russian study demonstrate how, at the period at which they were fought, it was essential to fight a decisive battle against the enemy's main forces, if one hoped to be victorious in the war as a whole. Of course, in order to win the war, victory in battle had got to be combined with the seizure of the strategically important areas of the enemy's homeland, as was demonstrated in an earlier chapter; but at this point in the argument we are concerned with only the first of these two factors: the destruction of the enemy's forces.

The wars of Prussia/Germany show quite clearly the validity of the converse of this proposition; for where the enemy's main forces were *not* in fact destroyed or rendered impotent, Prussia/Germany ended by *losing* the war. Thus, neither in Denmark in 1848 nor on the Western Front in 1914 nor on the Eastern Front in 1941 were the enemy's main armies destroyed in battle. In 1848 there was no major battle of any kind; in 1914 there were important actions, in which the enemy forces suffered heavy casualties, but in which the Germans also suffered heavily. Consequently, when allowance has been made for this, it will be seen that the French, the Belgians and the British were no less

capable of resisting Germany at the end of September 1914 than
they had been at the beginning of August.

The same phenomenon is observable in 1941. The Red Army
unquestionably suffered enormous losses during the first few weeks
of the fighting; but these losses, however big, were simply never
big enough to knock Russia out of the war. Accurate figures for
Soviet casualties are very hard to come by; but it is generally
accepted that, in prisoners alone, something of the order of 3
million effectives were lost to the Soviet fighting strength by
December 1941. Losses in tanks, artillery and aircraft are also
known to have been heavy: a Soviet source admits that, merely on
the first day of the fighting, 1200 Soviet planes were destroyed.[9]
The fact remains, however, that Stalin's Russia, despite these
appalling casualties and tremendous losses, was still capable of
continuing to resist; and Hitler's forces therefore failed in their
aim.

The above is a description of what happened in those wars
which Prussia/Germany lost. By contrast, in those wars which
Prussia/Germany won, the main forces of the enemy were
invariably brought to battle, and invariably smashed. I use the
word 'smashed' advisedly. After Duppel , after Könniggrätz, after
Metz and Sedan, the main forces of the enemy, which had been
engaged in those four battles, were no longer capable of offering
any resistance; and if any obstacle subsequently impeded the
German march to victory (as it did *not* after Duppel or after
Könniggrätz, but as it *did* in 1870), the defeated armies played no
part in erecting it. We must therefore suppose that another lesson
that would be drawn by our imaginary defence planner is that the
enemy's main forces must not only be defeated but totally
liquidated. Only thus, it seems, can one ensure victory.

But if this is true, and if the liquidation of the enemy's main
forces is the chief objective for a would-be victor to aim at, a look
at the history of Prussia/Germany appears to show that an actual
battle is a risky means of doing this. However carefully one plans
one's battle, it is always possible to lose it; and in those wars which
are the object of our study the Germans frequently did so.
Furthermore, even their resounding successes (Duppel, Könniggrätz, Metz, Sedan and Tannenberg) were won rather as a
result of their enemy's incompetence than of their own military
brilliance. Admittedly, in these five battles there must be added
to the enemy's incompetence his marked inferiority in weapons

and equipment (Duppel and Königgrätz, in particular, were largely lost through this); but it is a poor way of ensuring victory to have to rely for success in war on the defects of one's opponents.[10]

A study of the wars of Prussia/Germany must surely therefore prompt the thought that the best way of liquidating the enemy's army is not to fight it at all. Instead one should aim at rendering it militarily impotent by swooping down on it before it has managed to deploy. Even better, naturally, would be to make one's swoop before it had even mobilized.

Admittedly, the wars of the nineteenth century appear to demonstrate that this is not really practicable. As we have seen in earlier chapters, all the Powers in the course of the nineteenth century tried very hard to accomplish it. In other words they tried to complete their mobilization, concentration and deployment faster than their enemy. Some partially succeeded, in the sense that some intending belligerents managed to complete their preparations for their war a day or two earlier than their future enemies succeeded in completing their counter-measures. None, however, managed to be sufficiently successful to allow him to invade his enemy's country and stop the latter from even starting his mobilization. This was as true of the middle of the nineteenth century, when all parties to an impending war did the bulk of their mobilization, concentration and deployment after the war had officially begun, as it was in 1914, for example, when all parties had more or less fully mobilized before hostilities started.

The march of progress moves onwards, however; and by the time that we get to the Second World War things had considerably altered. Hitler in Poland in 1939, Hitler again in Russia in 1941, and the Japanese in the Pacific in the December of that same year, all struck at their enemies with forces which were fully deployed at a time when the opposing forces were not even fully mobilized, and when their enemies' strategic deployment therefore had scarcely even begun. From this device the attackers derived enormous military advantages; because the defenders' capacity for resistance was obviously very much less than it could have been; and the speed with which Hitler beat the Poles, and the Japanese beat the Americans and the British, was largely due, say modern Soviet strategists, to this particualr circumstance.[11] Furthermore, these same commentators do not merely remark on the fact of the speed of the victory, but claim that the device which led to the speed was a notable step forward in the art of war.[12]

The lesson, therefore, to be learnt by our imaginary defence planner is that, in so far as it is possible to get a powerful army across the frontier and into the enemy's territory before he has completed his deployment, this is a marvellous method of winning a war. It is an even more marvellous method if the attacker's forces can be got into the enemy's territory before he has so much as mobilized. A commander with his forces caught off balance can hope to redress the issue; a commander with virtually no forces at all (because those forces have not been mobilized) is in a really hopeless position.

Highly desirable though it may be, however, to pre-empt the intended enemy's mobilization, the history of war appears to indicate that there is only one means of doing this: that is by the achievement of surprise. It need hardly be said that tactical surprise is quite insufficient for this purpose; strategic surprise is necessary.

By the expression 'strategic surprise' is meant the achieving of surprise at the strategic level; and by 'strategic level' is meant, or at least is meant when the Russians use the expression, 'from and including army group level upwards' ('army group' here being a translation of the Russian expression *front*).

Tactical surprise has often been achieved; strategic surprise, seldom. This is because the number of troops required for strategic operations is so enormous that it is virtually impossible to conceal their presence from the enemy. Strategic surprise has consequently only been attainable when the purpose for which the troops have been assembled has been managed to be disguised, and the intended enemy lulled into false security. How this was done in the Second World War has already been discussed above.

But the dissembling of the purpose for which the troops have been collected is only one of the ways in which strategic surprise can be accomplished. Their purpose may have been wholly and completely concealed, yet still strategic surprise may not be attained; because in the event the impending attack has been revealed to the enemy in other ways.

One way by which it might be revealed is by the attacker indulging in old-world courtesies and issuing a formal declaration of war. This need not necessarily give a great deal of notice, but at least it is bound to give some. That, no doubt, is why neither Hitler nor the Japanese issued any declarations of war at all, but simply struck like thunderbolts.

Another way by which this might happen is as a result of espionage. Enemy agents by one means or another may get a sight of the plan of the intended operation, and proceed to forewarn their Government. Thus, for instance, the German plan for a surprise attack on Belgium in 1940 fell into the hands of the British and French; and the Allies were forewarned as a result. As it so happened, however, this circumstance, which might have proved fatal to Hitler's plans, was rendered null by his General Staff's discovery of the leak, and the consequent switch of direction of the attack to the area of the Ardennes.

Despite this lucky chance, which retrieved the situation for the Germans, the general principle remains good that one's own intentions are capable of being discovered by enemy agents; and that therefore the question of security and of counter-intelligence must be of prime importance for the securing of strategic surprise. In this connection the matter of how many copies of one's various plans are produced and circulated is itself of the utmost significance. Hitler's staff are said to have produced twenty-one copies of Plan 'Weiss', nine copies of Directive No.21 (Plan 'Barbarossa'), and thirty copies of the directive for the strategic concentration and deployment rendered necessary by 'Barbarossa'. These numbers, in Soviet eyes, were a very great deal too high.[13]

According to Soviet writing, however, the real genius of both the German and Japanese High Commands lay in their ability to recognize that their basic hostile intention towards another country (that is to say, their intention to commit aggression) was almost bound to be detected; that strategic surprise in its fullest sense was therefore an impossibility; and that it was consequently absolutely essential for them to deceive their victim at least in respect of the place and time of the attack, and in respect, too, of the way in which the attack would be conducted. The various means by which such deception can be implemented are not really relevant to this present chapter. They are, however, discussed in Chapter 12.

Despite what has been said earlier, the achievement of surprise, even the achievement of strategic surprise, is not an end in itself. In order to win the war, other things are necessary than just catching one's opponent on the hop. Catching him on the hop can usually be relied upon to produce initial successes; but the intial successes thus produced have got to be exploited. This can only be done if the invading forces possess the cardinal military virtues of speed, manoeuvrability and weight of blow.

The wars of Prussia in the nineteenth century cease to be relevant at this point, because in none of them did Prussia manage to surprise her enemy strategically. Indeed, to be fair to Moltke, he did not even try to. He did not think it was possible; and, in view of the way in which war was waged in his time, he was probably right. Imperial Germany certainly surprised the French in 1914, but even then only in respect of the direction in which her main blow would be launched, not in respect of whether or not the blow would be launched at all.

It is therefore really to the Second World War that we must look for examples of strategic surprise that are relevant to this present section. Such examples are Hitler's campaign against Poland in 1939, his campaign in Western Europe of 1940, his campaign against Russia of 1941, and the Japanese campaigns in the Pacific of 1941–42. These examples show very clearly, however, that the attainment of surprise is not of itself sufficient. In order to achieve victory the surprise, when attained, has got to be properly exploited.

This is because surprise, of itself, does little. Surprise will neither destroy the enemy's armies nor occupy the 'key' to his country. It is human beings who must do these things; and strategic surprise can only provide them with the necessary pre-conditions. Of course, if they are seeking to win their war without any particualr time-limit, they are perfectly able to achieve their aim without gaining strategic surprise. This book, however, is focused on those countries which *are* constrained by a time-limit, which not only want to win their war quickly, but very quickly indeed, and which also want to be sure they are going to win it. For such countries the gaining of strategic surprise is, we have now decided, an indispensable necessity.

But we then return to our earlier assertion that strategic surprise *of itself* does very little to assist them to achieve their aim. All it can do is to offer them opportunities; and it then depends upon their generals, and upon those generals' troops, as to whether they take full advantage of these opportunities. Many famous generals, it is worth recalling, have signally failed to do so, even though furnished with splendid armies and magnificent equipment. For instance the Wehrmacht, as it existed in the summer of 1941, was one of the finest armies that this world has ever seen; yet although, when it invaded the USSR, it achieved strategic surprise, the record of history shows how dismally it failed to take proper advantage of it. In particular it failed to destroy the main forces of the Red Army within the time laid down for their destruction in Hitler's directives; and it also failed to seize those vital areas, those 'keys' to the country, possession of which was deemed by Hitler to be essential, if the USSR was to be stopped from recovering from its heavy initial losses and from continuing with the war.

Strategic surprise will make its greatest contribution in the first few hours of the war. After that, unless heavy and remorseless pressure is exerted upon the enemy without respite, the strategic surprise will begin to lose its effect. In other words, after the first few hours the enemy will start to recover from his surprise, unless he is heavily pressured; and in order to exert that heavy pressure, the initial successes must be fully and effectively exploited.[14]

A proper exploitation is only possible, if the invader's initial offensive is speedy and very weighty. Consequently, speed and weight of blow are two of the essential qualities for any aggressor.

In modern war, a third essential quality is mastery of the local air space; and there are a number of other qualities, such as a co-ordinated use of Fifth Columnists, which, though not absolutely essential, are nevertheless highly desirable. These various qualities, however, are going to be dealt with later; and at this present juncture we will therefore assume that the intending aggressor is already in possession of them; because that will allow us to confine ourselves to a consideration of weight of blow and speed of the offensive as a means of achieving a proper exploitation of the initial strategic surprise.

Unfortunately, 'speed' and 'weight of blow' are merely relative expressions, because what is 'speedy' to a tortoise is 'very slow' to a hare. In the military field this sort of relativity is easily detectable. In 1066, for example, King Harold of England marched his troops from York to London in 5 days; and the general opinion of military historians is that his troops moved very fast. Such a march, however, is as slow as the slowest tortoise when compared with the speed that could be expected of a modern motorized column. Guderian's *Panzers* in the summer of 1940, to take

another example, advanced to the Channel at an average speed
of about 49 km per day. This has always been reckoned to have
been very fast. Yet in the summer of 1941, when racing across
Russia, although their average speed in the initial period was
approximately what it had been in 1940, it is clear to any
impartial observer that it was not nearly fast enough. The 'key' to
the enemy's country, the area around the Urals, lay more than
2000 km ahead; therefore, in order to seize it within the
prescribed period, an average speed of about 100 km per day was
necessary. Guderian's *Panzers* consequently moved too slowly;
though the same speed, if attained in a campaign in Flanders,
would obviously have proved sufficient.

There is the further paradox that, although we have just
concluded that Guderian's troops were not sufficiently speedy, at
the same time we are bound to admit that they went far too fast
for the rest of the Nazi armies. These, the bulk of Hitler's forces,
consisted of the infantry divisions, the horse-drawn artillery and
so on: as we have seen already, they all moved very slowly. For
each kilometre they advanced, they lagged further behind the
armoured forces moving with what, by comparison with them,
was lightning speed, but which, by comparison with what was
required to fulfil the task allotted them, was a slow dawdle.

But if speed is thus revealed to be a highly subjective
expression, the same thing is also true of 'weight of blow'. The
forces amassed by Hitler to conquer Poland in 1939 are usually
reckoned to have hit the Poles a very weighty blow. Those forces,
according to Soviet sources, numbered 54 divisions with a total
complement of 1,300,000 men.[15] For the invasion of Russia in
1941 Hitler employed, again according to Soviet sources, 190
divisions (including those of his allies) with a total complement of
5,500,000 men,[16] or, in other words, about four times the size of
the force he had employed in Poland. It presumably therefore
delivered four times as weighty a blow; yet all military historians
agree that this blow was not weighty enough.

At first sight one is led to conclude that the weight of the blow,
in the sense of the number of divisions required by the attacker, is
a fairly simple function of the size of the enemy's forces. The
bigger the latter, the greater the number of divisions that the
aggressor needs. This, however, is far too facile a conclusion.
Although it is true that the size of the enemy's forces is an
important factor when it comes to determine what size of force

one needs oneself if the attack is to be weighty, nevertheless the size of the enemy's territory is a determinant at least of equal, and possibly of greater, significance.

This is because the bigger the country, the greater its chances of finding the means to recover from an initial strategic defeat, and continue with the war. After the defeat of Napoleon III at Sedan in 1870, for example, Gambetta made heroic efforts to form new armies that could take the field with a reasonable chance of success. Furthermore, he formed them; though they were all defeated. Nevertheless, as a consequences, until Paris had fallen, the Prussian position could never be reckoned secure. In the event, as we have seen, Gambetta failed; but it was the size of France that allowed the attempt to be so much as made. In the war in the Pacific in 1941 the huge distances separating Japan from her principal enemy's heartland in America were too great to be overcome even by the dazzling initial strategic successes which the Japanese unquestionably obtained. It was therefore possible for the United States to recover from Pearl Harbor and her other defeats, to amass in safety the resources required to continue the war, and then to proceed to do so and to defeat Japan. By contrast, it was not merely the inadequate military precautions taken by the Dutch Government prior to Hitler's invasion in 1940 that led to the speedy and total conquest of Holland, but also the comparatively scanty extent of her territory, which allowed the Nazis to get right through it and then turn round and envelop and absorb it, all in the course of a day or two. They thus rendered it impossible for the Dutch commanders to continue their resistance (except, of course, in exile, which is what they did).

Even this, however, does not answer our question completely; because still the question of what is a 'big', and what is a 'small', country remains unsolved. Or rather it remains a matter of opinion. Belgium must seem a big country in the eyes of San Marino: in the eyes of the Soviet Union she would appear tiny. Since this book is devoted to Soviet thinking it is the USSR's opinions which concern us; and the Soviet Union's views on the bigness and smallness of countries appear to be as follows: the USSR is a big country; the United States of America is a big country; various other countries, such as Canada, may be big territorially speaking, but since they are militarily feeble, they do not count. China, on the other hand, despite her present military weakness, probably *does* count. All other countries, in any case, appear to be reckoned small countries, with the possible exception of France.

I say 'with the possible exception of France'; because General Ivanov has an intriguing paragraph on the subject. On p. 350 of his *Nachal'nyi Period Voiny*, he says, speaking of the Second World War:

> When big States possessed of high military economic potential and broad territories ... embarked on war against the aggressor, the blitzkrieg totally failed, despite big strategic successes won by the aggressor in the opening period. However even for big States the results of the first massive blows were always grievous; and for some, for instance France, they were catastrophic.

To what extent this single paragraph, which is the only one with which I am acquainted that points in this particular direction, is to be taken as representative of the modern Soviet view of the matter, I do not pretend to know. I can do no more than draw attention to it, repeat that I know of no other like it, and leave my readers to draw their own conclusions. My own conclusions, for what they are worth, is that France may be reckoned a big country by some Russians; but that the only countries which *all* Russians unhesitatingly agree to be big countries are the United States of America and the USSR, and also presumably China.

We have thus reached a position where, if we have correctly calculated the USSR's opinion on the matter, the size of the forces necessary to deliver a weighty blow on the intended victim is a function both of the size of the victim's forces and of his territory. The smaller those forces and the smaller the size of his territory, the smaller the number of troops one needs for the attack. The larger the forces and territory, the greater the number of troops the invader must have.

On the other hand all the above, however academically intriguing, has got to be heavily qualified in respect of the USSR. This is because the Soviet Union believes it highly desirable to deliver as weighty a blow as possible on each and every occasion, and against any and every enemy. In Soviet thinking the concept of economy of effort has little place. Whereas to an Englishman the taking of a sledgehammer to crack a nut is a wrong decision and a sign of mental immaturity, to a Russian the opposite is the case. In Russian eyes the cracking of nuts is what sledgehammers are clearly designed for.

Furthermore, the history of the Soviet Armed Forces demonstrates unmistakably that Russian generals, when faced with nuts, instinctively reach for sledgehammers. The Soviet Army sledgehammered its way to victory in Georgia in 1921; it did it again in Finland in 1940; and it was surely by use of the sledgehammer that, in 1944–45, the Soviet advance through Eastern into Central Europe was chiefly accomplished.

In this respect, however, it should be remembered that in none of these operations was there any danger of any consequence from other points of the compass. In other words the USSR did not have to keep tied up along its frontiers a significant proportion of its armed forces to guard against other enemies. In 1939–40 the Soviet Far Eastern Army was certainly tied up in keeping watch over the Japanese; but in 1939–40 the forces available to Marshal Timoshenko formed a sufficiently big sledgehammer, by comparison with the Finnish forces, to make the retention in Manchuria of Marshal Zhukov's Far Eastern Army a matter of no importance.

This brings us back to the main point: the USSR packs as big a punch as it can; and it has not yet had to fight a war where it has been obliged to pull its punches. Nor, in the present condition of the Chinese forces, is a war against NATO likely to prove an exception. The forty or so divisions which it keeps on the Chinese frontier are fully sufficient, in the present circumstances, to repel a Chinese attack; while forty or so divisions, if subtracted from the total number of the Soviet Army's divisions, still leaves a sledgehammer of formidable size with which the Soviet commander-in-chief could have a crack at NATO.

Leaving aside the Soviet viewpoint, however, and returning to the lessons of history, these show that there is no one single, absolute, immutable figure determining the number of divisions and the quantity of equipment that are needed for a weighty blow. What has to be provided is enough men and material to smash the enemy's forces and to occupy his vital territory. What quantity this will be, must therefore depend considerably upon the latter's size, bearing in mind any possible reduction due to the 'key' to his country being near the frontier.

This is an important consideration in respect of a country like

France. France is much more 'chewable' than her actual size would lead us to expect; because her chief economic regions, upon which depends her military power, are horribly near those frontiers of hers across which, throughout so many tempestuous years, her principal foe has glowered at her. Once those regions have been seized by an invader, her sole chance of continuing the war is to buy abroad the requisite material and bring it in through her western ports. She could do this without difficulty in 1870; she could not do it for long in 1940; and it is highly unlikely in this missile age that she could ever do it again.

The same sort of thing is true of Communist China. The principal industrial region of China lies in the north. This area forms a huge salient, jutting upwards and outwards into Soviet and Soviet-controlled territory, so that the USSR and the Mongolian People's Republic surround it on three sides. This salient is obviously highly vulnerable, and was proved to be so in 1945, when the Russians attacked the Japanese there in the campaign which forms the subject of the next chapter.

However, although the loss of this territory would be a heavy blow for Peking, it is most improbable that it would be sufficiently heavy to topple the Chinese Government. The sort of war that is planned by China at present depends much less on sophisticated weapons, and therefore less on industrial output, than does that of more developed nations; and it would consequently be wrong at the present time to call this area the 'key' to China. But although this region is not at present absolutely vital for the existence of China, it nonetheless constitutes a pertinent example of how the location of an important area can reduce the value in strategic terms of the size of a country as a whole. In other words China, as she is today, can only be called a big country; however she would, strategically speaking, be a very much bigger country, if her most important industrial region were not militarily so exposed.

We thus find that a principal lesson of the 1939–45 period is that a war or campaign can only be won in its opening phase by first securing strategic surprise, and then by immediately exploiting that surprise effectively. The means for effective exploitation are speed and weight of blow. Both these terms are subjective expressions; and it is essential to relate them in every case to the size of the enemy's armed forces and the extent of his territory.

By the end of the Second World War much experience had been gained in the use of the latest military technology, especially tanks and aircraft, for the purpose of winning wars in their opening phases. None of the attempts had been successful; none of the wars had been won. On the other hand the aggressor nations had succeeded in winning in their initial periods three major campaigns; while a fourth, the most important (Hitler's campaign against Russia), had at an early stage in its development been none too far from success. What lessons, therefore, can be learnt from these defeats and victories that could be used by a future aggressor to ensure that he succeeded where Hitler failed?

The most important, obviously, is concerned with air power. It proved to be essential to secure command of the air, and to secure it right from the outset, if the attacking troops were to achieve their speedy victory. By contrast, when command of the relevant air space was held by the defender the attack was doomed. These were the two absolutes. Between them were to be found the varying degrees of air mastery, or the lack of it, which in turn dictated the extent to which the aggressor's mobile forces were in fact able to move. The history of 1939–45 shows very clearly that what is really wanted for full and unqualified success in any *Blitzkrieg* is complete strategic, operational and tactical air mastery. It is difficult to see how, even today, a war could be won in its initial period unless this prime condition, or something very like it, can be met.

The second lesson to be learnt from past experience is that it is not sufficient to win command of the air: this, once gained, has got to be exploited. If the aggressor's armies are going to be able to win their war very quickly they must be able to look to their air forces for help with the following tasks:

(1) Stopping the enemy air force from interfering with their movements. This should follow automatically, if command of the air has been won: nevertheless, it does not always do so. It is generally accepted that the Luftwaffe secured strategic command of the air right at the start of the attack on Russia. This, however, did not prevent the Soviet air force on very many occasions from acquiring *tactical* air mastery at important points on the battlefield, and thereby exerting an adverse influence on the conduct of 'Barbarossa'. Those who

doubt this should read with close attention the many passages in Guderian's *Panzer-Leader* (Michael Joseph, 1970) and also in Halder's diaries which testify to its truth. Nor are these by any means the only witnesses.

(2) The second task that must be imposed on one's own air force, after mastery of the air has been won, is the stopping of the enemy from bringing up reserves and from sending reinforcements to a threatened area.

(3) The provision of direct support to the advancing ground forces is the third of the air force's tasks. In the Nazi campaigns of 1940 and 1941 this support was usually given in the shape of immediate fire power. The Luftwaffe, in other words, acted as a kind of mobile artillery which was particularly valuable on the Eastern Front, where the lack of integral SP guns was so often felt very keenly by the Nazi armoured formations. The role of mobile artillery, of course, is not the only one which a modern air force could play in a *Blitzkrieg* of the 1980s; but the sort of roles that air could play today will be discussed later. Here, it is sufficient to make the point that, in the *Blitzkrieg* of the 1930s and 1940s, the general principle that the aggressor's air force, having first secured command of the air, should use that command to support his ground forces was one that was generally observed; and that when in fact it was not observed, the attack was greatly hindered.

It is sometimes argued that it is not invariably necessary for command of the air to be won by one's own forces: it is claimed that it is usually sufficient to deny that command to the enemy. This seems to me to be wrong. If this is the most that can be achieved the planned operation is most unlikely to be more than marginally successful; and wars are not won in their opening phase as a result of marginal successes. What is needed is that the aggressor should reap the maximum possible advantage of whatever tactical successes his forces may have won. To use the Russian, and for that matter the German, expression, tactical success must be converted into operational and strategic success; but this involves rapid and bold manoeuvre, and also relentless pursuit. Neither bold manoeuvre nor relentless pursuit can be expected by any commander, unless the skies above him are filled with his own planes.

In appropriate circumstances local command of the sea may

also be necessary for the success of certain operations; but the whole history of the Second World War demonstrates in addition that sea mastery is not attainable without prior command of at least the local air space. On this point Soviet strategists are in agreement with Western strategists.

The growth of air power in the twentieth century provided the means, in the Second World War, for useful operations to be undertaken by the various airborne forces. In 1940 in the Low Countries, selective parachute drops were extremely valuable in helping the Wehrmacht to conquer Belgium and Holland; and although the Soviet attempts at this kind of operation on the Eastern Front can scarcely be considered successful, this was largely because, as the Russians point out, the USSR at that time did not have suitable aircraft. On the other hand they had no doubts whatsoever as to the value and desirability of the operational concept, supposing that they could have implemented it.

The introduction of helicopters into modern armies, and the consequent development of the heli-borne landing, were further innovations in military practice which have been much appreciated by the Russians. However their significance will be assessed in Chapter 10.

Although the full flower of airborne operations has bloomed since the end of the Second World War, General Ivanov is highly appreciative of what the Germans managed to achieve with them in the course of the war in question.[17] He thought they were particularly good when dropped in the immediate rear of the enemy when one's own troops were attacking; though they did really need air support, and often air supply. In Ivanov's view they proved to be tremendously effective at disrupting the deployment of the enemy's main forces; because by their disruption they forced a change of deployment plan on the enemy commanders. Such a change, in Ivanov's view, inevitably led either to a total failure by the enemy to deploy at all; or else it led to partial and inapposite deployment, with the result that the enemy had to fight his battle at a considerable disadvantage.

A further lesson learnt from the Second World War, at any rate by General Ivanov, was that where the terrain was unsuitable for tanks (as it was, for instance, in Holland), airborne landings under favourable conditions could be used as an effective substitute. That is to say that whereas, for example, the German victories in France in 1940 were won by an armoured *Blitzkrieg*, it was the mass use of paratroops that gave them victory over the Dutch.

The next point to be noted is that during the course of the period under study the importance of what may be broadly termed 'Fifth Column activities' increased considerably. In the Franco-Prussian war the *franc-tireurs* were a considerable nuisance to the German armies, though it cannot be said that they were sufficient of a nuisance to affect the outcome of any of the German operations. In the First World War they proved to be considerably less effective than had been intended and foreseen by many; on the other hand, in the Second World War their importance rapidly grew, Hitler's invasion of Norway, for instance, is an excellent example of the help that can be given to an invading force by citizens of the invaded country who are sympathetic to it; and the wars that have taken place since 1945 have rammed this lesson home. Since the Soviet Union has ready-made a considerable number of bodies of potential Fifth Columnists, in the shape of those Communist parties of Third World and Western countries which are not by nature Maoist, we must expect this point to be fully appreciated by our imaginary Soviet defence planner.

The Russians have also noted that in those wars of our period which were won, and also won very quickly, sufficient ammunition had been pre-stocked to last through the whole war. This was true of the Prusso-Danish War of 1864; it was also true of the Austro-Prussian War of 1866; and it was nearly true of the Franco-Prussian War. It also surely must have been true of the Soviet campaign in Manchuria of 1945, if we are to judge by what we are told in Soviet sources concerning the amount of ammunition transported to the Far East before the war began (3¼ million shells and 410 million rounds of small-arms ammunition between 1 December 1944 and 31 March 1945 alone), and compare it with what we know or can deduce concerning Soviet ammunition expenditures during that campaign.

The advantage to the attacker does not really lie in the benefit deriving from actually having the ammunition already manufactured, so much as in the extremely serious disadvantage that may arise if the ammunition is *not* pre-stocked. This disadvantage is inherent in the fact that, if enough ammunition to last the whole war is not available before the war breaks out, the tempo of advance of the attacking force may be slowed down through the lack of it. Once this happens the whole character of the war may change; and what once started as a mobile war may quickly become positional. This is obviously fatal for a *Blitzkrieg*. One consequence of this change is that the types of ammunition which were planned for use in the original mode of warfare are often no longer suitable for the new conditions. Therefore it is not merely a question of manufacturing more ammunition, but of changing the jigs in the ordnance factories to produce new types of shell. The First World War is a splendid example of this state of things, because there, by the time that the 'race for the sea' had been completed, all the armies on the Western Front had tons and tons of shrapnel, which was excellent for mobile warfare but not for positional. They were, however, vilely short of the high explosive (HE) shell that was required for the war of the trenches.

Another lesson that we should learn from history concerning the waging of *Blitzkriegs* is that an accurate forecast of loss rates is never possible. The Nazis ended their campaign in France and the Low Countries with far fewer losses of men and equipment than they had ever expected; on the other hand, in the USSR their casualties exceeded their expected rates by a fatally wide margin. In 1940, on the one hand, their error in forecasting merely meant that their victory was that much easier; on the other hand, in 1941 their error cost them the war.

The conclusion to be drawn from this particular lesson is that the numbers of men and weapons and equipment that should be made available for the intended *Blitzkrieg* must be far higher than those theoretically arrived at during the preliminary planning sessions. Listen to the figures that your planner gives you, and immediately double them. Double them again for safety's sake, and add 20 per cent for luck. In the case of ammunition, add at least 50 per cent on top of that – the Yom Kippur War has provided us with a new perspective on ammunition expenditures. This approach is likely to prove fruitful.

It may be that, in the upshot, these vast accumulations of men and munitions will prove to be unnecessary, and that the war will be won with minimal loss, as was Hitler's war in Poland. That does not matter. If one sets out deliberately to start a war, the important thing is to win it. The collapse of the Reich in 1945 is the clearest indication one could hope to have of the fate that befalls cold-blooded aggressors who end up by being defeated.

The next lesson that should be drawn by a would-be attacker from the various attempts at *Blitzkreig* in the Second World War is that the attacking force must be all of a piece in respect of doctrine, training and equipment. Hitler's Wehrmacht was not. In 1940 this was of no importance, because neither in France nor in Norway in 1940 was the *Schwerpunkt* of the Nazi attack confronted with serious resistance. In 1941 the resistance was stout; and, in addition, the tremendous distances imposed their own sort of resistance to Hitler's forces. Consequently we may say that, on the Eastern Front, it proved to be a serious mistake that only a part of the Nazi forces were equipped and trained for a *Blitzkrieg*, while the rest were trained for traditional war only, and had only traditional weapons. Nor must it be inferred that this particular error was the fault of Hitler or Keitel or Halder or von Brauchitsch. Guderian himself had gone on record as saying that, so long as the armoured formations were properly equipped and trained for their particular function, there was no need for the rest of the army to be motorized.[18]

This view was wrong. Whether, of course, it would ever have been possible for German industry to have provided the material for a fully motorized army of 180 divisions is more than doubtful. What we learn from history, however, is that until this condition could be fully met the Nazi leaders had no business in ordering an attack on Russia.

The error was further compounded by the lack of a unified doctrine of *Blitzkrieg* at the highest levels of the Wehrmacht. Hitler concentrated on the psychological side; Guderian concentated on the armoured *Schwerpunkt*; while other senior Nazi, generals such as Keitel, von Brauchitsch and Halder failed to concentrate on any aspect, for the simple reason that none of them had ever really studied the *Blitzkreig* and did not know what it meant. There was thus introduced into 'Barbarossa' a muddled direction at the highest levels which is most unlikely to be found in, for instance, the Soviet Army of today.

History also teaches us that there is a need for accurate intelligence – accurate intelligence about everything. The size of the enemy's forces, the nature of his reserves, his roads and railways and the lack of them, details of his topography, the morale of his civil population, and so forth and so on. The list is endless. But what is important above all else is accuracy. Better to admit to a total lack of knowledge about a particular subject (the effectiveness of the enemy's tank guns, for example) than to posit data which turn out to be wrong. For plans based upon faulty data are themselves bound to be faulty; and such are the complexities of modern war that a *Blitzkrieg* based on a faulty plan is almost bound to fail. It really is no longer possible for the local commander to remedy on the spot errors which have been programmed into the heart of the operation. It was not even possible as long ago as 1941; and that was not the least of the causes of the failure of 'Barbarossa'.

The next lesson to be learnt concerning *Blitzkriegs* is the importance of supply. If supply falters the *Blitzkrieg* falters too; and against a determined and competent enemy a faltering *Blitzkreig* is highly likely to fail. The problems of supply are obviously legion; but two points concerning it emerge from the Second World War. The first is that if the territory of the intended enemy is small it may be possible by careful and intelligent pre-stocking to avoid the worst of the supply problems altogether. By contrast, if the enemy territory is large no such solution is possible; and the task of maintaining the tempo of the advance becomes logistically very formidable.

The second point is that the logistician's problems, of whatever kind they may be, will be greatly eased if the weapons and equipment of the forces he serves are standardized. Hitler's 2000 separate *types* of motor-vehicle are logistic nonsense. A wise war-lord, planning the *Blitzkrieg* of the future, will reduce the number of types of weapons and equipment to the minimum consonant with efficiency.

Next, the enemy whose country is to be attacked and conquered must be 'chewable'. We have referred earlier to the concept of 'chewability'. We defined it as a combination of the size and quality of the enemy's troops, the quantity and quality of their weapons and equipment, and the size of that portion of his territory which is of economic significance. Poland and Western Europe were proved to be 'chewable' by Nazi Germany; the USSR was not. Nor was the USA by Imperial Japan. In the modern world the question is not what territory is 'chewable' by Germany or Japan, but what is to be regarded as 'chewable' by the Soviet Union. In the final chapter we shall try to establish which territories those are. It is a fair guess that, at any rate, they include Western Europe.

The final lesson from the wars of our period that is likely to be assimilated by the Soviet military is that the most notable successes of the Wehrmacht in respect of winning campaigns in their initial period all stemmed from a consistent and effective formula. This formula consisted of using all available men and materials for a very heavy initial blow, delivered along a limited number of carefully selected axes. In Hitler's attack on France in 1940, for instance, the armies assigned to the critical sector, that of the Ardennes, were all drawn up in one single echelon, with no army as second echelon, and only a small reserve. Thereby, the weight of the initial blow against the French 2nd and 9th Armies was rendered the maximum possible.

This in turn permitted the Germans to hit their enemy over the whole depth of his operational positions; while at the same time they employed the Luftwaffe for delivering powerful strikes at his principal rear installations. Consequently, the crucial sectors of the enemy's war potential (his armies, his airfields, his ports, his factories, and so on) were all being hammered simultaneously right at the very outset of the campaign. A major advantage to be derived from this procedure was that the enemy's troops in the forward areas could not be transferred from one sector to another to parry a new threat, nor could his reserves in the rear areas be brought forward to reinforce those who were under heavy pressure, nor could the men at the front be re-supplied. When this procedure worked well, as it did in Poland, as it did in France, and as it did in the first few weeks in Russia, German success was virtually assured; but in order to be able to implement it the Nazis needed previously unheard-of quantities of 'planes and tanks.

According to General Ivanov's analysis from which the above is taken, the Germans' operational objectives were to achieve 'the destruction of the main groupings of the enemy's armed forces and the seizure of his economic and administrative political centres and territories'.[19] Their preferred method of destroying the enemy's forces was by encirclement, as a preliminary to their total destruction.[20] Usually, the German encirclement operations were preceded by others designed to cut up and shatter the enemy's strategic front; while the encirclement itself was accomplished either by means of the double envelopment, or by the cutting off of the resisting enemy groupings and the squeezing of them up against the sea or some other natural obstacle.[21]

The success of this German formula was rendered even more probable by a skilful use by the Wehrmacht of two other tools, both of which are given considerable prominence by Soviet writers. These are the use of airborne landings and the Fifth Column.[22]

With regard to the former, Ivanov writes that they helped considerably in 1940 to ensure the success of the Nazi seaborne landings in Denmark and Norway. These airborne landings, however, were only at tactical level. On a much larger scale were those in Belgium and Holland, which resulted in, among other things, the seizure of bridges across the rivers Maas, Waal and the Lower Rhine, the capture of the vital fort of Eben-Email, the occupation of a number of airfields, and the prevention of the creation of a firm defence by the Dutch Army at the eastern and southern approaches to the Hague.

Airborne landings, General Ivanov concludes, proved very valuable. When used in co-operation with other arms they could dislocate the enemy's strategic deployment, disorganize his defence, sow panic among his civil population and even among his troops, and help their own ground forces to maintain a high tempo of advance. They could also be used most successfully in the pursuit of a beaten enemy, especially if they were to be dropped across the path of his retreat. It was best not to use them on their own, but in co-operation with the ground forces; and then they could play a most effective part in the destruction of the retreating foe.

The 'Fifth Column' was also a useful tool in the hands of the Nazis. Its core was the German ethnic minorities in the countries Hitler intended to attack. There were about 3000 such people in Poland; 2000 in Denmark; and a further 3000 in Holland. In addition, there were natives of these and other countries who were Nazi sympathizers, though in no way ethnic Germans. The whole 'Fifth Column' in each country was controlled by Nazi agents.[23]

In the opening phase of each campaign these persons had considerable success in removing obstacles placed by the defending forces in the path of the advancing Germans, in preventing the blowing up of bridges, in destroying important telephone lines (and even sometimes railway lines) that were needed by their own country's armies, and in spreading panic among the civil population by circulating false rumours. It is worth remembering that

Guderian's advance through the Ardennes was considerably facilitated in its first few hours by the activities of such people; and one of the lessons to be learnt from the period we are studying is how much harm they can do. A well-co-ordinated war plan by an intending aggressor who was intent on winning in the 'initial period' would certainly try to capitalize on any available 'Fifth Column'; and if no precautions against it were to be taken by his prospective victim, the latter's chances of survival would be reduced significantly. This is another lesson that the Russians have learnt.

Finally, mention must be made of something which General Ivanov does *not* mention, and that is the use by an aggressor of enemy nationals wearing enemy uniform. In 1941, for instance, Nazi Germany used ethnic Russians speaking Russian as their mother tongue and organized in units wearing Soviet uniform. These units captured at least one important bridge in the early days of the war by marching up to it and pretending to the guards that they were Red Army soldiers retreating from the advancing Germans. They were allowed across; and when they were across, they attacked and killed the guards.[24]

NOTES AND REFERENCES

1. The Prusso-Danish War of 1864 was punctuated by two periods of truce. The figure given for the length of the war refers to the actual fighting.
2. We are here talking about the winning of wars by countries which *need* to be victorious quickly, as Prussia/Germany has always done. There are, of course countries, such as traditionally Britain, which *need* their wars to be long, if they are to win. Such countries and their war-making are not discussed in this book.
3. Bismarck, *Reflections and Reminiscences*, vol. 2, p. 10 (Smith, Elder, 1898).
4. Barry A. Leach, *German Strategy Against Russia, 1939–41* (Clarendon Press, 1973).
5. See, for instance, V. A. Anfilov, *Proval 'Blitzkriga'* (Nauka, 1974) pp. 33–4.
6. Marshal V. D. Sokolovskii, *Voennaya Strategiya* (2nd edn) (Voenizdat, 1963) pp. 23–36.
7. *Marksizm–Leninizm o Voine i Armii* (Voenizdat, 1968) 5th edn, pp. 10–26. The US Air Force have produced a version in English, entitled *Marxism–Leninism on War and Army* (*sic*), available from the US Government Printing Office.
8. Richard M. Titmuss, *Problems of Social Policy*, in the *History of the Second World War* series (HMSO, 1950).
9. *50 Let Vooruzhennykh Sil SSR* (Voenizdat, 1968) p. 259.

10. For the defects of the Danish weapons, see the account given by a German staff officer who was present, Col R. Neumann, in his *Rapport sur l'Attaque des Retranchements de Duppel du 15 Mars au 18 Avril 1864*. This French version of his German original was translated by E. Heydt, and published in Paris in 1865 by J. Corréad.
11. See, for instance, S. P. Ivanov, *Nachal'nyi Period Voiny* (Voenizdat, 1974) ch. 9.
12. Ibid., pp. 14 and 142.
13. Ibid., p. 167.
14. For a Soviet exposition of this point, see Col-Gen V. S. Popov, *Vnezapnost' i Nieozhidannost' v Istorii Voin* (Voenizdat, 1955, pp. 10–11).
15. Ivanov, op. cit., p. 222.
16. *Istoriya Vtoroi Mirovoi Voiny; 1939–1945* (Voenizdat, 1974) vol. 4, p. 21.
17. Ivanov, op. cit., p. 233.
18. *US Infantry Jownal*, 1937 (p. 516).
19. Ivanov, p. 219.
20. Ibid., p. 225.
21. Ibid.
22. Ivanov has a section on each (pp. 233–4 and 235–6 respectively).
23. Ibid., p. 235.
24. See, for instance, Albert Seaton, *The Russo-German War 1941–45* (Arthur Barker, 1971) p. 103.

9 Soviet practice, having absorbed these lessons: the Manchurian Campaign of 1945

The campaign in Manchuria is an excellent example of the way in which the Soviet Armed Forces like to start their wars. Firstly, they chose an enemy and a theatre of war that were 'chewable'. Their enemy was Japan; and, according to their own account of the matter, they outnumbered their intended enemy by approximately 1.2 : 1 in men, 4.8 : 1 in tanks and SP guns, 4.8 : 1 in artillery and 2.5 : 1 in aircraft.[1] These are overall figures. As will be seen later, much higher ratios of superiority were obtained by the Soviet Armed Forces at the crucial points of attack.

So far as the theatre of war was concerned, this was certainly a large area, totalling approximately 1,300,000 sq. km according to Soviet sources,[2] which is somewhat larger than the territories of France, Belgium, Holland, Luxembourg, West Germany, Denmark and Italy put together. From the point of view of the size of the enemy's territory, therefore, the Far Eastern theatre of operations was markedly less 'chewable' than was that of Western Europe which Hitler so successfully conquered in the summer of 1940.

However, this comparison of territory is not nearly so simple as it sounds. The total width of Manchuria is indeed of the order of 1200 km, as Marshal Zakharov says:[3] and if the Russians had been advancing straight across it, in the way that the Wehrmacht advanced through France, it is obviously 1200 km that the Red Army would have been obliged to cover. In fact, however, one of their *fronts* (army groups) started from Manchuria's western frontiers, another from its eastern; and the two met in the middle in the area of Changchun and Girin. As a result, neither *front* had to advance for more than 800 km, which made things a great deal easier for them, and made the whole theatre thoroughly 'chewable' from the geographical point of view.

The next concern of the Russians was to secure strategic surprise. In this they succeeded completely. They secured it not only at the strategic, but also at the operational and tactical levels; and it was of the very greatest benefit to them.

It was not, of course, really possible for them to secure a total surprise, and make the Japanese believe that they would not attack them at all. Once the war with Germany was coming to its end, and once the Japanese forces were slowly, but inexorably, losing in the Pacific, a Soviet entry into the war against them must obviously have been regarded as probable. So that all that the Russians could hope to achieve was to mislead their intended enemy with respect to the date, the time and the place of the attack.

These things, however, they succeeded in doing brilliantly. For a long time after the Stavka, the supreme war-fighting organ of the Soviet Armed Forces, had taken the decision to begin their war in the summer or autumn of 1945, the Japanese continued to believe that the USSR could not possibly attack them until some time in 1946. Even when they had corrected their error, they still believed that a Soviet attack could not possibly be made on them before September 1945, at the earliest.[4] As we all know, however, the attack was launched in August of that year.

Furthermore, it was not merely with regard to date and time that the Soviet leaders deceived the Japanese; they did it also with regard to the place at which the main attack would be delivered. Wherever the Japanese General Staff expected the Soviet main blow to fall, they certainly did not expect it to come across the Great Khingan Mountains.

How did the Russians succeed so well with their deceptions? We will begin our answer by investigating their method of deceiving with regard to date. The Soviet opening gambit was to denounce the non-aggression treaty which the USSR had signed with Japan in April 1941. This treaty carried the provision that, although its duration was only for 5 years, it would be renewed automatically unless either party gave formal notice, a year before the expiry date, that it was not going to renew it. On 5 April 1945 the Soviet Union gave that formal notice. It is hard to see why. Presumably, either the Russians believed that their action would so alarm the

Japanese Government that it would see it no longer could avert defeat, and so would seek an armistice; or else they followed their extraordinary bent of being legalistic, even under circumstances where legalism can have no effect on the outcome of an issue whatever. This is a common trait of Soviet officialdom. What is obvious, however, is that this opening gambit of the Russians must have reduced to some extent the overall likelihood of their gaining strategic surprise; and I do not count it as one of their methods of doing so. I include it merely for the record, for the sake of completeness.

There was, however, one positive step which was taken by the Soviet Foreign Office for the purpose of deceiving the Japanese with regard to the date of the attack; and that was by refraining from issuing a formal declaration of war until after the war had started. Legalistically speaking, this statement is not quite true. The Russians started military operations at 10 minutes after midnight, 9 August 1945, and at 5 p.m. on 8 August Molotov told the Japanese Ambassador in Moscow that a state of war existed between their two countries. Consequently, some small advance warning does appear to have been given. However, it must be remembered that 5 p.m. Moscow time represented 11 p.m. Tokyo time, so that the actual amount of the warning is reduced to some 70 minutes. Even that amount of warning, however, was never actually received by the Mikado's Government; because although Molotov promised the Japanese Ambassador that he would personally undertake the transmission of a message to Tokyo, he did not do so. Or if he did, it was certainly never received there. The insistence on issuing a declaration of war that in practice was totally meaningless is an interesting example of that Soviet passion for legalism to which I have referred earlier.

To turn from the diplomatic to the more mundane military level, it needs to be said that the Stavka planned to use over 1½ million men in their war in Manchuria. Since there was nothing like that number of soldiers already deployed in the Soviet Far East, and most of those had had no actual battle experience, it follows that very large numbers of troops had got to be transferred from Europe. Of these, the whole of one army, 5th Army, together with a large number of independent tank, artillery, air, engineer and other units and formations, were destined for Primore, the strip of Soviet territory which lies between the Sea of Japan and the frontier with Manchuria. The prime means of transport was the railway system. The railway that had to carry the troops who were to be deployed in that area runs very close to the frontier, so close indeed that the Japanese could easily observe them. This circumstance alone ensured that an attempt to deceive the Japanese into believing that the Soviet Armed Forces were not intending to attack them was doomed to failure.[5] Even so, the attempt was actually made. The troops, on arrival, built defence works; and the local Japanese commander was invited to swallow the notion that the purpose of sending these big reinforcements was defensive, not offensive. They were there, he was to suppose, to protect the Primore area from an attack by the Japanese.[6] As a further attempt to mislead Japanese Intelligence, Marshal Meretskov, the *front* commander in this area, forbade his troops to be quartered in inhabited localities or to have any contact whatever with the local population, and, in addition, insisted that all troop movements should be done during the hours of darkness.[7] In the same vein, Trans-Baikal Front, during the final stages of its approach march from Mongolia, always moved by night; while during the day its units and formations concealed themselves from Japanese reconnaissance by hiding themselves in trenches, which were appropriately camouflaged.

Nevertheless, neither these nor any other measures, however carefully undertaken, were likely to persuade the Japanese that no attack was impending. What needed to be done, therefore, was to deceive them in respect of its date, its time and its place. With regard to the first of these requirements, the Soviet choice of August as the month for starting their war was particularly valuable. August in Manchuria is the month of rains. During that month, therefore, movement becomes very difficult: in particular the earth-track roads turn into treacherous quagmires. Consequently it might be regarded as a working hypothesis that it would be a bad month for tanks and trucks to be covering very long distances. It was certainly taken as their working hypothesis by Japanese Intelligence who, as time went by and the extent of the Soviet build-up started to become apparent, revised their estimate of 1946 as the earliest date for a Russian attack, and instead forecast the autumn of 1945, with their preference going to September.[8] They rejected August precisely because of the rains. Hence this helped the Russians to secure strategic surprise when they struck in August.

It ought to be said, however, that it is most unlikely that the

procurement of strategic surprise for the Soviet offensive was the
sole reason for the choice of August as the month in which to
commence it. The need to launch it as soon as possible in order to
forestall the Americans was almost certainly the primary motive;
while the surprise obtained by attacking in August was probably
regarded as little more than a welcome and additional bonus. In
this connection it is worth noting that the weather was not what
had been expected on all three Soviet *fronts*. 6th Guards Tank
Army, for instance, attacked in blazing sunshine and were sorely
tried by the heat.[9] It was not until several days later than this
formation reached an area where the seasonal rains were falling
and the floods were out. In the case of 6th Guards Tank Army,
therefore, it is highly probable that it was not the weather but the
choice of terrain, that singularly inhospitable, difficult terrain
across which this army chose to advance, that secured strategic
surprise. But we shall come to terrain later.

The choice of August was supplemented by a number of other
measures. No aerial reconnaissance of Japanese positions was
allowed,[10] nor was that form of ground reconnaissance so much
beloved of the Russians, the reconnaissance in force (*razvedka
boem*).[11] Officers' reconnaissance was permitted, provided it
stayed on the Soviet side of the frontier, though even then the
officers had to wear private soldiers' uniforms and to practise
camouflage.[12] Naturally, this led to the information regarding the
enemy which was available to the Soviet generals being of rather a
low quality; indeed 5th Army was so ill-informed about the
precise location of the enemy's defences that it renounced the
heavy artillery bombardment that traditionally precedes an
attack, for the simple reason that it had no proper notion of
where its targets were. General Krylov congratulates himself on
having at least secured some compensation, in that the absence of
a preliminary bombardment naturally favoured surprise.[13]

Although it is obvious that the renouncement of preliminary
artillery bombardments increases the chance of surprise, it is
clear from this and other examples that it was not only the
question of surprise that determined whether or not to resort to
them. In view of what I have said earlier about the enormous
importance the Soviet Armed Forces attach to securing surprise,
this may seem odd; but there are in fact a number of counter-
vailing factors.

One is that Soviet preliminary bombardments are almost

always heavy and very short. Thirty minutes is a favourite duration. Because they are heavy, the defenders are likely to be stunned; so that although they may realize that the bombardment means that an attack is in the offing, they will probably be unable to take any effective action. They will thus be in the same state as if they had been totally surprised. If all goes well, therefore, the Soviet commander will be in the happy position of having achieved a considerable degree of destruction of the enemy's defences and also the surprise he wanted.

The second is this business of destruction. If the enemy has constructed heavily defended positions, the attacking forces must obviously wish to weaken them before the offensive starts. Despite examples to the contrary, surprise is usually not of itself sufficient to allow the attackers to capture fortifications of this nature, if they have not been weakened by preliminary shelling and bombing. It is for this reason, therefore, that 2nd Far Eastern Front renounced all hope of achieving surprise and concentrated instead on destroying the Japanese defences on the far side of the Amur River before their attack commenced. By contrast, Trans-Baikal Front, which was attacking across terrain where there were no fixed Japanese defences, opted for surprise and renounced a preliminary bombardment.

But the whole of Trans-Baikal Front did not conform to this practice. That was because 36th Army, one of the armies belonging to this *front*, was confronted by a different set of circumstances. 36th Army's job was to attack Hailar; and in front of Hailar the Japanese, for reasons we shall come to in a moment, had constructed fairly powerful defensive positions. 36th Army, therefore, unlike the rest of its *front*, renounced surprise and opted for bombardment instead.

Measures to surprise the Japanese with regard to the date of the impending attack went so far as to involve the civilian population. This was particularly true of those areas that were near enough to the Japanese positions to be subject to visual observation. Consequently, the civilian population was not moved out of those areas, and the peacetime garrisons of the frontier zones carried on with their normal duties. The haymaking was done as usual.[14] In North Sakhalin, which was particularly liable to penetration by Japanese intelligence, the Soviet soldiers were allowed on leave to local leave centres right up to the night before the war began.[15] Here too the building of defensive works in positions where the

Japanese could see them was continued with great vigour right up to the 'off'.[16]

So much for deception with regard to date. As far as the time of the attack was concerned, the Russians stuck to the hour of their traditional preference. Whereas, for instance, the German Army has usually liked to attack about an hour before dawn, the Soviet Army, on the other hand, has preferred just after midnight. This means that their troops are obliged to operate for quite a long time in darkness; but they think that, despite the difficulties that this causes them, they gain on balance as a result of the confusion into which the enemy will have been thrown. In the case of the Manchurian Campaign, however, this particular factor was not operative in respect of 6th Guards Tank Army, for the simple reason that this army was advancing across empty desert at the time in question. On the other hand, in Primore 5th Army was directly engaged with the enemy only a very short time after midnight; and because it was round about midmight, because it was raining heavily, and because in any case a Soviet attack was not expected on the date in question, the Japanese soldiers in the forward lines were caught asleep in their beds.[17]

With regard to place, here deception was practised only by the Trans-Baikal Front. The other two *fronts* delivered their attacks more or less where expected; but their role was subsidiary. The main blow was to come from the west; and the main axis of this western attack ran across desert and mountain. A better appreciation of the difficulties will be gained from a look at the map. It will be seen that, with one exception, the whole first echelon of Trans-Baikal Front struck across difficult country. Indeed, the Japanese Headquarters regarded it as impassable for any large numbers of troops. They did not believe that an attack on them, except on a very minor scale, could be launched through the Great Khinghan.[18] They certainly did not imagine that any offensive was possible, the spearhead of which alone would consist of two mechanized corps, one tank corps, two motor-rifle divisions, two brigades of self-propelled artillery and four independent tank battalions.

Impressive though this deception was, it was not considered sufficient. The Japanese had clearly been expecting the main weight of the Soviet western offensive to fall upon Hailar. This ancient city lies on the traditional route from Mongolia into China. The approach to it runs through an easily traversible

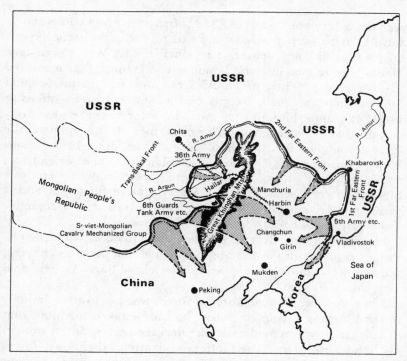

Soviet attack on Manchuria, 1945

valley; there is a good road, a railway and a river. All in all, it was
the route which, in the view of the Japanese High Command, any
self-respecting Soviet general would naturally wish to take. This
route therefore was heavily guarded by the Japanese who, before
the war broke out, had spent much time and effort in con-
structing permanent defences for its protection. If, then, the war
were to begin and no Soviet general with his attendant troops
were to advance upon Hailar, the Japanese would naturally begin
to wonder what was happening. And they might even take steps to
reconnoitre unlikely places (such as, for instance, the Khinghan
mountains) to see if it was by that route, however improbable it
must naturally seem, that the Soviet troops were coming. Such an
act by the Japanese would ruin the Russian plan, so they had to
be stopped from committing it; and by far the best way of
stopping them was to deliver the heavy attack on Hailar that the
Japanese were expecting. So one whole army, 36th Army, was
detailed off by Marshal Malinovsky to advance upon Hailar. It

was not a very good army. It had a first-rate army commander, but its troops were mostly second category with no battle experience. This did not matter. Its principal task was not to take Hailar, but to convince the Japanese commander that it *wanted* to take Hailar. Then he would feel confirmed in his original opinion that the main weight of the Soviet western offensive would fall upon him and his men. In order to make absolutely certain that he would indeed be confirmed in this opinion, the force despatched to attack him had got to be large. In fact, 36th Army consisted of 7 infantry divisions, 1 tank brigade, a considerable quantity of artillery and rocket launchers and one brigade of engineers. This was a pretty powerful force; and it turned out to be big enough to confirm the Japanese commander in his erroneous belief.

Having achieved surprise, the next thing to do was to exploit it. Proper exploitation, as has been explained in a previous chapter, requires a combination of speed and weight of blow. We will deal with the latter first.

Since the overall correlation of forces was not overwhelmingly in the Russians' favour, measures had to be taken to ensure that this situation was remedied at the decisive points. Soviet sources say that, just before their offensive started, their own forces consisted of 1,577,725 men, 5556 tanks and SP guns, 26,137 guns and mortars and 3446 combat aircraft;[19] while the Japanese had 881,000 men, 1115 tanks and SP guns, 5000 guns and 1800 aircraft.[20] This gives a ratio in favour of the Russians to the tune of roughly 1.8 : 1 in men, 4.8 : 1 in tanks and SP guns, 5.2 : 1 in guns and 1.9 : 1 in aircraft.[21]

Such ratios are useful, but hardly overwhelming. It therefore became the duty of the Soviet commanders to construct ratios that should prove overwhelming at the points where this was necessary.

They were given some help in accomplishing their task by the initial distribution of men and equipment decided upon by the Stavka. For instance, the allocation of tanks to the entire theatre was 5250; but this number was not divided equally among the three *fronts*. 1st Far Eastern Front, which was going to have to smash its way through prepared defences and chains of mountains, was allotted the bulk of the Soviet artillery, but only 1974 tanks and SP guns. 2nd Far Eastern Front, whose role was in any case minor, was also given only a few tanks, to the tune of

917. By contrast, Trans-Baikal Front, which was going to produce the armoured spearhead, was given 2359 tanks and SP guns.[22] This one *front*'s allocation represents more than double the entire Japanese tank strength in the whole of the Manchurian theatre, a strength which, moreover, naturally had to be dissipated in order to cover the various parts of the theatre.

In general, the shock groups of the three *fronts* are reckoned to have had the following superiorities along the main axes of their advance: 2.5 : 1 in men; from 5 to 8 : 1 in tanks; from 4 to 8 : 1 in guns; from 8 to 12 : 1 in mortars; and 3.6 : 1 in aircraft.[23] Where these figures give alternative ratios, the higher were always those along the main axes.

Having thus obtained a favourable correlation of forces the Soviet *front* and army commanders then proceeded, where necessary, to make these ratios even more favourable still. They did this by funnelling their forces towards the crucial points of their attack. Thus, Trans-Baikal Front s original deployment was across a width of 2300 km; the width of its front of advance was 1500 km; but its main blows were delivered across a sector that was only 400 km wide. On to those 400 km were channelled up to 70 per cent of the Front's infantry, 90 per cent of its tanks and guns,[24] and 74.7 per cent of the Front's aircraft.[25] (This gave it a superiority over the Japanese in this area of approximately 8 : 1 in men, 15 : 1 in tanks and SP guns, and an absolute superiority in aircraft.)

The same sort of thing is to be observed in the case of 1st Far Eastern Front. That *front* advanced across a width of about 700 km, but it fought its battles on a width of front of only about 100 km.[26] 5th All-Arms Army, which, together with 1st Krasnoznamennyi All-Arms Army, was responsible for delivering the *front*'s main blow, advanced on a front of 65 km; but when it came to attacking the enemy's prepared positions, its sector of breakthrough was down to a mere 12 km.[27] The divisional front for the breakthrough was 2.5 to 2.8 km; but the actual divisional attack was made on a front of only 1.1 km.[28] Furthermore, to each kilometre of actual attack was allotted 30 tanks and SP guns and an average of 200 guns and mortars.[29] In particular instances the number of guns and mortars was increased to 260 per kilometre of actual attack, and the tanks to as many as 40.[30]

Within 5th Army itself the same sort of thing is observable. The army attacked in two echelons, with the main blow in the first echelon being struck by 65th Rifle Corps under General Perekrestov and by 72nd Rifle Corps under General Kazartsev. To take the latter formation as our example of 'massing', we may note that, in the first place, it was reinforced for the purpose of the attack by 8 brigades of artillery (two of them of heavy calibre), 4 regiments of artillery, 3 batteries of artillery (of which 2 were super-heavy calibre), 2 brigades plus 2 regiments of rocket-launchers, 2 brigades of mortars, 2 brigades of tanks, 2 brigades of SP guns, and a regiment of engineers.[31]

As a result General Kazartsev had at his disposal 14,380 men; 1002 guns and mortars of 76 mm calibre or bigger; and 198 tanks and SP guns.[32] This mass of men and material was hurled at a sector of the Japanese defences that was just 5 km wide,[33] and it worked out at an average of 5.4 battalions, 218 guns and mortars and a trifle less than 40 tanks and SP guns per kilometre of sector of breakthrough.[34] The total number of Japanese defending this particular sector may be inferred as being one miserable infantry division plus one or two supporting units.[35] Soviet official histories say they were quickly overwhelmed; and we may well believe it.

Speed, we have decided, is the other necessary factor in exploitation. The Soviet speeds in Manchuria were very remarkable. Thus 6th Guards Tank Army covered some 900 km in 11 days; and this works out at an average of 82 km per day.[36] Even 1st Far Eastern Front, whose task was the penetration of prepared enemy defences and the crossing of mountains, advanced extremely rapidly. One of its constituent armies, a largely infantry army, averaged 16–22 km a day during a total of 5 days.[37] This was a highly creditable performance, given the circumstances.

Three factors contributed to the maintenance of such high speeds. One was the overall weakness of the Japanese resistance. They fought well in certain sectors, and those sectors were usually the ones where they were expecting a Soviet attack; but in other sectors their resistance collapsed speedily. Of course, it must be remembered that included in the Japanese forces were considerable numbers of the local populations from the various regions the Japanese had conquered; and that these could hardly be expected to fight heroically in defence of their conqueror's interests. Moreover, the Japanese lines of communication were under constant threat from guerrilla attack, though the threat was seldom very effectively implemented.[38] Furthermore, the quality of the weapons and equipment in use among the Japanese in Manchuria was generally significantly lower than that of the Russians. They had, for instance, no heavy tanks at all; while their medium tank was proof only against small-arms fire, and the gun it carried was only a 57 mm.[39] The Japanese infantry division numbered 15,000 men; but only 18 anti-tank guns were allotted to a division, and the calibre of these was only 37 mm.[40]

The second factor facilitating the speed of the Soviet advance was the creation of the forward detachments. These were created for every level from regiment to army. The forward detachment of the latter was likely to consist of about a couple of divisions with supporting arms, advancing on average about 30–40 km ahead of the main forces, which could thus continue to move forward in columns without having to deploy for battle except on rare occasions.[41] This was because the forward detachments were themselves strong enough to smash most enemy resistance; and since deployment for battle, and especially the deployment for battle of large numbers of troops, is an extremely time-consuming business, a great deal of time was saved as a result and the speed of the advance could be maintained. Indeed, in General Ivanov's view, the forward detachments were the chief reason why the Soviet advance was so rapid.[42]

But it was not only the armies that had these forward detachments; the corps and divisions did too. Thus the corps belonging to 6th Guards Tank Army each put out a forward detachment consisting of one motor-rifle regiment, one reinforced battalion (or, in some cases, regiment) of tanks and one regiment of field artillery.[43] This was for a formation operating in open terrain. A formation operating against fixed defences would be much more likely to create its forward detachment out of lorried infantry, SP guns, rocket-launchers, field artillery and a plentiful supply of sappers. One thing about them is certain. However they were constituted, they saved the main force time.

The third factor was the by-passing of pockets of enemy resistance. A forward detachment in certain circumstances, instead of stopping to obliterate a Japanese force that was resisting it, would move round its flanks and pass on. It was then the job of the first echelon, or occasionally of the second echelon, to mop this resistance up. Meanwhile the forward detachment was continuing its advance, and thereby applying pressure to the depth of the Japanese defences.

In the Manchurian Campaign, by-passing was done most frequently by Trans-Baikal Front; because it was the job of this *front* to advance as quickly as possible and hurl itself at Japanese Supreme Headquarters some 800 km away. Keeping going was therefore of the essence. On the other hand, 1st Far Eastern Front had the job of smashing through lines of prepared defences that the Japanese had been busily erecting along the common frontier: speed here was a less urgent consideration. Nevertheless, even here there are many examples of by-passing being practised by individual regiments or divisions.

The Soviet troops were fortunate enough to have mastery of the air from the outset. It was not hard to achieve this. The planes of the Japanese Air Force were technically inferior to their Soviet counterparts, and were inferior in numbers to them by a factor of about 2.5 : 1. This figure is correct, however, only in respect of the period before the actual fighting began. Once battle was joined on 9 August, the bulk of the Japanese aircraft in Manchuria were ordered to abandon that theatre of war and to fly to airfields in South Korea and Japan. The Manchurian skies were virtually clear thenceforward of Japanese planes, and Soviet mastery of the air was consequently complete.[44] Thenceforward, the Soviet Air Force could concentrate all its attention and all its resources on supporting the advancing ground forces.

All three Soviet fighting services participated in the campaign, and the efforts of all were co-ordinated for the purpose of winning victory speedily. There was thus no plan of naval operations that had a strategic purpose different from that of the ground forces, unlike the situation obtaining in the British Armed Forces in 1914 or the Imperial German Forces in the same year. In Manchuria, a principal assignment of the Soviet Navy was to assist the 2nd Far Eastern Front in its crossing of the Amur River. This was done by the Amur River Flotilla; and its chief tasks were to prevent the Japanese Navy from trying to disrupt the crossing, and to support the ground forces by bombarding the Japanese defences. These tasks it successfully accomplished. The Soviet Pacific Fleet had two main assignments: firstly, to mount the seaborne landings that resulted in the capture of the Kurile Islands, and secondly to co-operate with the ground forces in their advance down into South Sakhalin and their subsequent conquest of this area. These two assignments it successfully accomplished.

The tasks of the Soviet Air Force have just been discussed above.

Airborne landings were on a very small scale. None were attempted until after the Japanese Emperor had signed the Imperial Rescript of Surrender on 14 August. The first landing to be made was on 18 August, when 120 Soviet military personnel, including Major-General G. A. Shelakhov, the Chief of Staff of 1st Far Eastern Front, were parachuted into Harbin.[45] Their task was to negotiate the Japanese surrender with the Japanese generals on the spot. Subsequently, other landings were made; but they were all on a similarly small scale. Their purpose was to receive surrenders, to make arrangements for the stockpiling of the Japanese weapons which were subsequently to be given to the Chinese Communists, to prevent valuable raw materials from being shipped to Japan and so forth and so on. None of these landings played any part in winning the Manchurian Campaign.

As they had done in Finland, and as they were to do again in 1968 in Czechoslovakia, the Soviet Armed Forces attacked from more than one point of the compass. Of course, the geography of Manchuria made this very easy for them: it was possible to deploy a *front* to the north, another to the east and another to the west of Manchuria, and thus deliver three concentric blows upon the Japanese in the middle. Each *front*, moreover, could serve as the necessary anvil upon which the others could smash their defeated enemy. In Manchuria, therefore, the Russians were lucky, because circumstances conspired to facilitate the employment of a strategy they so strongly favour.

Before the campaign started in the Far East in 1945, the USSR had made preparations for ensuring supplies for its troops. This included sending 410 million rounds of small-arms ammunition and 3,200,000 shells to the Far East in the 4 months from the beginning of December 1944 to the end of March 1945.[46] No information is available on what further amounts were sent; but since the fighting lasted for only 9 days in most of the Far East theatre, and since the artillery was not much used, as compared with its use in such an operation as the storming of Berlin, we may safely conclude that the stocks of ammunition were fully sufficient for their purpose. In other words, the USSR had fulfilled the theoretical requirement to pre-stock sufficient munitions to last the whole campaign.

Finally, the Russians did undoubtedly benefit from the strong dislike of the Japanese evinced by most of the local population. It must be remembered that Manchuria was a Japanese colonial possession. They had conquered it only in the 1930s, and they had then proceeded to exploit its resources for the benefit of the Japanese war effort. They behaved like conquerors, and they were detested as such. On the other hand, it does not appear that Moscow succeeded in organizing a proper Manchurian 'Fifth Column' before the war began. Such acts of sabotage as occurred appear to have been spontaneous, not to have been planned with Moscow in advance. Even the mutinies of the colonial troops employed by the Japanese (Korean and Manchukuo units) seem to have been sparked off by the prospect of having to fight the Russians rather than as the result of any carefully worked-out agreement with the Stavka before the war began. It must be remembered that many of the local population had no more love for the Russians than they had for the Japanese; and that furthermore they had no love for Communism. Only the Chinese Communists made any attempt to co-ordinate their efforts with those of the Soviet forces: this they did by starting guerrilla activities against the Japanese 2 days after the Russians began their attack. If one accepts the view of the Soviet historians, these activities contributed little towards the Japanese defeat. Chinese historians naturally might think otherwise; but I unfortunately have had no access to Chinese accounts. The general conclusion to which I must come, in the light of the sources available to me, is that this element in the recipe for a foolproof *Blitzkrieg* victory was present only in part in the Manchurian Campaign.

Nevertheless, it was present to a certain degree, and the other elements were present fully and completely. It is, therefore, as a result of the presence of these elements, as a result of the implementation of the various measures that have been discussed in the preceding paragraphs, that the Soviet Armed Forces, according to their own historians, succeeded in that almost impossible military enterprise, the winning of a war in its 'opening phase'. From this it follows that they claim to having won it before their enemy had completed his initial process of mobilizing, concentrating and deploying.

This is not really true. The Japanese Army had been at war for some 3½ years before the Russian attack; and its mobilization, concentration and deployment had long since been completed. In 1941 the overall deployment had included the stationing of a strong force in Manchuria to guard against a Soviet attack. No such attack materialized; so as time went by and troops were needed elsewhere, the Japanese forces in Manchuria were greatly reduced in strength.

It was only in the early summer of 1945 that any measures were taken to reverse this trend: existing divisions then were moved from China to Manchuria and new divisions were formed.[47] New defensive works were also ordered, but these were not even expected to be ready before November at best. By early July the Japanese 39th Division did indeed arrive in Manchuria from China, but most of its equipment was sent by train and never arrived at all. The 39th Artillery Regiment had not one single gun.[48] The formation of 148th Division was finished only on 5 August. Its authorized strength was 12,000; its actual strength was 9800. It had only 30 per cent of its establishment of rifles, 10 per cent of its machine-guns, 30 per cent of its vehicles and 20 per cent of its guns. Its training was poor.[49] As for 138th Division, this, by the time of the Soviet attack, had about 80 per cent of its authorized establishment of personnel, but no small-arms and no artillery whatever.[50]

I may therefore be making a distinction without a difference when I say that the war was not won in its 'initial period', on the ground that the Japanese mobilization, concentration and deployment had been completed some years before. It is clear from what I have written above that in 1945 the Japanese forces in Manchuria were not properly deployed; and that furthermore a number of the Japanese divisions were not even properly mobilized, because they were still short of their full wartime establishments of personnel and weapons when the Russians struck. This circumstance greatly reduced the effectiveness of the Japanese resistance; and it is hard to deny that in the spirit, even if not in the letter, of the meaning the phrase 'the initial period' the Russians did accomplish what they always claim to have done.

We thus have an example of a Soviet campaign that comes very close to realizing the theoretical concepts of 16 years before. Some things were still not possible, because of the lack of the requisite technology. The USSR in 1945 had no long-distance transport planes that could carry airborne divisions into the

Japanese rear. That strand of the concept of the 'deep battle' could therefore not be implemented. Nor was it possible to 'hit the enemy over the whole depth of his defensive position', as the famous plan requires. There were no missiles then; the ranges of the guns were too short; and the scanty quantity of bombers with which Marshal Vasilievsky was endowed had neither the range nor the power to do much destruction. They did what they could. Finally, the subversion from within, the creation within the enemy State of a strong feeling of defeatism together with the creation of a strong Fifth Column to harvest the fruits of that defeatism and at the same time to engage in implementing a carefully prepared plan for sabotage was only partly realized in the Manchurian Campaign, as has already been explained above.

The Manchurian Campaign must be regarded as an interesting development of the conceptual thinking that had planned the strategy for the Russo-Finnish War of 1939–40. It also possesses very clear links with the strategic thinking of the 1930s, both Nazi and Soviet. Only the unavoidable handicaps imposed by the technology of the time prevented it from being implemented exactly in the way that had been dreamed of by the Tukhachevsky school. Modern technology has removed those handicaps completely.

Since in the Manchurian Campaign the Russians not only secured victory but secured it in the 'initial period', a recapitulation of the principal elements in their highly successful strategy is probably desirable. They may be summarized as follows:

(1) Manchuria was 'chewable';
(2) the Russians secured from the outset complete mastery of the local air space;
(3) they secured complete surprise at the strategic, operational and tactical levels;
(4) they exploited that surprise by concentrating on the principal axes of advance sufficient forces so as to acquire along those axes a tremendous superiority in men, weapons and equipment. The highest degrees of concentration were constructed on the principal axes of the three *fronts*; and a particularly high degree of concentration was constructed on the principal axes of the principal *front*, Trans-Baikal Front;
(5) the Russians also achieved a high speed of advance – this, it

will be remembered, is the other essential element in any effective exploitation of any initial surprise that may be secured;

(6) because of the strategic surprise that the Russians secured, and because of the fact that they effectively exploited it, they hit the enemy's forces when an important proportion of them were not fully mobilized nor properly deployed;

(7) the Russians obtained close co-ordination between their three Services;

(8) they stockpiled in advance sufficient amunition and reserve equipment to last the whole campaign.

On the other hand, it is important to remember that certain elements of the Russians' favourite operational concept could not be realized in the Manchurian Campiagn, mostly because of the absence of the requisite technology, but also for other reasons. Those missing elements were:

(1) Airborne landings in the enemy rear, designed to link up with the advancing ground forces – in 1945 the USSR did not possess the transport planes of a sufficient range and size for such an operation, and there were no helicopters.

(2) Hitting the enemy an initial and simultaneous blow over the whole depth of his position. Some attempt at doing this was made by bomber aircraft, but the distances were too great and there were not enough such aircraft to accomplish it properly. Artillery was obviously hopelessly inadequate for the purpose, and in 1945 the Soviet Armed Forces were not equipped with missiles.

(3) A pre-planned programme of disruption, sabotage and the spreading of false rumours and defeatism by a well-organized local 'Fifth Column'. Such activities of this nature as did in fact take place do not appear to have been concerted in advance with Moscow, nor do they seem to have contributed much to the success of the Soviet offensive. The same remarks apply, *mutatis mutandis*, to the guerrilla operations launched by the Chinese Communists.

It must be expected that in any war begun by the USSR against NATO these defects would have been remedied.

NOTES AND REFERENCES

1. S. P. Ivanov, *Nachal'nyi Period Voiny* (Voenizdat, 1974) p. 287.
2. Marshal M. V. Zakharov, *Finale* (Progress Publishers, Moscow, 1972) p. 39.
3. Zakharov, op. cit., p. 39.
4. G. H. Lensen, *The Strange Neutrality* (Diplomatic Press, 1972) p. 148.
5. General N. I. Shtemenko, *General'nyi Shtab v Gody Voiny* (Voenizdat, 1968) pp. 347–8.
6. Krylov, *Navstrechu Pobiede* (Nauka, 1970) p. 124.
7. Marshal R. Ya. Malinovsky, *Final* (Voenizdat, 1966) p. 322.
8. Lensen, op. cit., p. 158.
9. Zakharov, op cit., p. 130.
10. Ivanov, op. cit., p. 268.
11. Zakharov, op. cit., p. 135.
12. *Voenno Istoricheskii Zhurnal*, No. 9 (1975) p. 16.
13. Krylov, op. cit., p. 435.
14. Malinovsky, op. cit., p. 124.
15. Ibid., p. 123.
16. Zakharov, op. cit., p. 102.
17. Marshall K. A. Meretskov, *Serving the People* (Progress Publishers, Moscow, 1971) pp. 350–1; see also Krylov, op. cit., p. 435.
18. Many Japanese officers have testified to this effect. See, for instance, Malinovsky, op. cit., p. 203. Materials shown me by the Japanese Embassy in London agree with Malinovsky's account.
19. *Istoriya Velikoi Otechestvennoi Voiny Sovietskogo Soyuza 1941–1945*, vol. 5, (Voenizdat, 1963) p. 551.
20. Ibid., and Malinovsky, op. cit., pp. 67 and 548.
21. *IVOVSS*, vol. 5, p. 551. Other Soviet sources give slightly different figures, but none that affect the substance of our argument.
22. *Istoriya Vtoroi Mirovoi Voiny 1939–1945* (Voenizdat, 1980) vol. 11, pp. 194–7.
23. Marshal I. Kh. Bagramyan, *Istoriya Voin i Voennogo Iskusstva* (Voenizdat. 1970) p. 343.
24. Ivanov, op. cit., p. 290.
25. Malinovsky, op. cit., p. 116.
26. Ivanov, op. cit., p. 290.
27. Krylov, op. cit., p. 429.
28. Ibid.
29. Ibid.
30. Ibid.
31. Ibid., p. 436.
32. Ibid., p. 437.
33. Ibid., p. 436.
34. Ibid., p. 437.
35. *VIZh*, No. 8 (1975) p. 83, gives the total force opposing the whole 5th Army as 'three infantry divisions plus a few supporting units'. I have attempted a rational sub-allocation.
36. Bagramyan, op. cit., p. 355.

37. *VIZh*, No. 8 (1975) p. 88.
38. *VIZh*, No. 4 (1967).
39. Malinovsky, op. cit., p. 67.
40. Ibid.
41. Ivanov, op. cit., p. 295.
42. Ibid.
43. Bagramyan, op. cit., p. 344.
44. *VIZh*, No. 8 (1975) p. 68.
45. For details of this operation, see Malinovsky, op. cit., pp. 273–6, and elsewhere.
46. *IVOVSS*, vol. 5, p. 559.
47. This section is drawn from *Records of Operations Against Soviet Russia*, Japanese Monograph No. 155 (Office of Chief of Military History, Dept. of Army, undated US Publication drawing on Japanese sources).
48. Ibid., pp. 19–20.
49. Ibid., p. 32.
50. Ibid., p. 48–9.

10   The new ingredients: air mobile forces and rockets

It was 23 years after the Manchurian Campaign before the USSR again embarked on war. This second military operation was the Soviet invasion of Czechoslovakia, which began on 21 August 1968, and which was all over and done with, so far as concerned the possibility of effective Czech resistance, a mere 24 hours later.

The near quarter of a century that separated these two wars or campaigns had been noteworthy for, among other things, a quite remarkable improvement in aviation technology. During the Second World War it was the old-fashioned, propeller-driven aircraft that was the standard component of the respective combatants' air forces; by 1968 propeller-driven aircraft were being fast consigned to the museums. Among other things this resulted in the greatly improved performance of transport aircraft. The technical advances that produced this improvement are not, however, to our purpose: we are concerned only to note that by the end of the 1960s transport aircraft could carry very much bulkier and heavier loads than had been possible during the Second World War: they could also carry them further and much more quickly. This permitted the transport of men and equipment on a scale unknown to the commanders of the 1940s and 1950s.

These remarks are particularly applicable to the operations of the Red Army. Generally speaking, Soviet aviation technology had lagged behind that of the West during the period in question; but by 1968 it was catching up fast. Furthermore (and very much more to our purpose) it was by then able to undertake a whole range of military operations which it could not have tackled earlier. This was made possible not only by the improvements in fixed-wing aircraft, but also by those in helicopters.

We noted in the preceding chapter that airborne landings were really used very little during the Manchurian Campaign; and that those that took place were undertaken with conventional transport aircraft using conventional airfields and airstrips.[1] Such landings are vulnerable. If to this vulnerability is added the Soviet air forces' lack of ability in the Manchurian Campaign to offer proper support to airborne landings because of the enormous distances, it is quite understandable that there were very few such landings; that those that took place were small; and that not one single one of these was undertaken until the war was virtually over.

On the other hand, the whole 'feel' of the Stavka's plan for its Manchurian Campaign indicates very strongly that the Soviet commanders would have liked to have mounted many more airborne landings than in fact they did. If only the Soviet technology of the period had made the launching of this kind of operation a more practicable proposition than it actually was, then, one feels, the USSR would have launched a great many more of them. We should, however, note – because it will become highly relevant later in this chapter – that the airborne landings which the Soviet commanders did contrive to launch were all aimed at Japanese 'nerve centres' rather than at Japanese units. What we mean by 'nerve centres' will be described in detail below.

For the moment, however, we are concerned only to point out that during the 23 years that elapsed between the Manchurian Campaign of 1945 and the Soviet invasion of Czechoslovakia in 1968 the Soviet Armed Forces had acquired the technology necessary to allow them to accomplish in practice, and on a very large scale, what the Soviet military thinkers of the 1920s and 1930s had always hoped and planned to do, but had never been able to achieve through lack of means. There had, of course, been notable Soviet experiments during the 1930s in the art of projecting troops by means of 'planes to a considerable distance into the enemy's rear; but these had all been comparatively small-scale undertakings, and the troops had all been dropped by parachute.

Admittedly, the manoeuvres at Kiev in 1935 and those in Belorussia in 1936 had seen the successful dropping of 3000 men by parachute, accompanied by a conventional airborne landing of a further 8200 men, together with artillery, light tanks and other equipment.[2] This, however, was the high-water mark of what was achieved in practice before the war. The lack of suitable aircraft ruled out further progress on these lines. The concept, however, remained firmly rooted in the minds of Soviet strategists.

In view of all this, it must be reckoned only natural that the Soviet operations in Czechoslovakia and Afghanistan should allot an important role to airborne landings. There was no reason inherent in either of these operations to compel the Soviet planners to go in for tricky para-drops; and in both cases airborne landings, using fixed-wing aircraft on conventional landing grounds, were the order of the day. In addition, in Afghanistan helicopters were to be used widely; but in Czechoslovakia there was simply no need for the employment of this type of aircraft; and furthermore in 1968 Soviet interest in helicopters was not so very widely developed. It was the American use of helicopter-gunships in the later stages of the Vietnam War that caught the Russians' attention; so that the HIND, for instance, did not come into service until the 1970s.

Nevertheless, the failure to employ helicopters during the Czech invasion of 1968 must not be taken as implying that the Russians regarded the airborne element in this operation as secondary: on the contrary, the part it played was crucial, just as the part that it played in the Afghan invasion was crucial.

We must therefore take it for granted that, in any operation of whatever kind in which the Soviet Armed Forces may be engaged in the future, a vital role will be allotted, wherever practicable, to the projection forward of forces by means of airpower (and in suitable circumstances by seapower) deep into the enemy's rear. The purpose of the undertaking will be to paralyse vital nerve-centres, and thus bring the operation to a successful conclusion much more quickly and much more surely than one could expect it to be done otherwise. This kind of projection of force forward is, in my humble opinion, an almost essential ingredient in any strategy that seeks to win wars in their opening phase, and seeks to be sure of doing so. Since at no time in the past history of warfare has this method ever been available, except on the somewhat limited scale of the German invasion of Holland, I have decided to regard it as being one of the ingredients, one of the absolutely essential ingredients, hitherto missing from the strategic recipe that shall render the *Blitzkrieg* infallible.

This may seem to be a gross over-estimate of the potential of this kind of operation: in reality, however, it is not. The object of a campaign as a whole is to destroy the enemy's power to resist. Hitherto, this could only be done by battles; and we have already discussed the considerable defects of a battle as a means of doing it. In particular, one may end up losing the battle; and then the enemy's power to resist will be strengthened, not destroyed.

Now, however, by means of airborne operations, it has become possible to end his resistance by means other than by battles, or, rather, so to weaken his power to resist that the fighting of the battle becomes a mere formality. Of course, as we have said already, the airborne operation cannot be launched unsupported: it will need to be mounted in conjunction with one by the ground forces if it is to be successful. Soviet strategists know this as well as we do. But they also know that the launching of an airborne operation *in addition to, and in conjunction with*, an offensive by their ground forces increases the chances of success for the latter to a significant degree. This is because of the ability of the airborne operation to sever those vital nerve-ganglions that make it possible for the enemy's forces to continue with their resistance.

The analogy is with rat-catching. The purpose of the airborne operation is the projection of force forward, by means of aircraft, to a vital nerve-centre. This nerve-centre is then put out of action, or, if required, is converted to serve the purposes of the aggressor. In either event the enemy is severely crippled. Because the aggressor is transported to the attack in aircraft, he can leap over the enemy's perimeter defences, and pounce down on his target like a cat. And, like the cat, he will probably hunt at night.

But perhaps a dog tackling a rat is a better illustration for my purpose. If a rat is allowed to get himself organized and into a good defensive position, he can give a formidable account of himself against any cat or dog. An accomplished ratter, in order to prevent this happening, will therefore seek to grab him by the back of the neck. Cats and dogs alike will try to do this. Their purpose is to grab him from behind, aiming to break his spinal cord; and if they succeed in their purpose, the rat is dead.

Surprise, speed and decision are therefore essential; and these must be supported by weight of blow. If these four qualities are absent, what is likely to happen is that the would-be ratter will get badly bitten and the rat will manage to escape.

In Czechoslovakia in 1968 these four qualities were duly present and Czechoslovakia did not escape. In Afghanistan in 1979 reliance was placed on the Afghan army, and Soviet weight of blow was somewhat lacking. The result was a rather messy operation which, although it succeeded in removing Amin and establishing a Soviet presence in the principal Afghan cities, has not yet succeeded in its main objective, which was to secure the acquiescence of the Afghan people to the rule of Afghan Marxists.

Three additional comments in connection with this subject: firstly, the weight of blow must come from the ground forces, who are to mount an offensive by land in conjunction with the airborne operation. It is not possible to land airborne troops in anything like sufficient quantity to be able to rely on them alone to provide the necessary weight of blow, except against a puny enemy. Secondly (and here the analogy with ratting breaks down), these airborne troops will have a twofold task. One of these will be the one we have already discussed: the destruction of the enemy's command-and-communication centres and strategic depots, thereby making the enemy defence a matter of hasty improvisation by junior commanders at the periphery. But a second task is likely to be the seizure of enemy airfields, as a means of permitting the airborne landing of substantial quantities of their own ground forces. To borrow a metaphor from earlier warfare, their job will be to overpower the guards, raise the portcullis, let down the drawbridge, and thus admit their comrades into the enemy's castle.

My third comment is an amplification of my description of the objective allotted to these airborne operations. I described it as being the swift paralysis of vital enemy nerve-centres. The expression 'nerve-centres' must not be interpreted too narrowly: obviously, command-and-control centres and capital cities can all be envisaged as 'nerve-centres' without any difficulty;. but the phrase should be given a wider application, and embrace such things as ports, airfields and supply depots. Of course, I have included mention of these things in what I have written earlier, but I have mentioned them only marginally. Given the sophistication of modern war, however, these are surely 'nerve-centres' as much as any other; and it is not improbable that airborne landings or heliborne landings might be used by the Russians to paralyse them.

In any case, it is obvious that the type of target to be selected by the Russians will depend upon the aims of the campaign as a whole. In 1945 in Manchuria, for instance, the aims that were set the Soviet commanders were the seizure of South Sakhalin and the Kurile Islands, the bringing to an end of the war against Japan, the giving of aid to the local national-liberation movements (Chinese, Korean, Vietnamese, etc.), and, in addition, the seizure for the benefit of the Soviet Union of Japanese stocks of raw materials and of industrial machinery located in Manchuria.

As a consequence, the Soviet airborne landings that did in fact take place during the Manchurian Campaign were aimed at hastening the capitulation of important Japanese headquarters; at preventing the Japanese from destroying important Manchurian industrial centres in a kind of 'scorched-earth' policy; and also at stopping the removal to Japan from Manchuria of valuable raw materials.[3] Others were aimed at seizing ports that would prevent the Americans from shipping arms to their allies in China and Korea; while the one in South Sakhalin must be regarded as having had, in addition, a strictly military significance, as it made a contribution to the defeat of the Japanese forces, which were still resisting the Russians at the time. This airborne landing was overshadowed, however, from the point of view of military significance, by the two seaborne landings that were mounted during this operation, which helped considerably towards the speedy ending of Japanese resistance.[4]

The Soviet airborne landings were very small, ranging from 120 to a maximum of 500 men; and only about 20 of these landings were ever mounted. They were none of them para-dropped nor heli-borne; but all were landed by ordinary transport aircraft on conventional airfields. Their escort of fighter aircraft was rather scanty.[5] Their targets were places like Harbin and Changchun, Lushun (Port Arthur), Talien (Darien) Taichara. Of these, Changchun and Harbin were military headquarters; while the others were ports, industrial centres and so on. A Soviet map, showing the locations of the most important of the airborne landings and the dates on which they were undertaken is included in Marshal Zakharov's *Finale* (in between pages 68 and 69).

In Czechoslovakia, on the other hand, and also in Afghanistan the aim of the campaign was to get rid of a government that had become obnoxious to Moscow, and replace it with one more acceptable. Since governments live and have their being in the capital cities of the countries they rule, it was only logical that it should have been Prague and Kabul that were the main targets of the Soviet airborne forces in 1968 and 1979 respectively. As we all know, the forces in question were successful on both occasions.

On the other hand, success in this sort of operation does require that the airborne forces should receive help from within the victim country. In other words, some sort of Fifth Column needs to be in existence. In both Czechoslovakia and Afghanistan such Fifth Columns did indeed exist; though the term 'Fifth Column' is perhaps not wholly appropriate in the case of Afghanistan. This is because Amin, the political boss who was to be deposed, was extremely unpopular with his own people; and many of those Afghans who helped to topple him were no doubt motivated by anti-Amin, rather than by pro-Soviet, sentiments. This contrasts sharply with the situation in Czechoslovakia, where Dubcek was highly popular with the overwhelming majority of his own people, and where those who conspired to bring him down were wholly unrepresentative. To such people the term 'Fifth Column' may properly be applied.

It must not be forgotten, however, that in 1968 and 1979 there were also a number of Soviet 'advisers' stationed in the victim countries before the operations began. These rendered invaluable additional assistance to the incoming airborne forces.

On the other hand, the success of the airborne operation is simply not sufficient to ensure the success of the campaign as a whole. The efforts of the airborne forces must be complemented by those of conventional ground forces in considerable numbers. Otherwise it is always possible that the armed forces of the victim country will come to their senses, recover from their surprise, and proceed to liquidate the airborne troops that have taken possession of their capital. Arnhem showed very clearly what happens to airborne forces that do not receive support from conventional ground forces.

In Czechoslovakia, therefore, and also in Afghanistan, Soviet ground forces in considerable numbers entered the country by road. Their task was twofold: they had to suppress any attempt by the armies of the victim countries to repulse the invasions, and they also had to seal off those countries' frontiers with the outside world. Once these two things had been done the task of suppressing anti-Soviet movements within the countries could proceed methodically and at leisure.

But although in the cases of Afghanistan and Czechoslovakia their capital cities were the Soviet airborne forces' logical targets, different considerations would naturally prevail in the event of an attack by the Warsaw Pact on NATO. For there the principal military goal would be the destruction of NATO's ability to resist the invading armies. Such an ability rests upon the NATO troops already deployed, and upon the supply and reinforcement of them once the battle has been joined. Consequently, the logical targets for Soviet airborne landings in a campaign of this nature would not be capital cities, but military command-and-control centres, communications centres, nuclear installations, supply depots, ports and airfields, and the like. However, although the targets would be different the principles underlying the operations to seize them would be the same as those underlying the Czech and the Afghan operations.

Mention has been made earlier of Soviet admiration for the German strategy of hitting the enemy over the whole of his operational – and also if possible his strategic – depth right at the start of the war. This hammering, in other words, has got to be undertaken at the self-same moment as the ground forces move to the attack. In 1941 the Wehrmacht was unable to apply that formula properly, because a very great many of the desired targets were too far behind the Soviet front line for the Luftwaffe to be able to reach them. On the other hand, in the West in 1940 the desired targets were mostly within range of the Luftwaffe; and these targets were therefore duly hit. However, the resultant damage, though serious, was very seldom fatal, because the German planes of those days could not carry a bomb-load of sufficient capacity to achieve the necessary degree of destruction, nor could they drop their bombs with sufficient accuracy.

Today, however, we live in the missile age, which means that the modern equivalent of the bomb can be delivered over any distance. Hitler invading Russia in 1980 could destroy targets in the Soviet Union, however far back in the depths of that country its rulers might have located them. By the same token, a Warsaw Pact commander engaged in invading NATO territory could hit military targets in Germany, France, Holland, Italy, Belgium or Britain, or the United States or Canada for that matter; and furthermore he could hit them in the first few minutes of the war. In addition his missiles would be much more accurate than the bombs of the Nazi air force.

The destructive power of the Luftwaffe's bombs, moreover, would be far outdone by the destructive power inherent in the Soviet rockets. It is not the purpose of this present essay to examine the question of whether the Russians, in the event of them attacking the NATO Alliance, would decide to use nuclear weapons: we are here concerned only to state the self-evident proposition that they have nuclear warheads available, if they care to use them; and that they also have chemical and conventional warheads. There is in existence today, therefore, the technical means for hitting the enemy over the whole of his operational/strategic depth with deadly blows of enormous destructiveness: consequently the task which the Nazis in 1940 were able to accomplish only very partially can now be accomplished with complete finality, if the attacker wishes to do so.

Furthermore, the Soviet armed forces have just come up with a new concept, the operational manoeuvre group. It envisages large Soviet formations, possessing their own organic air, and of the size of a strong division on each main axis, operating behind NATO's main defensive belt by the end of the first day of the main battle. Their purpose will be, to quote a recent Polish journal, 'to switch the focus of the fighting into the depths or rear of the enemy . . . to achieve chaos and disorganization, and to limit the freedom of manoeuvre and the effectiveness of the enemy's action'. These formations, together with the missiles and the helicopters, could pose such a threat to NATO's nuclear installations and other 'nerve centres' as would be far from easy to counter.[6]

NOTES AND REFERENCES

1. *Voenno-Istoricheskii Zhurnal,* No. 9 (1975) p. 54.
2. *Sovietskaya Voennaya Entsiklopediya,* vol. 2 (Voenizdat, 1976) p. 287.
3. S. P. Ivanov, *Nachal'nyi Period Voiny* (Voenizdat, 1974) p. 297.
4. *VIZh,* No. 9 (1975) p. 54 and Zakharov, op. cit., pp. 173–4.
5. *VIZh,* No. 9 (1975) p. 54 and Ivanov, op. cit., p. 297.
6. This is taken, by kind permission, from an as yet unpublished manuscript by C. N. Donnelly.

11   The Soviet invasions of Czechoslovakia and Afghanistan

We now turn to consider in greater detail the invasions of Czecho-slovakia and Afghanistan, in an attempt to see to what extent the practice followed the theory. We will start with Czechoslovakia. But before we continue with the military aspect of the 1968 invasion, we must first examine its political aspect.

Just as the Russo-Finnish War and the Manchurian Campaign were both preceded by intense diplomatic activity on the part of the USSR, so too was the invasion of Czechoslovakia in 1968. This political background has been exhaustively studied by the most eminent Western specialists; and some have picked on one thing as the cause of the Soviet intemperance, while others have picked on others. Professor Gordon Skilling, in a massive but admirable survey of these various views, concludes that there are many plausible Western theories as to the whys, the whens and the wherefores of the Kremlin's action; but that it is quite impossible for anyone in the West to decide which one is right.[1]

Luckily, it makes no difference to my thesis whether the Russians sent their troops into Czechoslovakia because they believed that the Czech Communist Party was no longer going to be able to continue its autocratic rule, but would have to submit to some degree of genuinely democratic criticism; or because they believed that Czechoslovakia might leave the Warsaw Pact; or because the Soviet leaders had all gone mad, and were impelled by some totally unreal fantasy, such as that Dubcek was the illegitimate great-nephew of the late Tsar Nicholas II, and was being groomed to proclaim himself Lord of Moscow, with the help of that other and very influential Romanov, the present First Secretary of the Leningrad Party Regional Committee.

Any of these things may, or may not, have been the cause of the

Czech invasion. Here, we are concerned only to note that quite a lot of time elapsed between the first brush between Moscow and the Czechs, which dates from March 1968 when Novotny resigned, and the advance across the border into Czechoslovakia of the troops of the Warsaw Pact in August of that same year. In other words, there was a period of about 4 months when the Soviet Union *refrained* from sending in troops.

Furthermore, even when the crisis deepened, the USSR was not particularly eager to use armed force. If things may be said to have become serious by about June, at the end of which month the Russians were provoked to fury by the famous manifesto, 'Two Thousand Words', nevertheless this still means that nearly 9 weeks elapsed between then and the moment when the soldiers of the Warsaw Pact were ordered to march in.

Moreover, not merely did time elapse, but the Kremlin made considerable efforts to reach an agreed solution. Two summit meetings were held, one at the end of July at Cierna nad Tisou, and the other at Bratislava on 3 August. At these two meetings the USSR was represented by Brezhnev and all his most senior colleagues. At the end of the second meeting it seemed that a solution had been found. The communiqué of the Bratislava meeting was widely interpreted in the West as meaning that Czechoslovakia and the Soviet Union had reconciled their differences. *The Times*, for example, described the text of the communiqué in the following headline: 'Bratislava powers agree on right to be different.'[2]

Between 3 August and 21 August, the day of the invasion, something clearly happened to convince the Kremlin that armed force would have to be used. What that was, does not concern us here: here, we are concerned only to note that the USSR, though fully determined to get what she wanted by hook or by crook, would have far preferred to have got it by crook, if possible; that is to say, she would have far preferred to have got it by diplomatic negotiation. And in this she was merely following a pattern that she had followed in the cases of Finland and Manchuria.

The task confronting Soviet diplomacy was not, however, confined to negotiation. It was also its job to make preparations for a possible failure to reach agreement, and for the *putsch* that would then be necessary. In particular, it was the job of Soviet diplomacy under this heading to isolate Czechoslovakia; firstly by acquiring for the USSR as many active allies as it could; and secondly by persuading other countries to give no help to the Czechs (and in this connection it was particularly important that the NATO countries, and especially the United States, should confine themselves to moral support for Dubcek and his followers, and should not attempt to furnish troops or send in arms and equipment).

The Kremlin realized that the advance of Soviet forces into Czechoslovakia might make the NATO governments wonder where those Soviet forces would stop. It is for this reason that it ordered its ambassadors in the most important of the NATO countries to inform the governments to which they were accredited that the Soviet forces would stop at the NATO frontiers and would under no circumstances cross them, unless the NATO Powers themselves took military action.

But the key factor was the attitude of the United States. As the crisis progressed the reactions of the White House were watched with great anxiety by the Soviet Union. Rumour in Moscow has it that a prime indicator of the degree of seriousness with which the American Government was treating the Soviet Czech dispute was what the American President did each successive Friday evening. If he stayed in Washington for the weekend it was assumed he was taking things seriously; but if he went off to his ranch in Texas it was assumed that he was not. As it so happened, President Lyndon Johnson departed for his Texan ranch on Friday 2 August telling reporters he was leaving Washington and did not expect to be back until September except perhaps for the occasional quick visit.[3] This, it will be noted, was the day before the signing of the unsatisfactory (from the Soviet viewpoint) Cierna agreement. By his departure, the American President gave a very clear signal to the hawk-eyed watchers in the Kremlin that the United States was relaxed, and quite unready to take momentous decisions swiftly.

Once military measures had been decided upon, Soviet strategy followed its familiar pattern, the same pattern that had already been followed in the Russo-Finnish War and the Manchurian Campaign. The same attempt to get what was wanted by negotiation; the same refusal to flinch from the use of force when negotiations failed; and the same preliminary isolation of the intended victim; the same insistence, once the decision to use force had finally been arrived at, on the need to gain surprise at every level, particularly the strategic, and on the need to see that the accompanying attack was weighty and very fast.

Speed was of the essence. As has already been said, it was vital for the Russians that the Western countries should confine themselves to moral support for Dubcek, and should not attempt to send in troops to encourage Czech resistance. The quicker the Warsaw Pact forces could complete their military activities, and could crush, and be seen to have crushed, any potential effective Czech opposition to their movement, the less likely it was that Western governments would order their military commanders to support the Czechs.

It is a fact of history that the Soviet grip was fastened on Czechoslovakia within less than 24 hours. Various forms of opposition, and even outright hostilities, did indeed manifest themselves later; but the civilian protests in Prague, though superb propaganda, could do nothing whatever to expel from their country the forces of the Warsaw Pact. Like it or not, within 24 hours the Czech people had lost their war, and the Russians and their allies had won it.

As for weight of blow, the Czech forces at that time consisted of about 250,000 men.[4] Various estimates regarding the strength of the Warsaw Pact forces have been given in Western sources: the one most generally accepted today is 600,000 men. Even supposing, therefore, that the Czechs had fought the invaders, which in actual fact they did not, they would have been opposed by well over twice their number. A 2 : 1 superiority in men, especially in conditions of the attainment of surprise, is a formidable opposition for an army to face. As we all know, the Czech Army did not have to face it, because the Czech Government ordered its forces not to offer resistance; but even had the latter done so, it is just not possible to imagine that they could have offered resistance for long. The improbability of their doing so was rendered still more improbable by the routes chosen for the invasion by the Soviet General Staff. These thrust into Czechoslovakia from the north, the east and the south; so that the Czech armed forces, had they wished to resist, would have had to fight a war, not on two fronts, but on the frightening total of three. The Japanese in Manchuria, it will be remembered, had also to fight on three fronts; and so did the Finns in 1939. This threesome-ness, this *troika*, of Soviet invasion routes is probably no more than a pure historical coincidence; but it seemed to be rather an intriguing one, and I have therefore ventured to draw my readers' attention to it.

The key element, however, was the gaining of surprise; because the sole danger of effective Czech resistance lay in the granting to Dubcek's Government of substantial military support by the NATO countries. It was, however, reasonable to assume that, if the Western world were taken by surprise, then the collective Western leadership, under those circumstances, would not have time to agree a policy, and to put that policy into operation, before Czech resistance was finished. Consequently, it was a matter of the very greatest importance to keep the whole world guessing as to whether the Soviet Union and her allies would invade Czechoslovakia or not; and to encourage that considerable and influential section of Western public and professional opinion (as well as a section of Czech opinion) which believed that she would not.

Consequently, the order to invade was given at a time when many extremely competent observers believed that the danger had considerably diminished, if not completely vanished. The exercise which the Warsaw Pact had been conducting along the borders of Czechoslovakia, and which provided the excuse for the bringing together of such a large number of troops, had by then been ended; and the troops themselves appeared to be dispersing to their camps. It was precisely at this moment, when Czech vigilance and world vigilance had begun to relax a little, that the Russians struck.

Nor was this the only means by which the Soviet Union secured surprise in 1968. For the Russians guessed that a main indicator for the Western world as to the likelihood of an actual invasion was the Group of Soviet Forces in Germany (GSFG). They, it was supposed by NATO governments, would have to do the invasion, if there was to be one; and hence their movements, or lack of them, were regarded as the criterion. If they moved in strength, an invasion was thought by the Western world to be likely to be imminent; if they stayed in their barracks, it was thought that it was not. In the event, however, it was the large body of troops engaged in the exercise who did the actual invasion; while Soviet forces in Germany stayed in their barracks. As a result, the Western world was effectively surprised.

We have no means of knowing by precisely what methods the

mastery of the local air space was secured for the Warsaw Pact forces at the time of the Czech invasion; we only know that they secured it, and that the mastery in question was total. This allowed the Warsaw Pact to make seven airborne landings, according to foreign reports.[5] The most important of these, obviously, was the one on Prague. Not only was it the most sensational, but it was also the one of the greatest military importance. Its success allowed the capital to be seized, and the potential leaders of Czech resistance to be arrested, and all within an hour or two of the start of the campaign. Dubcek himself, for instance, was arrested as a result of this landing. The landing itself was very greatly facilitated by the fact that the Russians, through their control of the Warsaw Pact, knew the correct landing procedures at Prague airport. The planes they used were civilian ones taken from Aeroflot; and therefore, provided the proper procedures were used by them, the electronic interrogators of the Czech airport control would have no reason to suspect that things were amiss. Had military planes been used, the outcome might perhaps have been different; because the robot scanners would not have so readily accepted them. But military planes were *not* used at the *beginning*. *The first* planes to land were Aeroflot civilian airliners, precisely in order that the robot scanners should have no cause to demur. It was only after they had landed successfully that the military planes came in. As for the other six landings, their purpose was, by seizing vital military communications centres, to render doubly certain the non-resistance of the Czech armed forces.

Other factors which Soviet doctrine deems to be necessary for securing victory include, as we have seen already, the launching of the offensive in an unexpected place, the delivery of blows over the whole depth of the enemy's defences, the use of what we in the West would describe as a 'Fifth Column', and the mounting of airborne and seaborne landings.

We have no means of knowing whether the particular axes chosen for the Soviet invasion routes were unexpected by the Czech authorities; but since the whole invasion was unexpected this seems a minor matter. On the other hand, it was of considerable importance that the blows of the Warsaw Pact forces should be struck more or less simultaneously across all of Czechoslovakia, because this made it far less likely that any Czech resistance, if it should prove to be forthcoming, would be effective. The choice of routes for the invading ground forces, coupled with the airborne landings, satisfied this requirement, except for that part of Czechoslovakia which lies to the west of Prague. An early task for the Pact forces was therefore to move to the western frontier as quickly as they could: in particular, their job was to discourage and, if necessary, resist any military move by NATO. The Soviet forces reached that frontier in less than 24 hours; so one is bound to admit that they successfully accomplished their mission.

We may end this section by saying that the invasion of Czechoslovakia by the Warsaw Pact forces in the summer of 1968 was a splendid example of that most successful of all forms of warfare: the war that achieves its political objectives with scarcely a shot being fired. If ever a war has been won in its initial period, this war is it. The Czech forces were in no way fully mobilized, for the Czech reservists had not been recalled to the colours; while those already serving were mostly in their barracks. Furthermore, neither the Czech Army nor the Czech Air Force was deployed to resist aggression from its fraternal allies. If the Czech armed forces were neither fully mobilized nor properly deployed, they clearly come under the classic definition of being still in the 'opening phase' of the 1968 war; and the Soviet armed forces have therefore got to their credit the distinction of having won *two* wars in their 'initial periods', the war the subject of this present section and that against the Japanese in 1945. This is, of course, provided that you accept that 'war' is a proper description of each of them.

The diplomatic background to the Afghan invasion differs from that to the Czech in certain particulars. In the former case there was no manipulation of international tension because, there being at the time of the Soviet invasion no perceptible international tension with regard to Afghanistan, the USSR was not required to manipulate. A second difference is that in 1968 the Soviet leaders had had prolonged negotiations with the Dubcek Government, in the hope of avoiding the need for its forcible overthrow. In 1979, however, there were no such prolonged negotiations. Hafizullah Amin, the Afghan leader whom the USSR was soon to depose forcibly, only took over the leadership in September 1979. During the 3 months of power that was to be all he was to have, he never engaged in negotiations with the

Russians of the kind that Dubcek engaged in. All that happened in the case of Amin was that his standing with the Russians went lower and lower, until in the December they removed him.

A third difference is that, in the case of Czechoslovakia, Soviet diplomacy worked very hard to isolate that country politically and militarily, and, in particular, to ensure that the West would not come rushing to its rescue. In 1979, however, the Russians knew that Afghanistan was already isolated politically and militarily long before the invasion. The resignations from CENTO of Iran and Pakistan, which took place in the March of that year, removed the last possible springboard for any Western military rescue. It was by then evident that, in any case, the West had not the ability to mount a rescue, and probably not the will. The West's leader, the United States, was in a presidential election year, which rendered her much less able than usual to take quick and far-reaching decisions. This was true of 1968 also. In addition, in the case of Afghanistan, the United States was embroiled in a quarrel with Iran over the American hostages held in the Teheran embassy. Furthermore, President Carter had announced emphatically that he would not use force as a means of resolving this quarrel. Such a statement, admittedly, has nothing to do with America's *capacity* for action; but it did say something with regard to her *willingness* to act. It was likely to have been interpreted in the Kremlin as meaning that in respect of Afghanistan (with which at that time the USA had no ties at all, whether military or political) the American willingness to act must be reckoned minimal. Since in addition her capacity to act effectively to defend the Afghans could be seen, beyond any doubt, to be absolutely nil (except by nuclear war, of course), Brezhnev had good reason to believe that Afghanistan was completely isolated.

Moreover, there was an additional reason why he should hold the belief he did. It was neither a king nor a 'bourgeois' republican ruler whom the Russians wished to depose, but an Afghan Marxist. It was hard to see why the Western countries should be particularly interested in the fate of a Marxist, especially one so cruel and tyrannical as Amin had proved to be. If, therefore, he could be removed from power by Soviet troops acting in conjunction with Afghan troops, and with the Afghan people applauding the tyrant's downfall, and if moreover this could be done quickly, it was reasonable to expect that the

Western countries would not show much displeasure.

Brezhnev's calculations may not have been completely accurate; but it is certainly true that Afghanistan was isolated, in the sense of being bereft of foreign aid that could be militarily effective, at the time when the Russians struck. This, then, is an extremely important *similarity* between the 1968 and 1979 invasions. The one isolation may have come about as a result of Soviet diplomatic activity; the other, almost fortuitously: the important point is that both Czechoslovakia and Afghanistan were completely isolated, completely helpless militarily by the time that the Russians struck. This, it will be remembered, was the tactic that Hitler used to employ; and it is one more piece of evidence to show how effective the Nazi tactics were, and also how much the Soviet tactics resemble them. We must therefore expect that the political and military isolation of the intended victim will be a feature of any future attempt by the Russians to invade and conquer another country, whichever that may be.

Having thus, as they thought, isolated Afghanistan, the Soviet leaders then proceeded to launch their military coup. Since the purpose of the coup was to depose the existing leadership, it was the Afghan capital city that was the target of the airborne landing. Provided that this succeeded, which it did, the change of leadership could be effected quickly and easily; and in fact it was a matter of a mere 3 days before Amin's resistance had been crushed, and he himself executed.

A section of the Soviet airborne forces had in the meantime rushed north along the road from Kabul and secured the Saglan Tunnel. This carries the road under the mountains of the Hindu Kush, and it was the only point along the road network where Afghan opponents of the Soviet intervention could have caused really serious disruption to the subsequent invasion by land. The latter began on 29 December, and had achieved its main objective by the end of the month. That objective was to secure the continuance in office of the new Marxist Government, headed by Babrak Karmal. For that purpose they needed to be able to dominate Kabul and the other cities; and therefore they needed Russian troops either in, or very near to, them. Events have shown that they have only partially achieved their purpose, because, although they have got their troops into the required positions, they can hardly be said to *dominate* the Afghan cities. They can admittedly prevent their opponents from dominating them, but that is as much as they can manage at present; and, in order to achieve their objective in full, they will need to have many more troops.

This brings us to the chief point of criticism of the Soviet handling of the military operations: the failure of the Soviet forces to deliver a sufficiently weighty blow. The previous occasion on which they committed this particular military error was in 1939, when the Russians invaded Finland. They erred then, because Stalin believed that the Finns were incapable of offering resistance; and that therefore a comparatively small army was all that would be necessary. He was proved wrong. In 1980 the Russians erred, because they intended to persuade the world that it was the Afghans themselves who deposed Amin, with the Soviet Union doing no more than lend 'fraternal aid'.[6] For this to be convincing, the 'fraternal aid' had got to be very limited; and consequently it was the Afghan Army that was going to have to do the donkey-work. The Soviet leaders mistook the extent to which the Afghan Army was willing to act as donkeys; and this error of theirs was responsible for the error concerning the weight of blow.

This, however, was their only mistake concerning the military handling of the operation. In other respects it was handled extremely well. The airborne forces were allotted the correct targets and duly seized them; the ground forces moved in rapidly and occupied their allotted positions. Owing to the geography of the country it was not possible to mount the invasion from opposing points of the compass; but in view of the Soviet mastery of the air this hardly mattered. Surprise, that major Soviet military virtue, was, however, secured. This was done by a combination of factors. Firstly, the divisions used for the invasion by road were not, as might have been expected, Category A divisions, but comparatively low-grade Category C divisions which were below establishment. Since there were no Category A divisions in the area near the Afghan frontier, a Soviet invasion of Afghanistan did not appear to be imminent. This was the first means of securing surprise. Then, however, the Category C divisions were suddenly mobilized. This process began on 18 December, and only 10 days later, on 28 December, these low-grade divisions had completed their mobilization and had already crossed the border into Afghanistan. The speed with which they did these things was the second means of securing surprise for the

Russians. It is important to note that, because they secured surprise, and advanced speedily and decisively, low-category divisions were sufficient to do the job. This is a most important point, to which we shall return later. The third means of securing suprise was aimed, presumably, exclusively at the West. Just as the Russians delayed their invasion in 1968 until President Lyndon Johnson had gone off on his vacation, just as the Egyptians in 1973 chose the Israeli holy day, Yom Kippur, as the date for the start of their attack on Israel, so, in 1979, the USSR chose the Christmas holidays for the date of their attack on Afghanistan. From the beginning of the weekend before Christmas until a day or two after New Year's Day, the Western world in modern times has been accustomed to relapse into torpor. An endless round of boozing and guzzling and recovering from boozing and guzzling overtakes it; and the world could go up in flames, for all it cares. The Russians know this. To my mind, therefore, it seems extremely significant that the first of the airlifts occurred on the Friday immediately preceding Christmas (21 December); while the major ones that followed were on 25 and 26 December respectively. This was the third of the means whereby the Russians achieved surprise. If to that we add the fact that it was not only Christmas, but the Christmas of an American election year, and a Christmas dominated, in any case, by the American quarrel with Iran over the Teheran hostages, one is bound to conclude that the thing must have seemed to the Kremlin an absolute snip.

The Afghan operation is not yet over and done with. Indeed, at the time of writing it is still very far from being over. Consequently it is still not possible to assess it properly. What we can say, however, is that the standard ingredients of the Soviet military recipe were mostly present. The Russians achieved surprise; they had total air superiority; they acted quickly and decisively; they selected the correct targets. Admittedly they failed to deliver a sufficiently weighty blow; and this appears to be embroiling them in unpleasant military consequences. That mistake, however, resulted from a political error, from an incorrect political appreciation of the attitude of the Afghan Army. On the other hand, if the political appreciation had been accurate, who knows what might have happened? One possible consequence is that there might have been no invasion. Or else there might have been an invasion mounted by the whole of the

Soviet Army. One thing alone is certain; and this is that Brezhnev's error is of the same nature as Hitler's error when he embarked upon 'Barbarossa'; and the consequences of that were far from pleasant for the maker of it. We should also note that Brezhnev & Co. committed another political error, when they quite misjudged the world's reaction to what they intended to do. In particular, their misjudgement of the reaction of Third World countries is likely to cost them dear.

On the other hand we would do well to remember that the Soviet invasion of Afghanistan has shown that, provided strategic surprise can be achieved and then exploited speedily, the 'military keys to a country' can be seized by a not very large force of low-category troops. A picked force of high-grade troops will be needed for a part of the operation (the seizure of a vital communications centre or a bridge or an airport or, in the case of Afghanistan, a road tunnel; but low-category troops are sufficient for the rest, provided only that they move quickly and that strategic surprise has been obtained. It may be objected that this was true in Afghanistan, because the Afghan Army was a somewhat unsophisticated body and because the Afghan Air Force was mostly in the hands of the Russians; but that it would not be true of NATO, where things are different. Certainly the NATO air forces are not in the hands of the Russians, and the NATO armies are sophisticated in respect both of their weapons and their training; but can we be sure what the result would be if they were all utterly surprised? A man caught with his trousers down is not in a condition to fight properly; and we all agree that, if we do have to fight the Russians, we shall need to be able to fight them at the top of our form. So this is a matter on which it might well be profitable to reflect a little.

The second point that emerges from this present chapter is that the Russians conquered Czechoslovakia in the 'initial period' of their invasion (in the sense that none of the Czech armed forces were deployed against their invaders). We should note how easy a victory the Russians had as a result; and we should then reflect what an appalling price the USSR might have had to pay if the Czechs had in fact resisted. The political price she had to pay was in any case heavy enough; but if her armed forces had been obliged to kill Czech soldiers in pitched battles in Czech cities, then, although the Soviet Union would unquestionably have been victorious, she would have had to have paid a political price that would have been very nearly unbearable. So once again we see the value of winning in the 'opening phase' of a war.

NOTES AND REFERENCE

1. H. Gordon Skilling, *Czechoslovakia's Interrupted Revolution* (Princeton University Press, 1976) pp. 713–58.
2. *The Times*, 5 August 1968.
3. See, for instance, the *Washington Post*, 16, 20 and 21 August 1968.
4. *The Military Balance, 1968* (ISS, 1968) p. 2.
5. See, for instance, the map on p. 199 of Friedrich Wiener's *Soldaten im Ostblock* (J. F. Lehmann's Verlag, 1972).
6. For 'wars of fraternal aid' see P. H. Vigor, *The Soviet View of War, Peace and Neutrality* (Routledge & Kegan Paul, 1975) pp. 56–8.

12 The Soviet view of surprise attack

It has now become a main theme of this book that surprise attack at the strategic level is an essential ingredient of any endeavour to win wars in their opening phase. It therefore follows that we must examine in detail the Soviet view of this subject; and this we shall do in this chapter.

Surprise attacks at the strategic level are possible even after a war has started: 'Overlord,' the code name for the allied landings in Normandy in 1944 is only one of several impressive examples. This book, however, is concerned exclusively with the actual beginnings of wars and their immediate sequels; and consequently the sort of strategic surprise to which this chapter is mainly devoted will be that associated with the start of a war, though 'Overlord' and similar operations may naturally be used to shed additional light on particular aspects of our subject.

Since war between NATO and the Warsaw Pact will be the principal theme of this chapter, it would be as well to remind the reader that there can be three types of war of this kind; namely: one begun by NATO on the Warsaw Pact; one begun by the Warsaw Pact on NATO at a time of acute international crisis, when war is reckoned by the Soviet leaders to be the least bad policy option open to them; and war begun by the Warsaw Pact at a time and date of their own choosing, under conditions of minimal international tension, so that the war does indeed erupt on the world out of a clear international sky. A moment's thought should be enough to convince the reader that only the third of these types of war can possibly come as a surprise to NATO: the other two, virtually by definition, must be ones which NATO expects.

It is, of course, true that there is a fourth type of war: all-out nuclear war between the Super-powers. From one point of view it is correct to say that this is the type which, if any can, will guarantee surprise. The aggressor pushes the button; the missiles fly; very soon after, with minimal warning, the victim country is hit. It was not for nothing that Sokolovsky insisted so vehemently in his *Military Strategy* that for surprise accompanied by huge destruction nuclear war is un-surpassed. Sokolovsky penned that comment in the 1960s; it remains valid to this day. On the other hand, we have already mentioned that we are not concerned in this book with war of this nature. Consequently, although in theory we ought perhaps to devote the bulk of our attention to all-out nuclear war as being especially suited to the securing of strategic surprise, the fact remains that, so long as neither of the Super-powers acquires a first-strike capability, such a war should not form a part of this book, for the reasons we have already given. That having been said, we can now turn to the actual subject of this chapter.

We should begin by reminding ourselves that the Soviet Union showed little interest in surprise attack before the Second World War; and that such interest as she did show was confined to the tactical level. It was the events of the Second World War that compelled her interest in surprise attack at the strategic level. In particular, it was the German campaign in Poland in 1939, the campaign against Western Europe of 1940, the Japanese campaigns in the Pacific in the winter of 1941; but above all, and naturally quite dwarfing the rest in its significance for the Russians, it was Hitler's campaign against the USSR which he code-named 'Barbarossa'. Finally, certain aspects of the Allied invasion of Normandy in 1944 command the respect and attention of Soviet strategists, as do certain aspects of the Egyptian attack on Israel in 1973; but these are secondary.

The German campaign in the West in 1940 clearly showed that strategic surprise could be valuable. Its attainment by the Nazi ground forces, together with the securing by the Luftwaffe of virtually complete air mastery, were the chief factors that brought about the Fall of France. On the other hand it could be argued by a Soviet analyst (and many Soviet analysts *did* so argue) that the only reason the Germans won was that their defeated enemies were 'bourgeois' countries which were, by the nature of their 'class' society, more interested in destroying Communism than in resisting Nazi Germany. In any case, by the mere fact of them being 'bourgeois', they were necessarily effete.

However, this view was quickly rendered untenable by

'Barbarossa'. Admittedly, Nazi Germany did not bring about the destruction of Communism in Russia; but it came very close, uncomfortably close, to doing so. Of course, it failed in the end; but it came so near to achieving its purpose that among the Soviet military the question inevitably posed itself: How was it that it did so? Why did Barbarossa come so frighteningly near to success? The Soviet military then went on to ask themselves four supplementary questions: What were the causes of Barbarossa's failure (the *real* causes, not the propaganda causes)? And why, by contrast, was the German assault on France so highly successful? Could it be said that the Nazi leaders had invented a recipe for speedy victory, which might indeed suffer from certain defects – might even suffer from major defects – but which was nevertheless basically sound? Because if this were true, if the basic concept could be shown to be sound in its essentials, it was then presumably only a matter of effecting certain improvements to that basic formula in order to render the latter virtually foolproof. In which case, what were those improvements?

In trying to discover the answers to these questions the Soviet analysts came to the conclusion that strategic surprise was indeed a most valuable weapon, which any intending war-maker would be wise to include in his arsenal. It can confer, they decided, immense advantages on the attacker (or, for that matter, on the defender in the appropriate circumstances): in particular, it allows the attacker to gain his victory with smaller forces and even with forces of inferior quality than he would need if surprise proved unattainable; while furthermore it allows him to do this with fewer resources in weapons and equipment than are enjoyed by his intended enemy. This, it should be remarked, is not a peculiarly Soviet view of the matter; the German assessment is similar. General Halder, for instance, says in his diary (entry for 20 January 1940): 'More may be expected from an attack with small forces, using maximum surprise, than with larger forces, but against an enemy poised for defence'.[1] The truth of this dictum was admirably proved in France in 1940.

Of itself, however, surprise can achieve nothing. It can only confer the right conditions under which great achievements can become possible. It therefore follows that surprise must be exploited, and exploited to the maximum degree possible, if a great victory is to be won. This point, however, has been noted in an earlier chapter; there is no need to say more about it here except to emphasize that, for proper exploitation, air mastery is essential.

It should also be emphasized, with regard to the question of air mastery, that the Russians agree with this proposition. In the modern age, they say, no offensive operation of any significance, whether by land or by sea, has any hope of success without air mastery.[2]

The Russians have also come to the conclusion that it is very difficult for surprise to lead to a quick victory over an enemy possessed of big expanses of territory. This is because, by trading space for time, the enemy can manage to recover from this surprise and fight on and defeat his attacker. Of course it does not follow that he will necessarily do so; but he does at least have the possibility of doing so, which another endowed with a very small territory simply does not possess.

This advantage, conferred by nature upon a big country, is magnified even further if the country in question is geographically virtually featureless. If, that is to say, it has no high mountain barriers, no impassable swamps, no broad oceans within easy distance of the aggressor's original point of attack, there is then no anvil upon which the aggressor's hammer can fall and flatten his foe. By contrast, if the small country is possessed of such natural obstacles it is especially vulnerable to the use of strategic surprise.

Western Europe, by consequence, is almost an ideal target for a surprise attack, because its size is relatively limited in the context of modern military technology, and because it has a number of natural obstacles against which an attacker can pin the defender's forces and then destroy them.

It is, of course, patently obvious, but should perhaps be included for the sake of completeness, that the success of an attack will be even greater if it can be directed upon a defending force composed of second-category formations. This is what the Germans did in France in 1940. Success will also be likely if the attack can be directed at a boundary between two formations or, even better, at a boundary between two formations belonging to two quite different nationalities. That is to say, if you are fighting a coalition enemy, you should aim to split the coalition.

This point of view is ardently supported by Soviet military writers, including so great an authority as General Radzievsky, a man with a glittering record in the Great Fatherland War and one who, until his recent illness and subsequent death, was Head of the Frunze Military Academy. Here is what he has to say about the subject:

> In the offensive operations of the Great Fatherland War the main blow was most often aimed at the weakest, most vulnerable spot in the enemy's defences. Such spots were usually sectors held by small quantities of men and equipment, with poorly planned and poorly constructed defence works, and with ill-trained troops of low morale. Other weak spots in the defence were axes along which the enemy had not deployed large operational and strategic reserves. The weakest spots were always reckoned to be boundaries and flanks, especially when these were weakly guarded, and also sectors defended by troops of low fighting capacity. We also regarded as weak spots in the enemy's defences those sectors which he considered to be difficult of access from a tactical point of view. These sectors he usually held with the minimum quantities of men and equipment. An attack on such a sector was a complete surprise for the enemy; and, as a result of the surprise gained, our forces gained tremendous advantages, despite the fact that they were attacking over difficult terrain.[3]

From all this it follows that the ideal theatre of war for a Soviet commander is Western Europe; and the ideal foe is an enemy force composed of several nationalities.

China, by contrast, comes into a different category. It is, on the one hand, possessed of a formidable 'anvil', the ocean, within manageable distance of the Soviet and Mongolian frontiers; its capital, Peking, is only about 500 km from Mongolia; in the west there is to be found an additional useful 'anvil' in the shape of mountains; while it remains, one supposes, always possible for the Soviet and Mongolian armies to repeat their exploit of 1945, and invade North China from three directions, and then encircle and subsequently destroy the enemy forces deployed there. On the other hand, China is a huge country. From this it follows that the vulnerability of China to a Soviet strategic surprise attack is of a different order from that of NATO in Europe. Nor is the Chinese People's Liberation Army a coalition army.

It is reasonable to conclude from this assessment that the USSR is more likely to be planning to attack NATO than China, always supposing that she is planning to attack either of them. We may also conclude that the Soviet generals, having agreed that surprise is vital for the success of such an attack, will devote a great deal of time and effort to finding out how to secure it. In recent years they have been doing exactly that. The development of Soviet military thought with regard to the concept of strategic surprise is shown very clearly by the following:

In 1930, before the Second World War and before, therefore, strategic surprise had become a preferred ingredient of Soviet strategy, Soviet writers declared that surprise was to be attained in the following manner:

(1) by concealing one's movements;
(2) by a good choice of place for the blow to fall;
(3) by the speed and energy with which the blow itself is delivered.[4]

At some time in the 1950s the recipe was changed and surprise was then said to be attainable as follows:

(1) by keeping secret one's intended operation and the preliminary preparations for it;
(2) by falling upon the enemy unexpectedly;
(3) by deceiving the enemy with regard to one's own intentions;
(4) by attacking the enemy where he least expects it;
(5) by the decisiveness of one's actions and by clever manoeuvre;
(6) by employing weapons and methods of fighting which are new to the enemy.[5]

It will be observed that only the last of these nine methods shows any degree of sophistication. It is the only one that indicates any awareness of the lessons taught by the Second World War. The rest are either statements of the obvious or elaborations upon statements of the obvious. In 1976, however, there appeared an important article on surprise, written by Lt Gen M. M. Kir'yan, a senior member of the Voroshilov General Staff Academy. He declared that 'Surprise is one of the most important principles of military art'; and he went on to say that it is to be achieved;

(1) by deceiving the enemy concerning one's own intentions;
(2) by the use of new weapons, and by the employment of methods of warfare unknown to the enemy;

(3) by the correct choice of axis for the main blow, and by the correct choice of time for its delivery;

(4) by unexpected strikes by air, artillery and tanks, and by the sudden use of firepower of all kinds;

(5) by speed of manoeuvre and decisiveness of action, and by forestalling the enemy in the delivery of one's blow, thus making it harder for him to take counter-measures;

(6) by deception and camouflage;

(7) by the clever use of terrain, of weather conditions, of the seasons of the year and time of day.

General Kir'yan observes that surprise brings the greatest rewards when exploited with daring and initiative (*initsiativa*); and he also states that the significance of surprise increases steadily as a result of the development of new weapons. He cites aircraft and the nuclear missile as examples of the truth of this latter saying.[6]

A careful analysis of Kir'yan's list shows that it can be divided into four categories. One is concerned with camouflage and deception. This is a very important category. The success of 'Overlord', for instance, was in considerable measure due to it. Indeed, in the case of 'Overlord' it was very largely by the multiple use of deception, supported by extensive camouflage, that von Runstedt was led to believe that the main Allied assault on the Continent would come in the area of the Pas de Calais; and that, furthermore, he was made to go on believing this for 30 days after the Allied forces had stormed ashore at Normandy. In other words, even although it was incontestable that enemy forces had invaded Normandy, it was still possible to make him believe that this was only a feint; that the main attack would come in the Pas de Calais; and that, as a consequence, the main attack would come later than in fact it did. One can therefore say that he was thoroughly deceived both as regards place and time.

The means by which he was thus deceived included such things as radio deception, dummy landing-craft in and around Dover, heavy bombing of the area of the Pas de Calais designed to simulate the softening-up bombardment traditionally preceding a large-scale seaborne invasion of enemy territory, misleading lights in south-east England designed to indicate massive military activity there (whereas in fact there was none of any significance), and a total blackout in south-west England designed to conceal the military activity that mattered. This blackout by night was of course coupled with strict camouflage by day. Finally, there were the dummy Signals messages which were designed to convince, and did convince, the Germans that there was a US Army Group stationed in East Anglia and therefore poised to land in the Pas de Calais. No such US Army Group existed; but the German generals believed that it did, and that was all that mattered.

The Soviet campaign in Manchuria in 1945 offers another effective example of work in this category. Although the Russians could have had no hope whatsoever of keeping concealed from the Japanese the build-up of their forces, they were determined to succeed, and did succeed, in keeping the Japanese guessing as to the time and place of their attack on them. Full details are to be found in Chapter 9, where the Manchurian Campaign is analysed in depth. Here it is sufficient to point out that, for a long time, Tokyo was under the illusion that a Soviet attack in Manchuria was simply not possible for more than 8 months after the actual date when the attack in fact occurred and furthermore that, even when the Japanese General Staff had realized that they were badly wrong in their assessment, their revised estimate was still erroneous to the tune of nearly a month. With regard to the place at which they expected the attack to be delivered, they were badly at sea here, too.

The means by which the Russians induced these pleasing errors in the Japanese mind has also been examined in Chapter 9. Secrecy, camouflage, movement by night and deception are among the most important. These, it will be noted, figure prominently in General Kir'yan's list.

To return to that list, the second category of measures for securing surprise which can be extrapolated from it is that concerned with speed of manoeuvre and decisiveness of action as a means of prolonging, and indeed reinforcing, the effect of the initial surprise. Once the enemy has been thrown off balance, fast and decisive action by the attacker will make it extremely difficult for him to recover. Hitler's campaign in the West in 1940 provides superb confirmatory evidence. So too does the whole long series of operations launched by the Russians on the Eastern Front in 1944/5.

With regard to the first example, the Nazi generals themselves accept this verdict. It was, they agree, to a large extent the unremitting maintenance of their armoured offensive that got their *Panzers* to the Channel coast in a miraculous 10 days. It was the same unremitting maintenance of that armoured offensive that brought about the fall of France only a very few weeks later.[7]

In the second example, by 1944 the Red Army had reached a stage where it could keep the Nazis on the run. To quote their own description,

> The Soviet art of warfare rose to a still higher level in 1944. The various operations were begun, one after the other, along different axes and then merged into a simultaneous strategic offensive on an enormous front, which led to the complete rout of the most important enemy groupings.[8]

Admittedly, German sources do not describe this phase of the war in terms so flattering to the Russians; but the fact remains that on 1 January 1944 the front line ran from a little west of Leningrad more or less straight down south to the Black Sea; while less than a year and a half later the Russians were in Berlin. In order to get there they had had to travel a distance of 700 miles or more. If this cannot be allowed to be described as 'fast and decisive action', which made it 'extremely difficult for the enemy to recover', then the English language has lost its power to convey the meaning required.

The third category of measures includes all those where surprise is obtained as the result of the choice by the attacker of a particular area, a particular season of the year, or a particular day or time of day that will be least expected by the enemy. Of course, there are usually very good reasons why the enemy should *not* be expecting the attack on that particular sector or at that particular time of day or season of the year: the terrain is terrible; it is mid-winter and there is 20 feet of snow; or it is midsummer, the monsoon is beginning, and the roads are under water. All that this really means, however, is that the attacker who secures surprise by this method will have to pay a price. It was the view of the Germans, as also of the Russians, that the price is usually well worth paying, in view of the results achieved. Thus the German attack through the Ardennes in 1940 was launched over terrain which was much less conducive to rapid and easy movement than the plains a bit to the north; yet it was precisely because the terrain in the Ardennes was difficult that the French and British focused their attention on the northern plains and left the defence of the Ardennes sector to second-category formations.

Similarly, in Manchuria in 1945 the Soviet Trans-Baikal Front, which was responsible for launching the main attack, charged at the Japanese Kwantung Army across a considerable stretch of desert and a range of mountains. The *front*'s spearhead was 6th Guards Tank Army, and it was this army's tanks and SP guns, which together numbered more than 1000, which roared through the Great Khingan range and scuppered the Japanese.[9]

The surprise obtained by this method, by attacking where least expected, can be powerfully reinforced if the attacker deludes his victim by launching a second attack. This attack should be launched in the very sector where the defender has been *expecting* his enemy's main blow to fall. In 1940, for instance, some Nazi forces *did* attack through the northern plains – that is to say, through Belgium and also Holland. What is more, in order to make it seem plausible that this attack was the main attack, the forces that delivered it were powerful. They consisted of twenty-eight divisions, including three *Panzer* and one motorized. It goes without saying that these resources could have been used to make the blow to the south considerably stronger than it actually was; in particular, the three *Panzer* divisions would have been of the greatest use to von Kleist. If, however, these resources had actually been allotted to the group of armies that went through the Ardennes, it is highly likely that the plan would have been detected; and that the Franco-British Commander-in-Chief, General Gamelin, would have re-deployed his forces to prevent it. As things were, however, the Nazi force that invaded Belgium was of sufficient size and had sufficient armour to delude General Gamelin into the fatal belief that this was indeed the principal thrust, coming in the place and with the type of force he had so sagaciously predicted.

The same sort of thing took place with the Russians in Manchuria. Their main thrust was to be delivered across hundreds of miles of desert and a range of mountains. The Japanese did not believe this possible. But in order to lull the Japanese generals into a still firmer grip on that fatal belief, Marshal Malinovsky ordered the whole of one of his armies, 36th Army, to advance along the only route that the Japanese did believe possible, and which they had therefore lined with strong defences to trap the expected enemy. This was the route through Hailar. It was the old caravan route, the only really practicable route for entering Manchuria from the west; and this was the one which, in peacetime, was invariably used by travellers. In the old days, of course, the going was mostly by camel; but long before the war the track had been improved into something more nearly resembling a road, a railway had been built, there was also a river; all in all, it was the obvious place for an invading army to aim for.

Marshal Malinovsky, as we have seen, had no intention of doing the obvious; but he did realize that it was absolutely essential for the obvious at least to *appear* to be done, if the Japanese were not to become suspicious and to look for his main thrust elsewhere. Consequently, he obliged the Japanese generals by using the whole of one army for an advance on Hailar; in other words, he used force of a reasonably impressive size to attack where the Japanese expected him to. It was not a very good army; most of its units were second-category formations; but it had an excellent army commander with a first-class record of fighting the Germans; and in terms of numbers it was really quite impressive. It mustered a total of seven infantry divisions and a tank brigade, together with a number of artillery units and other supporting arms. When it advanced on Hailar, therefore, it was big enough to confirm the Japanese generals in their belief that this was the main thrust. It was not, of course. What was actually advancing upon these Japanese generals was something nearer Falstaff's army than a crack Soviet formation; and it seems to have suffered a considerable number of casualties as a result. That, however, to Marshal Malinovsky was totally irrelevant; from his point of view the only thing which mattered was that 36th Army's casualties had helped to secure the surprise he sought for the main thrust of his offensive.

To return to General Kir'yan's list, it will be seen that he has another category, his third category, of methods for securing surprise which he describes as 'the correct choice of axis for the main blow and of the time for its delivery.' I will subsume that category under the category we have just been discussing; because by 'correct' he must surely mean not only the time and direction that shall lead to important strategic results, but also those that shall help to secure surprise. Otherwise, he has no business in including them in that particular article.

We therefore pass to the fourth category of General Kir'yan's measures; and this consists of new weapons and new strategies and tactics. The new strategies and tactics need not necessarily be kept for new weapons; Hitler gained his greatest successes with weapons that dated from the previous war, the aeroplane and the tank. The Nazis, however, devised new methods of using these already existing weapons; and it was the new methods, not new weapons, which gave them their famous victories.

But it was really not even the actual new methods that brought about these sensational triumphs; rather, it was the surprise that their newness effected. I speak as one who has had personal experience of being on the receiving end of the German *Blitzkrieg* when I say that, for instance, in the case of the Stukas, it was not the actual dive-bombing that caused the consternation and the drop in morale, but rather our total ignorance of what dive-bombing consisted of, and our total lack of knowledge of how to deal with the bombers. It was only as time went on and the Stukas' horrific screaming became familiar to us, that we grew aware that, firstly they caused far more noise than casualties, and secondly there was a point in the course of their dive when they were very vulnerable. This was when they had dropped their load and were pulling up and out of their dive, and their soft underbelly was for a moment or two exposed for all to shoot at. Once we had assimilated these two points the Stukas proved much less effective. Yet the Stukas' tactic had not changed a bit; they were doing exactly what they had done before; yet then, because that tactic was new, they had been astonishingly successful. In other words it was the newness, not the actual tactic, that had been the chief cause of their success. Go back 2000 years and the same sort of thing was happening. In 255BC, for instance, the Carthaginians won the Battle of Tunis by using elephants, a weapon of war which was then unknown to the Romans.

Naturally, I am not trying to argue that newness is all that matters. The surprise it causes is valuable; but, as we have seen already, surprise has to be exploited if it is to win victories. A good tactic will allow the newness to be exploited much more effectively than will a poor tactic (though to put it accurately, it will not be the newness, but the surprise caused by the newness, that will have this desirable effect).

On the other hand, an excellent example of a good tactic can also be found in the history of the German blitzkrieg. In this case it was the marvellous use of tanks. Here the strategy and tactics were themselves good; so that to the huge advantage that their newness gave them must be added that which derived from their own merits. The result was formidable. Even after the newness had worn off the essential soundness of that approach to armour always clearly manifested itself; but during that time when to the soundness of the concept was added the fact that it was a new concept and that its use in battle was a complete surprise, the effect on the enemy was shattering.

It is worth noting that this category, this method of attaining surprise by new weapons and by new methods, has been rated very highly by General Kir'yan. He puts it as high as No. 2 on his list. In view of the very important position he holds, and the influence likely to be exerted by the General on successive generations of students at the Soviet General Staff Academy, we would be wise to assume that, in a future war, new weapons or new ways of fighting, or not impossibly a combination of the two, are likely to be employed by the Soviet forces, and are likely to prove very dangerous.

Given, therefore, that the Soviet commanders see very great merits in securing surprise, and also given that Kir'yan's methods may well be those the Russians will use to secure it, what can we say about the specific measures for the securing of it that are likely to be taken by the Soviet forces in Europe? In particular, are there lessons to be drawn from the history of Soviet war-fighting that will help us to elucidate them? The next section of this chapter will try to answer those questions.

We may begin by saying that the highest degree of surprise in war is virtually unobtainable. This is when one State falls upon another, and the wretched victim has no idea that he is going to be attacked at all. In practice, however, it is almost impossible to assemble in readiness sufficient troops to win not merely the opening battle but also the war as a whole (an important point, it will be remembered) without the victim ever suspecting than an attack is to be launched. Not 'Barbarossa', nor even Pearl Harbor, managed to achieve that much.

In these two cases the Russians and the Americans were well aware that an attack was in the offing; their failure was merely to be not quite sure exactly when it would happen. Even in a third case, the case of Czechoslovakia in 1968, the Soviet invasion was always to be reckoned possible.

So even in 1968 one could not say that the Russians had

succeeded in doing the impossible. The degree of surprise they obtained was great, but it was still by no means total.

This in itself implies, however, and implies perfectly correctly, that a partial degree of surprise is usually possible. A would-be attacker can reasonably hope to mislead his opponent with regard to the time or the place of his impending offensive. If he is very efficient he may do both. The USSR, not normally given to praising Western military achievements, has always agreed that in this respect Operation 'Overlord' was remarkable. That such a vast armada of ships, such tons of stores, such thousands of men, could be brought ashore on enemy territory without the enemy being aware either of the time or the place of their landing makes it unarguable that this sort of deception of the enemy is a perfectly feasible affair. It needs to be remembered, however, that German aerial reconnaissance at the time of 'Overlord' was very feeble indeed; that this is true of the French aerial reconnaissance in 1940, and of the Japanese aerial reconnaissance in Manchuria in 1945.

Accepting that is so, we still see that the Russians are extremely interested in securing strategic surprise; so the next question is: how will they set about doing it?

The history of the operations of the Soviet Armed Forces led us to suppose the following:

1. SURPRISE AS TO THE PLACE OF THE ATTACK

The Russians have used two principal methods for achieving this:
(a) They have used camouflage and deception. They used these in the Great Fatherland War and they used them in Manchuria. They went to great lengths to use them properly, and they usually succeeded. In Manchuria, for instance, the advance of Trans-Baikal Front across the open desert was kept from the knowledge of the Japanese to a considerable extent as a result of effective camouflage and of movement by night. Certainly the feebleness of the Japanese aerial reconnaissance was an important contributory factor, but had there been no camouflage used by the Russians, and had they moved in the daytime, the Japanese must have detected them.

(b) Soviet generals have a very great liking for attacking the
    enemy in a place where the terrain is difficult. Being
    difficult, it will probably either be guarded lightly by the
    enemy or else with second-category formations. In either case
    the task of the attacking Russians is rendered easy. The Soviet
    Army used this method on many occasions during the Second
    World War, and we have already mentioned General
    Radzievsky's assessment of it. The most important examples
    for the period 1939–45 are probably Hitler's attack through
    the Ardennes in 1940 and the Soviet attack through the
    Great Khinghan Mountains in Manchuria in 1945.

2. SURPRISE AS TO THE DATE OF THE ATTACK

Soviet experience seems to show that they try to obtain this form
of surprise in either one of two ways: either by attacking when the
season of the year would appear to be unfavourable to the
conducting of military operations, or else by choosing a week or a
day when the intended victim is likely to be on holiday. The
Soviet attacks on the Germans during the four winters of the
Great Fatherland War are an excellent example of the first of
these two methods. In particular, the winter of 1941–42 was
extremely severe. It was surely the sort of weather when any
sensible army would follow classic military practice and go into
winter quarters. The Germans set about doing so;[10] the Russians,
on the other hand, did not. Instead, they mounted a series of
operations that was aimed at getting the Germans on the run.
Having fought the Nazis to a standstill in front of Moscow, they
embarked on a counter-offensive. There seems little doubt that
the Germans, when their drive on Moscow had been halted,
expected that all would become quiet in the east until the return
of spring. They were proved wrong. On 5 and 6 December 1941
very large Soviet forces struck at them.[11]

To take another example, that of Manchuria in 1945, one
reason for starting the Soviet offensive at the beginning of August
was that this was a month in which movement in that area was
very difficult, and so an attack would not be expected in
August.[12] As we now know, the Japanese were not expecting one.
So although the Russians had to pay a price in the shape of
difficulty of movement, they received in exchange strategic
surprise which they reckoned fully rewarded them.

As for the other method that we have mentioned, that of surprising the enemy as to the date of the attack by choosing a day when he is going to be away on holiday, this has been used frequently by the Soviet Armed Forces. The invasion of Czechoslovakia, for instance, was done at a time when President Lyndon Johnson was away on a summer vacation; and since the United States was the only Power that could cause the Russians difficulties, this was extremely important. Admittedly, Johnson did come back to the White House on 20 August, but his whole attitude, his decision to take a 2- or 3-week vacation during the Czech crisis, showed much more clearly than words could do that, in his eyes, the Czech crisis was very much a non-crisis. In addition, had he suddenly desired action, it would have been none too easy to take it, because August in the United States is very much a holiday month, and large numbers of officials are away from their desks.

When it came to the question of Afghanistan in 1979, the day chosen for the initial wave of the invasion was Friday, 21 December. For the Western world this was the beginning of the Christmas holiday, which in modern times has fused with the New Year's holiday to give 12 or 14 days of abstention from work. It is of course possible, but extremely difficult, to get important decisions taken during that period; it is still more difficult to get them taken quickly. The start of that holiday period is therefore an ideal moment for a military adventure; and the Russians chose it.

In the same vein, the Egyptians chose for their attack on Israel in 1973 one of the most sacred days in the Israeli calendar, when as many Israelis as possible would be at prayer. Actually, their being at prayer turned out to be something of a help for the Israeli military, because, the worshippers being assembled together in the synagogues, it was comparatively easy to spread the alarm and get them off to their units. Had the Egyptians postponed their attack until the day *after* the Jewish festival, the Israeli population would have been dispersed on the holiday beaches and other places where it would have been far harder to have got them alerted quickly, and would have taken very much longer to get them mobilized. Thus, as it transpired, the Egyptians were clever in their planning, but not quite clever enough.

The United States has also employed this gambit. In 1980, when the attempt was made to free the hostages held in Iran, a

Friday was chosen for the day of the rescue, because that day is the Muslim sabbath and, in so religious a State as the Islamic Republic, the Iranians were likely to be at prayer, and therefore less immediately able to take effective counter-measures.

This method of surprising the enemy with regard to the date of the attack has obviously therefore been widely accepted (and not only by the Soviet Union) as an excellent means of doing so. There is therefore no need to say more about it here.

3. SURPRISE AS TO THE TIME OF THE ATTACK

The effect of the surprise that has been gained by these methods can usually be made to be even greater by a suitable choice of *time*. An attack launched just after midnight, for instance, will stun the enemy far more heavily than one that is launched at noon. Another favourite hour is just before dawn. On the whole, however, the Soviet generals seem to prefer the middle of the night, despite the difficulties that darkness causes to the movement of their own troops.

They started their offensive in Manchuria at 10 minutes after midnight;[14] while in 1968 they moved into Czechoslovakia at 11 p.m. on the night of 20 August. It seems reasonable to conclude, therefore, that where the Soviet troop movements are aimed at securing strategic surprise, the hour just around midnight is the one they are likely to choose. Of course, if the Soviet generals (as a result, no doubt, of reading this book) perceive that their enemies have become aware that they have acquired this habit, they will naturally choose another hour in the future, because no habit is a surprise.

4. SURPRISE AS A RESULT OF NEW WEAPONS AND NEW METHODS OF WARFARE

The introduction of new weapons and new methods of fighting has also been mentioned earlier as an admirable way of increasing considerably the effect of the initial surprise. To date, however, the Soviet armed forces have not introduced any new weapons or new methods of fighting into any of the operations in which they have been engaged since 1941. It is true that they produced the 'katyusha', the multi-barrelled rocket-launcher; but this was not really a new weapon, rather a development of an old one; and in any case it was not used by the Russians in connection with strategic surprise. Its chief use during the Great Patriotic War was as a component part of a heavy barrage; and it was employed in orthodox, not in novel, fashion.

On the other hand the USSR has introduced one new element which it is extremely difficult to categorize. This is to use for an impending operation troops which seem, on the face of it, to be unsuitable for the task awaiting them. In the case of Czechoslovakia, for instance, it was widely expected in the Western world that the invasion, if it were to be done at all, would have to be done by the well-trained troops of the Group of Soviet Forces in Germany. If these men were to do it, the invading force would be all Soviet; consequently, no problems of political will and military resolution would arise. Furthermore, GSFG is a cohesive, admirably trained striking force – the sort of force one needs for this kind of enterprise. What one surely does *not* need is a multi-national, miscellaneous force, which cannot be expected to have the drive and precision that GSFG possesses. Yet speed and drive and precision were the very qualities that were obviously going to be needed, if Czechoslovakia were to be quickly seized and quickly brought under control.

Western observers therefore naturally said to themselves that a prime indicator of whether or not an invasion was going to be ordered was what happened, or did not happen, to the units of GSFG. If there were going to attack Czechoslovakia, they would have to change location; and a change of location therefore could serve as a warning of invasion. This point obviously had struck the Russians too, because the GSFG did *not* change their location; consequently no alarm bell rang in Western ears; consequently when the job was done by the multi-national, lower-grade force which had been on exercise near the Czech frontiers, a considerable degree of surprise was secured for the Russians.

A somewhat similar operational method was employed in Afghanistan. Although the West was well aware that, as early as March 1979, contingency planning had been undertaken with a view to a Soviet invasion if that were necessary, it was generally assumed that, if it came to an invasion, it would be first-category troops that would do it. As there were no such troops in the vicinity of the Soviet–Afghan frontier it therefore followed that, in the event of invasion, they would have to be moved from wherever they were to a suitable jumping-off point. That movement, in turn, would signal their intention to any interested observer, and so would act as a warning.

In fact, however, no such troops were used by the Russians at all. Instead, they mobilized a C-category division whose headquarters were near the frontier. The mobilization itself proceeded extremely quickly; many in the West were very surprised to see how fast it could be done. On the other hand, by conventional Western reckoning the Russians were going to have to pay a price for doing things in this fashion. Firstly, they were going to have to use C-category troops, whose lower standard of training might quite conceivably imperil the operation's success; secondly, those troops would not be ethnic Russians; and there is a widely held view among Western observers that troops from Soviet ethnic minorities are not wholly reliable politically.

Be that as it may, the Soviet commanders continued with their policy; and, as things turned out, the price they paid was negligible. Whatever the inferiority of these particular troops as compared with others in the Soviet Army, they proved to be fully competent to fulfil the tasks allotted to them. By the same token they proved to be sufficiently politically reliable. The Soviet commanders may even have been reckoning that the fact that they were Asian would prove to be a positive advantage, at least in the initial stages of the operation. They would not, it might be argued, seem to the Afghanis to be so much of a foreign conqueror as would European troops. In this connection the Soviet commanders probably remembered the success that has attended the use of Cubans in Africa. Of course if subsequently the kinship of the Afghanis with the Soviet Asian soldiers should bring about a danger of infection of the latter with the virus of Afghani Islam, this could be easily countered by bringing them back into the Soviet Union and replacing them with ethnic Russians. By that time their task would have been accomplished, and the Soviet grip on Afghanistan would have been sufficiently secured.

5. SURPRISE AS A RESULT OF COUNTER-ELECTRONIC WARFARE

Additional methods of securing surprise have been put forward by Soviet writers on the subject. Thus General Kir'yan ingeniously suggests that in the modern world of electronic reconnaissance, surprise can be obtained, at least theoretically, by 'blinding' that reconnaissance. Certainly it is true that none of the political leaders of the Western democracies are going to order military retaliation merely because their electronic screens are simply showing blank. They will only order military retaliation (and that with the very greatest reluctance) if reconnaissance reveals that that the Communist forces are engaging in actual aggression. But if, for whatever reasons (including because it has been put out of action) the electronic and other reconnaissance reveals nothing whatever, the political leaders will permit nothing whatever: they will wait and 'see what happens'. And 'what happens' in a few hours' time is likely to prove devastating. By then, naturally, it will be far too late to do anything effective about it. This will be all the more true, of course, if the attacking forces up to that moment have done nothing at all suspicious. If they have refrained from reinforcing, if they have engaged in no unusual troop movements, the surprise they achieve by the blinding of the screens will be doubled or even trebled.

But, continues General Kir'yan, it is not sufficient merely to 'blind' the enemy by putting out of action his technical means of reconnaissance: it is, in addition, essential that the attacker, in order to discover in sufficient time the forces and equipment that the defender would need in order to launch a retaliatory strike, must activate in sufficient time his own spare set of reconnaissance equipment and his own spare set of equipment necessary for destroying the enemy's command and control and his navigational systems. This all adds up to a very comprehensive programme; but for success in war such a programme, he thinks, is essential.

6. THE 'DEAD VOLCANO' METHOD OF SECURING SURPRISE

I am no military historian, but I believe I am correct in saying that this method has been used only once during the last 200 years of warfare. That was in 1940, when Hitler attacked France.

Of course, the phrase 'the dead volcano method' is an invention of my own. Neither Hitler nor any of his generals used any such terminology; and indeed, so far as I can see, they did not apply the method as a method. That is to say, they did not do what they did do consciously, as a deliberate means of securing surprise, and after carefully assessing its value for this particular purpose. Rather, they did what they did for other, administrative reasons; and the fact that they thereby secured surprise was merely a pleasing bonus. Nevertheless they did secure surprise, and very effectively too; so it is therefore obviously important for us to see how this was done.

The method originated in Hitler's decision to attack in the West in Novemer 1939. Preparations for the offensive reached an advanced stage, and among other things the necessary troops were deployed in their form-up positions. So far as concerns the area round the Ardennes, this involved the moving to positions around the German–Luxembourg frontier of a considerable number of divisions which were no longer needed in Poland. These troop movements were noted by French reconnaissance. But then the weather turned bad, so that air support for the ground offensive was going to be out of the question; yet a major element in the *Blitzkrieg* concept was the co-operation of the air and the ground forces. Hitler therefore ordered that the offensive should be postponed.

It was postponed to a date in January. It would have been plain silly to have returned the troops to their original quarters, if they were to be back within a couple of months. Therefore the troops stayed. But when February came the weather was still unaccommodating; so once again the offensive was postponed. And once again the troops remained in their new, advanced positions.

The British official history of the Second World War describes it thus:

In both November and January when the [German] attack was ordered, the Allies were promptly 'alerted' some days before it was time to begin; in May they were not. Why was this? In the original version of [the German plan of attack] six days were allowed for the approach-march and final concentration of attacking formations; the offensive was to open on the seventh day. In both November and January the Allies had been warned by the preparatory movement forward of the enemy's troops ... but the final version [of the plan] allowed for no such preliminary moves. They had indeed become unecessary, for on each of the previous occasions formations had begun moving forward before the order for the offensive was cancelled, and when it was cancelled the troops remained in the positions they had already reached. Thus of the six days' movement originally planned three had taken place. Moreover the fact that the Allies had ordered the 'alert' in November and again in January became known to the German Command and showed them that better disguise of their intentions and greater security were imperative if the Allies were not to be forewarned of an impending attack. In adjusting dispositions to the final plan, therefore, any necessary closing up was effected gradually, so that well before the offensive was ordered the attacking troops were already within easy striking distance of the frontier. . . . When the code word 'Yellow' was issued about midday on May the 9th they could attack at daybreak on the 10th, without further large-scale movements to forewarn the Allies. This time the Allies' 'alert' was only ordered after the enemy attack had begun.

We thus see that the Franco-British High Command were like those peasants who live and work on the slopes of a 'dead' volcano. At one level of their consciousness such people know very well that they are in mortal danger. Wisps of smoke can be seen from the cone of the volcano; occasionally the earth rumbles: Years ago, it is asserted by popular tradition, the thing erupted, killing hundreds of people and destroying their crops and their farms. But that was back in the past. The volcano has shown no signs of life since then, and may be considered 'dead'.[15]

Then suddenly this 'dead' volcano erupts. The wretched peasants are caught entirely by surprise. They have no defence; they can do nothing but run; and as they run the lava and ash sweep over them, and that is the end.

This supine attitude towards imminent danger is not confined to men. It appears to be endemic in the whole animal kingdom. Danger is that which moves. From this it follows that something which does not move must be innocuous. Of course that 'something' must remain immobile for quite a considerable time to be reckoned harmless; but once it has done so, once it has remained motionless for a sufficient period, even the most suspicious human or animal will cease to worry about it. It will

Soviet Blitzkrieg Theory

have become not merely a part of the landscape, but a *normal* part of the landscape. And normalcy is not dangerous. Normalcy is the familiar, the ordinary, the safe.

So it was not long ago with Etna; and so it was too with Mount St Helens in the United States of America. In the middle 1960s also, a similar sort of thing occurred in Wales, though then not with a volcano. Then it was an old tip, the debris of the local coalmine, which collapsed on top of the village of Aberfan. It had been there for years; therefore it was a normal part of the landscape; therefore it was not dangerous, and you could sleep safely in its shadow – until that day in 1966 when it tumbled down on the sleepers, and it was their last sleep on earth.

It is this 'normalcy' syndrome which alone explains the otherwise incredible blindness of the French senior commanders in 1940 to the danger inherent in all those hundreds of *Panzers* leaguered so near the frontier. When the *Panzers* first arrived in their positions they did indeed alarm the French commanders. But after 2 or 3 months or so they had become a normal part of the landscape. Therefore they were not dangerous. Therefore the German armies secured strategic surprise.

The rewards of a successful surprise attack more than compensate for the tremendous effort which will have had to have been made to secure them. This is how the Russians themselves speak of the nature of the rewards:

(1) The history of the Second World War shows that, by the use of surprise attack and by the all-out use of armed forces which had been already deployed, the aggressor could gain his initial goals, and sometimes even his final ones.[16]

(2) Experience shows that an aggressor who has achieved surprise with his attack and who exploits the power of those of his armed forces which have already been deployed, has achieved tremendous results at the start of a war. The States exposed to the German surprise attacks in the Second World War were either completely defeated, or else they capitulated without having exhausted all their powers of resistance (Holland, Belgium, France and others) or else they lost huge territories and the power to gain the strategic initiative.[17]

Surprise attack, therefore, has proved itself worthwhile.

NOTES AND REFERENCES

1. *The Halder Diaries*, vol. 1, p. 189 (T. N. Dupuy Associates, 1976).
2. On this point see, for instance, *Sovietskaya Voennaya Entsiklopediya*, vol. 2 (Voenizdat, 1976) p. 620; vol. 5, p. 520, and also S. P. Ivanov, *Nachal'nyi Period Voiny* (Voenizdat, 1974) p. 350.
3. General A. I. Radzievsky, *Proryv* (Voenizdat, 1979) p. 167.
4. *Bol'shaya Sovietskaya Entsiklopediya*, 1st edn, 1930, vol. 11, p. 674.
5. Ibid, 2nd edn, vol. 8, p. 253.
6. *Sovietskaya Voennaya Entskilopediya*, vol. 2, p. 161.
7. See, for instance, Major General F. W. von Mellenthin, *Panzer Battles* (University of Oklahoma Press, 1956) pp. 24–5.
8. *Bol'shaya Sovietskaya Entsiklopediya*, 3rd edn, vol. 4.
9. According to Soviet sources, 6th Guards Tank Army had for this operation a combined total of 1019 tanks and SP guns and 188 armoured cars *Voenno-Istoricheskii Zhurnal*, No. 3, (1977)).
10. On this point see *The Halder Diaries* for the early days of December 1941.
11. These are the dates given in *Bol'shaya Sovietskaya Entsiklopediya*, 3rd edn, vol. 4.
12. Another reason, of course, was that the Russians had got to hurry, if they were to get their troops into China and Korea before the Americans got there.
13. The rescue was begun on the evening of the Thursday, 24 April, but the actual operations that, it was hoped, would result in the freeing of the hostages were planned for the Friday, 25 April. As we all know, the President called them off.
14. M. V. Zakharov, *Finale* (Progress Publishers, Moscow, 1972) p. 39.
15. Mount St Helens in the USA erupted in 1980. It had not erupted previously since 1857. So 'dead' had the volcano come to be reckoned by those living around it that its first eruption of 1980, that of 26 March, caused little stir. There were no casualties – just a lot of steam and ash that were thrown high into the air. Clearly there was nothing serious; nothing to cause a right-minded person to leave home or take other precautions – and so there were plenty of victims available when Mount St. Helens erupted again almost 2 months later. The surprise was complete: the casualties were therefore heavy.
16. Ivanov, op. cit., p. 14.
17. This is taken from General M. M. Kir'yan, 'Vnezapnost' ('Surprise') in *Sovietskaya Voennaya Entsiklopediya*, vol. 2 (Voenizdat, 1976) pp. 161–3.

13 But what does 'surprise' consist of?

We ought now to be able to embark on our final chapter; but still this question of surprise needs more elucidating. We have established the importance that the Russians ascribe to the subject; we have examined the ways in which they seem to be trying to achieve it; we have seen that surprise of itself is virtually useless, and that to have any military value it must swiftly and effectively be exploited. What we have not yet done, however, is to see what surprise consists of, and from there go on to establish whether a commander needs to surprise the enemy totally and completely, or whether a degree of partial surprise can ever be sufficient for his purposes. If the latter, then can we say how low a degree of surprise will suffice for the commander to be successful?

In addition to the above, we should surely compare the theory of the matter with the practice. Is it true, as is often said, that the USSR was *totally* surprised in the summer of 1941? How exactly did surprise operate to confound the Israeli defence effort in 1973? Because if the surprise in neither case was total, and yet its effects in both cases were extremely damaging to those surprised, we may possibly be guilty in this book of conducting the discussion of this intriguing subject on too high and perfectionist a plane. If this is true, is it not then a necessary corollary that we may very well be deceiving ourselves when we assert with smug satisfaction that the Soviet armed forces are not, and never will be, capable of achieving a *total* surprise of NATO, because it may well be that all that is needed for their purposes is some degree or other of *partial* surprise.

It is, of course, true that total surprise is by no means inconceivable. An individual civilian can be surprised in the street and murdered, without having had even an inkling that death is about to strike. By the same token a small military unit can, as a result of an ambush or of a lightning attack by night, be wiped out before a single man has become aware of what is happening. Such an occurrence can really only be possible if the doomed unit in question has failed to take proper precautions – to conduct reconnaissance, to mount sentries, and so on. Nevertheless, it can happen, and it has happened.

Instances such as these, however, are all at the tactical level; and this book is concerned with strategy, and hardly at all with tactics. At the strategic level it is impossible to think of any instance of total surprise being actually effected. A platoon, a company, a battalion may have been surprised totally, but not an army.

What happens with armies is that their most forward elements (sentries, patrols, advance guards) may sometimes suffer total surprise, as may even perhaps the forward elements of the main body; but it is impossible to think of any army commander who was so totally ignorant of the incipient disaster that he himself and his staff and his nearer units were, as it were, overwhelmed out of a blue sky. This is true of an army commander in wartime; it is still more true of an army commander in peacetime, when the war has yet to break out.

In the twentieth century, and among the big industrialized nations, the rank of army commander has been a relatively low one. In time of peace in a democracy, no military decisions of any real importance are taken by generals, even by four-star generals. It is the politicians who take them. Such decisions include the decisions to mobilize and to permit the use of this or that level of weaponry. Even once a major war has started, then, at least in the principal theatres of war, it is the army group commander who has been the lowest military figure of any importance. For the purpose of this analysis, it is therefore the leading politicians with whom we shall be especially concerned in peacetime while in wartime it will be the army group commanders and the commander-in-chief.

What we are now saying about these people is that they, at any rate in the twentieth century and among the big industrialized nations, have always had some sort of warning (and usually quite a good deal of warning) about any impending attack. Where their country has been surprised, it has therefore been these people's errors of judgement in refusing to believe, or at any rate refusing to act on, the warnings that they have been given. The French and British Governments in 1940 were not totally surprised by Hitler's May offensive; the Soviet dictator, Stalin, had repeated warnings from the most varied sources concerning 'Barbarossa'; while in 1973 the Israeli Cabinet had been told by its own Intelligence that an Egyptian attack was imminent, but simply chose to ignore what it was told.

Since Hitler's attack on France in 1940, his attack on Russia in 1941 and the Egyptian attack on Israel in 1973 are the three chief examples of the 'initial period' with which we have been concerned in this book, it seemed right to select them for analysis now with regard to the nature of the surprise effected, which is the subject of this penultimate chapter. The analysis naturally will concern itself with as many facets as possible. For good measure, we shall include an analysis of 'Overlord'.

HITLER'S ATTACK ON FRANCE IN 1940

Prior to the attack, a reasonably accurate assessment of the number of Nazi divisions and of their deployment had been made by the French and the British. The main characteristics of the three German army groups were fully comprehended. In particular, the preponderance of armour in Army Group A was known, though the fact that it was located near the Ardennes puzzled the Allies somewhat. This was because General Gamelin simply refused to believe that a major armoured thrust through the Ardennes and across the Meuse was feasible. But if it was not feasible, it was obviously not very easy to say why the Nazi armour was deployed in that particular region. Weak aerial reconnaissance by the French Armée de l'Air (itself the result of Gamelin's personal order) did not help to dissipate the latter's ignorance.

One thing, however, is certain. The war had begun 8 months before; so both France and Britain were by then on a war footing. Total surprise (*really* total surprise) was consequently impossible. From this it follows that surprise in respect of *place* was also impossible, if by *place* we mean the overall theatre of war. If Hitler were to attack the French and British at all, he was obliged to attack them through some point or points on the western frontier of Germany. It did, however, remain possible for him to effect surprise in respect of the overall offensive. These things, as we know, he successfully accomplished. It was also possible for him to achieve surprise in respect of new ways of war-fighting which of course he did as well.

The result of his success in these respects was that the French Army was deployed badly to meet, not Gamelin's imagined threat, but the one that actually materialized. The result of this failure on the part of the French was that astounding catastrophe which we call the Fall of France. We therefore have here a surprise which, although it was far from total in the strict sense of that expression, was nevertheless sufficient to do the job.

Further north in Belgium, failure to ascertain beforehand the date of Hitler's attack, failure to ascertain with certainty that he would attack Belgium at all, was undoubtedly a contributory factor in bringing about the extremely rapid capture by the Germans of the key Belgian fort of Eban Email. It was of course the very rapid fall of Eban Email which in turn was a principal reason for the failure of the Belgian Army to delay the Germans longer at the frontier than in fact they actually did; and it was the consequent increase in the tempo of the German Army's advance which doomed whatever hopes of success the Dyle Plan might have had.

On the other hand, although surprise in respect of *date* and *direction* undoubtedly contributed greatly to the fall of Eban Email, so too did surprise in respect of *method*. It was the use by the Germans of paratroops, then wholly unknown as a tool of war, that contributed very significantly to the fort's capture.

So far as Belgium is concerned, therefore, we may say that surprise in respect of method was total, but that surprise in respect of date was only partial. Belgium's most powerful neighbours had been in a state of war with each other for over 8 months when the attack happened; it was plain to all, including the Belgian Government, that the attack might come through Belgium; it cannot therefore be said that the surprise was total, but it can be said that it was totally successful.

'BARBAROSSA'

In 1941 the Soviet leaders were told repeatedly that a German attack was imminent. Some of the information given to the Kremlin even predicted accurately its date. Students who want a detailed study of the extent to which the political and military leaders of the Soviet Union were informed about 'Barbarossa' should turn to A. M. Nekrich's invaluable monograph, *1941: 22 iyunya* (Nauka, 1965). Here it must suffice to say that not only was Soviet Intelligence itself informing Stalin that the German attack was coming, but so were foreign diplomats, and so too (and still more important) were the Soviet commanders of the frontier districts who could see and hear the gigantic preparations necessary for so massive an attack. The trouble was that Stalin, because of his personal preconceptions, wrongly assessed this information and believed it to be erroneous. Only at the end, only in the final hours before the 'off', did he give permission for certain limited precautions to be taken by the frontier districts.

We have here, therefore, an example not of total, but only of partial surprise; but we also have an example of a partial surprise which only failed to be totally successful because of the large size and utter flatness of Russia, the latter circumstance meaning that there was no 'anvil' within easy reach of the 'start' line upon which the Nazi hammer could smash the Russians. We should note that the surprise was partial in five respects:

(1) The decision-maker-in-chief (in this case Stalin) was surprised by 'Barbarossa' only because he refused to believe the various reports that were given to him. His military commanders on the frontier, however, were not surprised at all. They knew perfectly well what the Germans were up to; but they were prevented by Stalin's orders from making full use of that knowledge. Here we have one more example of certain citizens of a victim State being fully aware of what is about to happen, but of being unable to react effectively, because the key decision-makers simply refuse to accept it. The Israel of October 1973 is another classic example.

(2) The second respect in which the surprise achieved by 'Barbarossa' must be reckoned only partial is that, as we have seen, in the last few hours of peacetime Stalin did give grudging permission for certain precautions to be taken.

(3) Such surprise as was achieved was *not* in respect of place. The Soviet commanders knew perfectly well the sectors along the frontier which were to be the subject of the attack.

(4) They also knew approximately the date; so surprise here was also only partial.

(5) They were much more surprised by the new ways of war than they ought to have been. They had studied the lessons of the German campaign in Poland of 1939, and also those of the campaign in Western Europe of 1940; but for a variety of

reasons they had not really assimilated them. To a considerable extent they were victims of their own Bolshevik propaganda: they did not believe that 'bourgeois' countries could have any stomach for a war against Germany; and hence they under-estimated the quality of the Nazi victories. Consequently they were in no hurry to devise effective counter-measures. The lessons of the war against Finland were far more cogent in Stalin's eyes than those of the Fall of France; and therefore Soviet armoured formations, which had been disbanded in 1938 as a result of Stalin's reading (or, to be more accurate, mis-reading) of the lessons of the Spanish Civil War, were re-formed not in the autumn of 1940, as a clear study of the French campaign should surely have dictated, but only in 1942, after bitter experience had taught the Russians the need to re-create them.

Nevertheless, though the surprise achieved by the Germans was partial rather than total, its effects were terrific. On the first day over 800 Soviet aircraft were caught on the ground and destroyed;[1] while, because of wrong deployment, infantry units of the Red Army were caught without their artillery. As a result of these and other disasters, the German forces of Army Group Centre moved on remorselessly into Russia. By the end of September it had advanced approximately 500 miles, had taken prisoner about 600,000 Soviet soldiers, and had destroyed about 5000 Soviet tanks and several thousand guns. Furthermore, the Luftwaffe's heavy bombing of the Red Army's rear, itself made possible only by those crippling initial losses of the Soviet Air Force, rendered the question of reinforcement and supply particularly difficult for the Stavka.

THE SOVIET INVASION OF MANCHURIA IN 1945

Surprise as to the date and time of this attack was total. The Japanese, though they believed that an attack was probable, did not believe that it could be undertaken till a month later than it was. Surprise as to the place of the attack was at best only partial, because it was clear to everyone that this must come from the east, the north and the west, as indeed it did. Surprise generated by new methods of war-fighting was also only partial. To the extent that it was achieved at all, it derived from the success of the Soviet generals in pushing large armoured formations through the Khinghan Mountains. On the other fronts the methods of fighting were traditional. In any case, many would say that the pushing of large armoured formations through mountain ranges is not a 'new method of warfighting'. On the other hand it is impossible to deny that, however it may be categorized, the surprise it produced was real.

It should also be said that there would have been little surprise of any kind, if the Japanese had conducted efficient reconnaissance in the weeks before the attack. This they did not do. Tokyo was finding it increasingly difficult to continue the war against their existing enemies; they did not wish to add Russia to that already formidable list. Consequently, orders were sent to the forces in Manchuria categorically forbidding them from reconnoitring across the frontier, whether by land or air, in order, as they expressed it, to avoid 'provoking' the Russians. A similar order, it will be remembered, was issued by General Gamelin in early 1940, with similarly disastrous results. In the case of Manchuria the chief disadvantage of the Japanese order was that General Yamada, the Japanese commander-in-chief in the area, was quite unaware of the size of the Soviet forces advancing from Mongolia towards his western frontier, quite unaware of the amount of the Soviet armour, and quite unaware also, once the war had started, that his pet view had been proved to be wrong, and that big armoured formations were actually crossing the Khinghan.

Summing up, one is bound to declare that the surprise achieved in Manchuria was only partial in respect of place, very partial indeed in respect of new methods of war-fighting, but, on the other hand, virtually total in respect of the date and time of the commencement of the attack and of the direction of the main thrust. These three kinds of surprise were extremely well exploited, and the result was disastrous for Japan.

The chief causes of the Japanese defeat were the fact that it was their enemy who had the mastery of the air; the fact that their reinforcements, the trained divisions from China, had not completed their move to Manchuria before the Russians struck; the low quality of many of their troops already stationed in Manchuria; and their failure to expect that the Red Army would mount their principal attack through the Khinghan Mountains.

The reasons for their lack of air power and for the low quality of many of their troops do not come within the province of this chapter; but it was surprise that accounted for the Japanese lateness in transferring their good divisions from China, and also for their failure to assess correctly the direction from which the main Soviet blow would fall. Of these, the former is the more relevant, so far as concerns this book, because it appears to demonstrate that surprise in respect of date and time is capable of catching the enemy either not deployed or wrongly deployed; and that, when it does, the results can be catastrophic. But this is a thought that we shall be developing in the course of the final chapter.

THE YOM KIPPUR WAR OF 1973

The Israeli Southern Command Headquarters had no doubt whatever that an Egyptian attack was likely on or around 6 October. The Israeli Director of Military Intelligence did not, however, agree with them, nor did the Israeli Chief of Staff. The trouble was that, in the previous May, similar signs of an impending attack had been detected; and that, although the Director of Military Intelligence had dismissed these signs also, the Chief of Staff had not. He had therefore recommended to Mrs Meir that the Israeli forces be mobilized; and this was done.

In the event, however, no attack came. Consequently, when in October similar warnings were uttered, the Israeli Cabinet treated them as simply a cry of 'Wolf!' Mobilization places an enormous strain upon an always very shaky Israeli economy; no Israeli Cabinet will therefore wish to order mobilization unless the need is perceived to be inescapable. In October 1973 it was not perceived to be inescapable; and therefore it was not ordered. [2]

In one sense, therefore, the Egyptians did not succeed in surprising Israel at all: Israeli Intelligence knew perfectly well what was happening. In another sense, however (and in the only sense that matters), the Egyptians surprised the Israeli political decision-makers, and surprised them totally, in respect of the date and time of their attack, though not, of course, the place. It is a matter of semantics as to whether it can be said that they surprised them in respect of new ways of war-fighting, because what was new was not new *ways* of fighting, but the unexpected excellence of the Egyptian anti-aircraft weapons systems and the consequently minimal effectiveness, at least in the early stages of the fighting, of the hitherto unquestionably dominant Israeli Air Force. Israeli tank losses were also higher than had been expected.

On the other hand, the Egyptian forces did not exploit their surprise at all effectively. A Guderian or a Malinovsky would surely have wept to see the dilatoriness with which the Egyptians operated; and it is this dilatoriness which I believe must be accounted the chief cause of the Egyptians' subsequent failure.[3]

'OVERLORD'[4]

Largely as a result of the Allied plan of deception, code-named 'Fortitude South', and partly as a result of the much-reduced German ability to conduct effective aerial reconnaissance over Britain and the English Channel, the German commanders in 1944 were surprised both strategically and tactically. They were not surprised *totally*. Some information regarding the imminence of an Allied landing in Normandy was undoubtedly made available to them, but they chose to ignore it. Then, when unquestionably Allied forces had succeeded in getting ashore in France, the German commanders refused to believe that this was the main assault. For this the Allied deception plan was very largely responsible, while Allied mastery of the air – which was virtually total – prevented Nazi reconnaissance from detecting the plan's working.

SUMMARY OF ALL THE FOREGOING

We may sum up by saying that, in the case of Western Europe in 1940, the British and French forces had long been mobilized, concentrated and deployed; and that they were well aware of the existence of the German Army Groups A, B and C. Nevertheless, the Nazis succeeded in achieving surprise over them in respect of the date and time of the attack, of the direction of the main thrust, and of new methods of war-fighting. As a result of the surprise the Belgian resistance collapsed extremely quickly, while the Franco-British forces, being deployed to meet a main attack in the north, were wrongly deployed to meet the actual main Nazi attack, which came through the Ardennes. The faulty deployments were due to a faulty assessment by the Allied Commander-in-Chief, General Gamelin. It was he who was surprised more than anyone; and it was his surprise which wrought the Allied ruin.

Important additional reasons for the German success were the speedy winning of mastery of the air by the Luftwaffe, the new method of war-fighting which we know as *Blitzkrieg*, and the heavy bombing by the Luftwaffe of the rear areas (itself only made possible by their mastery of the air) which rendered impossible any effective and continuous resupply and reinforcement of the British and French divisions engaging the Germans. Altogether, the German exploitation of their surprise was both extremely speedy and extremely effective.

In the case of 'Barbarossa', our summing up will concentrate on the faulty deployment of the Red forces at the time of the German attack. Once again, the Germans achieved surprise in respect of the date and time of their offensive; and they did so purely because of the obstinacy of one man: the dictator Stalin. They also achieved surprise in respect of new methods of war-fighting. As a result of the surprise, numerous formations of the Red Army were trapped and either captured or annihilated; while large numbers of their aircraft were caught and destroyed on the ground. The Luftwaffe quickly attained air mastery to bomb into total ineffectiveness incipient counter-measures being taken by the Soviet generals. The Nazis exploited their surprise extremely quickly and extremely effectively; and they came remarkably near to defeating Russia.

The Soviet assault on Manchuria achieved surprise in respect of both date and time, largely because of the determination of the Imperial Government in Tokyo *not* to believe that the Russians would attack at a moment so desperately unfavourable to the Mikado's forces, stretched as they were by their disastrous war in the Pacific. Consequently, measures for the proper defence of Manchuria were not put in hand in time. The Russians also achieved surprise in respect of the direction of their main axis; though this was due as much to the Gamelin-like stolidity of the local Japanese commander as to anything else. He was, however, himself severely hampered by a ban put on aerial reconnaissance by Tokyo, which would not allow his aircraft to fly over Soviet or Mongolian territory for fear lest, if they did so, they would somehow 'provoke' the Russians. The latter, having achieved their surprise, exploited it very speedily and very effectively. The Soviet Air Force had from the outset complete mastery of the air.

The Israeli Cabinet, though not Israeli Intelligence, was surprised in respect of the date and time of the outbreak of the Yom Kippur War. It was also surprised by the effectiveness of the enemy's anti-aircraft weapons systems. The Egyptians obtained from their surprise a 5-hour start over the Israelis; in other words it was 5 hours from the start of the Egyptian crossing of the canal to the moment when the Israeli forces began to react effectively. Had the Egyptians exploited their surprise with greater speed and vigour than they did, they might have achieved victory. They did not do so. We should not, however, imagine that the Warsaw Pact would make so poor a use of a 5-hour start; but that is a point we shall be examining in the next chapter.

The Germans in 1944 were surprised at the date and time and place of the Normandy landings. They were also surprised by certain military technology, such as PLUTO and the 'Mulberry' harbour. The Allied air forces had from the outset complete mastery of the local air space; and this space they widened and deepened as the days and weeks went by. It cannot be said, however, that the Allies exploited the surprise they had gained sufficiently quickly or effectively to come within the purviews of this book. One reason for their failure was the admirable discipline and fighting spirit of the German troops opposing them; another was the nature of the terrain, the *bocage* country of Normandy, which provided enormous natural help to the defence. As against all this, it may be said that the Allies reached and crossed the Seine a good many days ahead of their pre-planned timetable; but in the context of winning in an initial period, it has to be accepted that the first Allied landings were on 6 June, that Paris was not liberated till 25 August, and that the Allied forces crossed the Rhine only 7 months later. I am not so foolish as to say that the Allied armies fought badly or were poorly commanded; I am merely saying that their rate of advance and the degree of their exploitation of their unquestioned initial surprise were not so great as to make 'Overlord' an example of any great relevance to the subject of this present book.

CONCLUSIONS

(1) We thus see that, for the purpose of achieving effective surprise at the start of a war (or, during wartime, at the opening of a new theatre of military operations), it is not necessary for the surprise to be total, in the sense of not one single enemy soldier having any idea of what is afoot. It is quite possible for the surprise to be effective, and even possible for it to be totally effective, if the senior enemy decision-makers can be hornswoggled. These decision-makers will be in peacetime the leading enemy politicians, and in wartime the enemy army group commanders and commanders-in-chief. If these can somehow be flabbergasted, the reaction of the enemy's armed forces will be nugatory.

History seems to indicate that this pleasing result can be obtained by psychological warfare as often as, if not indeed more often than, by purely conventional military means. Gamelin did not *want* to believe that the Nazi attack would come in the south; so he accepted evidence that confirmed this view and rejected what contradicted it. Stalin did not *want* to believe that Hitler intended his assault on Russia for 1941; he desperately needed it to be delayed for at least another 12 months. Consequently, he refused to listen to evidence that contradicted his thesis. The Imperial Japanese Government in 1945 simply did not *want* to believe that the Soviet Union would invade Manchuria at any time that year; consequently it grasped at whatever bits of 'evidence' the Russians kindly proffered it that tended to confirm it in its belief. Therefore it did not take the necessary military counter-measures in time to be of any use; and a defence, which must in any case have been extremely wobbly, was rendered completely hopeless. The Israeli Cabinet in 1973 did not *want* to believe the Intelligence reports. As events proved, there was nothing wrong with the reports; it was the Israeli Cabinet's assessment of them which proved to be defective.

In contrast to the above, von Runstedt in 1944 did not assess the Allies' intentions wrongly simply because he did not *want* to believe in an Allied landing in Normandy. He assessed them wrongly because of faulty Intelligence; and the latter was due to the Allied plan of deception, 'Fortitude

South', but also to the Luftwaffe's inability to conduct proper reconnaissance of the English coasts. Had proper reconnaissance been possible, 'Fortitude South' might well not have succeeded. It begins to seem as though lack of proper reconnaissance on the part of the enemy, in the widest sense of that word 'reconnaissance', is a key prerequisite for achieving surprise, however partial.

(2) Since the political leaders of any Western democracy never *want* to believe that war is imminent and, in addition, are always loth themselves to take the responsibility for ordering their forces on to a war footing, mobilizing the reserves and so on, it becomes attractive for any intending aggressor to reduce the likelihood of these necessary measures being taken by seemingly offering to 'negotiate' with his intended victim. Chamberlain believed that Hitler was a gentleman, and therefore he would not countenance measures that might be thought likely to 'provoke' him. He relied on negotiation. The French adopted a similar sort of policy; so did the Poles. Consequently, information that might have seemed to cast doubts on Hitler's gentlemanliness was simply automatically rejected by the Western leaders; while those who in fact did not actually believe in it mostly found it prudent, because of their electors' views on the matter, to speak and act at all times as if they did.

By the same token, if the Soviet Union is in fact planning a surprise attack on NATO, it is likely to time the start of it to synchronize with a period in international relations when there is great talk of detente. The Kremlin leaders would be speechifying daily about disarmament, about the Soviet Union's horror of war and its longing to see the Communist lamb lie down with the Capitalist lion. Under such circumstances Western political leaders would find it virtually impossible, despite the gravest Intelligence warnings, to order mobilization before the war began; yet as we all know, a non-mobilized NATO would be an important factor favouring a Soviet victory.

(3) History demonstrates that even partial surprise can be sufficient, if the aggressor gains the mastery of the air and exploits it speedily and effectively. The surprise may be partial in respect only of direction of the main attack, or of date and time, or of new ways of war-fighting, or of any combination

of these four; but it appears to be most successful when it results in the enemy forces being found to be deployed wrongly at the start of the war. The nineteenth and twentieth centuries provide overwhelming evidence in support of the correctness of Moltke's dictum, that he who is wrongly deployed at the start of a war never recovers (He must be presumed to have added 'when faced with a competent enemy').

(4) Total surprise, in any case, is a total illusion. Individual soldiers, or even a section or company, can be surprised totally, but armies cannot. Nor is it necessary that they should be. Total defeat can be inflicted on armies as a result of only partial surprise; and it is, of course, the total defeat of his enemy that the attacking general is seeking. (This is particularly true if the attacking general in question is a Soviet general.) Consequently, we in NATO should not sit back and preen ourselves because we have managed to convince ourselves (and probably quite correctly) that the Warsaw Pact is quite unable to achieve total surprise over us. As history demonstrates, partial surprise, if properly exploited, can serve its turn admirably; and we should therefore sit down and ponder much more deeply than we do over what forms of partial surprise the Pact *is* capable of achieving; and what would happen, what would be our reactions, if it did achieve it. We should also reflect that, with regard to surprise at the start of a war, the key figures in a democracy are the political leaders, very few indeed of whom *want* to believe that war is imminent or are willing to accept the political odium of ordering the necessary military measures before the war begins. Yet if they do not, the Russians gain a head start. It is with the effects of that head start that we shall be concerned in the final chapter. That chapter will be based on the assumption that the Pact's attack will be from a 'jump start', with the aim of achieving victory within the 'initial period' of the war; that this, by definition, means that the NATO forces will neither be fully mobilized nor properly deployed, and that this can only happen if the NATO politico-military leadership had been surprised as to the date of the attack (hence no mobilization) and also as to its main axis (hence incorrect deployment). It will also be based on the assumption that a key method of attaining these desirable

objectives is a sound knowledge of, and regular practice in, a form of warfare known as the 'encounter battle'. The essence of this form of warfare will be the subject of the first part of the next chapter; while the implications of a 'jump start' will be discussed in the second part of chapter 14.

NOTES AND REFERENCES

1. *Istoriya Velikoi Otechestvennoi Voiny Sovietskogo Soyuza 1941–1945* vol. 2 (Voenizdat, 1963) p. 16.
2. This material is based on Chaim Herzog, '*The War of Atonement*' (Weidenfeld & Nicolson, 1975).
3. There are those who say that it was never the Egyptian intention to exploit their surprise for the purpose of winning a total victory over Israel. In that case, I can only say that the basic Egyptian strategy must be reckoned faulty.
4. The material in this section is based upon L. F. Ellis, *Victory in the West*, vol. 1 (HMSO, 1962) especially pp. 159–60, 197–201 and 488–91.

14   A possible Soviet scenario for the perfect *Blitzkrieg*

Surprise is valuable only if it can be exploited; and the traditional method of exploiting it has been speed plus weight of blow. This was the Nazi tradition in the matter, and it has also been the Soviet tradition. Both agreed that the combination of speed and weight of blow were necessary in order to ensure success.

But a new idea appears to have dawned in the minds of Soviet strategists, or at least of those who have returned to the notion of the 'opening phase' of a war. They may be spurred by the immense difficulty of putting into practice nowadays the traditional concept of the *Blitzkrieg*; but there is no doubt that, for whatever reason, the 'opening phase' as a technical solution has caught their imaginations.

The immense difficulties referred to above are really very formidable. The Warsaw Pact's forces, on one scale, can be said to number $180^2/3$ divisions.[1] These are the total of all the divisions possessed by the Warsaw Pact countries; but for the purpose of mounting an attack on NATO it is not a very meaningful figure. In the context of a Soviet *Blitzkrieg* aiming at securing strategic surprise, all Pact forces to the east of longitude 40° can be omitted. If the *Blitzkrieg* succeeds they cannot arrive on the battlefield in time to take part in the fighting; and it is a successful *Blitzkrieg*, not the horrendous consequences of a failed *Blitzkrieg*, with which we are concerned in this chapter. This leaves for a possible Pact offensive the Soviet divisions at present located in the Belorussian and Baltic Military Districts, together with the Soviet and Polish divisions in Poland, the Soviet and Czech divisions in Czechoslovakia, the East German divisions, and the Soviet divisions that come under the heading of the Group of Soviet Forces in Germany. These, added together, amount to approximately 80 divisions. A formidable force! This large force, however, cannot be used for a surprise attack, because almost all the divisions in the Belorussian and Baltic Military Districts are well below full strength. In order to be useful for war, therefore, they would first have to be brought up to strength; and this very action would powerfully alert NATO. Hence there could be no question of achieving strategic surprise.

Of course, these formations could be of tremendous value to the Russians if the USSR did indeed unleash a *Blitzkrieg*, and the *Blitzkrieg* then bogged down. It is reasonable to assume that these divisions would start calling up their reservists at a moment timed to coincide with the start of the *Blitzkrieg* offensive. This would give the greatest chance to the latter of securing surprise. The speed of Soviet mobilization is such that these divisions could move westward and enter the battle in time to act as a third echelon; but it is hard to see how they could possibly arrive earlier. In other words, the divisions that we are talking about just cannot be used for adding weight to the proverbial initial weighty blow, if surprise is to be aimed for; and we are all agreed that Soviet strategy sets great store by surprise.

So we are left with the maximum weight of blow as being that which can be derived from the various divisions in Poland, Czechoslovakia and East Germany. These amount to a total of 62, of which 33 are Soviet, 10 are Czech, 13 are Polish and 6 are East German. Sixty-two divisions are by no means a negligible force; and if not quite the titanic thunderbolt of the old Russian tradition, they are no inappreciable substitute. On the other hand, their utilization for the initial blow raises a number of problems.

The problems here are concerned with the troops in Poland. They are in Poland, not in East Germany; and Poland has no common frontier with NATO. Consequently, in order to contribute their weight to the initial blow of the war, they have got to be moved westwards to positions located reasonably near the West German/East German frontier. The distance involved is something of the order of 250 miles.[2] They can start this journey after the war has begun, of course; but then they can only act as a second echelon. If they are to lend weight to the initial blow, they must cover that distance in peacetime, so that they are all deployed near the enemy *before* the battle starts. The movement westwards of some fifteen Pact divisions to totally new locations near the West German frontier would obviously alert NATO, and surprise would become impossible. The Russians might try achieving surprise by means of the 'dead volcano' method; but that would involve leaving about a dozen Polish divisions in East Germany at a time of ostensible peace – at a time, that is, when there was no avowable reason for the Polish presence. The relationship between Poles and Germans has always been one of hatred; and the tensions engendered within the Pact by any such stationing of Polish troops would seem to be too dangerous to be acceptable. In this instance at least, therefore, the 'dead volcano' method seems inappropriate.

It may be objected at this point that I have overstated the difficulties. A journey of 250 miles, travelling under peacetime conditions, can be accomplished within a time-frame of 10–15 hours. NATO has said that it needs to have a warning time of a minimum of 48 hours; so the 10–15 hours allotted for the journey to the frontier of the forces from Poland will, on this reckoning, still get them to their objective before NATO has reacted effectively. This may well be so.

If this solution is to be ruled out, however, because of the various difficulties we have just been discussing, there remains to the Soviet General Staff only one other means of launching their *Blitzkrieg* on NATO. That is to rely exclusively on the Group of Soviet Forces in Germany, together with the East German divisions and the Soviet and Czech divisions in Czechoslovakia. If the formations in Czechoslovakia are used for an attack on Bavaria, in order to prevent the Americans there from hurrying to the help of AFCENT, Marshal Ogarkov is then left with only twenty divisions with which to deliver his knock-out. At first sight this number appears to be inadequate.

Perhaps it is. Perhaps the optimum plan of attack requires the addition of the 15 divisions from Poland, despite the various difficulties we have already mentioned. Perhaps, on the other hand, this plan too is far from being the optimum, and the least bad method of attacking NATO is to mobilize the divisions is Western Russia and then, despite the loss of surprise, bear down on NATO like an avalanche. Perhaps ... perhaps! Luckily it is not the purpose of this book to try to assess the rival merits of all these various plans, but to concentrate its analysis on any one of them that aims to win its victory in the 'initial period'.

The third of these plans has no hope whatever of doing so; the second is not very likely to do so; the first must either succeed in doing so, or else be a complete disaster. So we will concentrate on that one. In addition to its many other merits it exemplifies in its purest form the striving of the aggressor for victory in the 'opening phase' of a war. Naturally what follows is a purely theoretical discussion: it is as well to make that clear at the very outset.

The plan rests upon a number of assumptions which can be shown to be widely accepted among Soviet strategists. These in turn are based upon two assumptions which are common to them all, and which we have already examined. They are:

(1) that the achievement of surprise of itself reduces *momentarily* the strength of the enemy resistance; and that the more complete the surprise, the less effectively *momentarily* the enemy will be able to resist; and

(2) that in order to transmute that '*momentarily*' into the much more satisfactory '*permanently*', the surprise has got to be exploited, as we have already seen.

Traditionally, that exploitation has been done by combining speed of advance with weight of blow. The precise proportions of the two elements in this traditional formula has usually varied according to the particular circumstances. No commander, or at least no British commander, has ever yet worked out a mathematical formula by means of which the speed would be pre-ordained to be so many miles an hour, while the weight of blow would be set as being so many men and weapons systems to each square mile of the battle area. What has happened in practice has been that each commander has advanced as quickly as possible, and with as many men and weapons systems as he could manage to assemble. Speed, men and weapons were all considered necessary; and all were required to be utilized to the maximum extent possible.

It does however follow, at least theoretically, that if one of these elements is augmented significantly, the other can be diminished. If, that is to say, the quantity of the aggressor's men and weapons systems could be increased till it outnumbered that of his enemy's by a factor of a thousand to one, the rate of advance could be slowed to a crawl and, providing his forces suffered no loss of morale or collapse of discipline (and under such favourable circumstances it is hard to see why they should), the enemy's defeat would be just as certain as if the advance had been rapid.

Military technology today, however, does not permit of vast, elephantine forces lumbering ponderously across enemy territory and subduing the enemy at leisure. Such an attractive target would unquestionably get clobbered; and the defence's means of clobbering targets are today extremely effective, and likely to get still more so as time goes on. Despite what theory suggests, therefore, this alteration to the formula is unlikely to prove successful; and a would-be victor of NATO must consequently look for others.

One possibility is to alter the values posited in our original equation. If, that is to say, instead of increasing the size of the aggressor's forces (the weight of blow), we increase significantly the speed of his advance, this should result in the size of his forces being able to be reduced. The argument goes roughly as follows: a speedy advance means less enemy resistance; a degree of surprise means less enemy resistance; surprise speedily exploited means *much* less enemy resistance. If, therefore, you can be sure of achieving surprise and exploiting it speedily, you know you will be faced with much less opposition. Consequently you will do less fighting. As a result, you will need a great deal less ammunition, fuel, replacements and reinforcements. Therefore, under these circumstances you have no need to burden yourself with the huge quantities of those four things, which you would indeed need, if you were to be faced with stiff resistance. Freed of this appalling supply burden you will be able to advance still faster; and by the very act of doing so you will reduce still further the enemy's ability to defend himself. The less he is able to defend himself, the fewer troops you will need. One might put it, as a purely theoretical hypothesis, that if it had originally been reckoned that a force of approximately 60 divisions would be needed to defeat NATO, given that strategic surprise had been achieved, and that the rate of advance would be of the order of 50 km a day, it should therefore be feasible to do so with only 35–40 divisions, if the speed of the advance could be doubled.[3]

Hitler's campaign in France in 1940 is highly relevant here. The crucial victory was won by a force of only 10 divisions. These were the *Panzer* and motorized divisions of von Runstedt's Army Group A. The other divisions of that Army Group were engaged only in mopping-up operations; they did nothing of any significance to shatter enemy resistance. The 17 divisions of Army Group C were concerned with blocking the Maginot Line, a fortress system whose garrison made no attempt to unblock itself. Army Group B was the group in the north with 28 divisions. These did have not merely an important, but a really vital, part to play; because their attack through Holland and Belgium was designed to deceive the French and British into thinking that it was through the northern plains that the main German thrust was coming. Without that successful deception, Guderian's attack was obviously doomed to failure. Even as it was, it was very seriously criticized beforehand by a number of senior Nazi generals on the ground that it was far too risky. So it was the 28 divisions of Army Group B and those 10 divisions of Army Group A that got the Nazis to the Channel.

What we seem to be saying, therefore, is that 38 divisions, being properly handled, having secured strategic surprise, and being able to advance at an average speed of 50 km a day, can defeat a force of 83 divisions.[4] This is not necessarily so. In 1940 there were a number of additional factors favouring the Wehrmacht. These were:

(1) It possessed from the very outset mastery of the air;

(2) It only secured strategic surprise because of the attack launched by Army Group B. That attack, mounted across the plains of Holland and Belgium, was intended to deceive the French and British into thinking that it was the main one. Had it failed to accomplish this, the offensive mounted by Army Group A would probably have been defeated.

(3) Since electronic reconnaissance had not been invented in 1940, it was easy for the Nazis to fool the French and the British about the direction of the main attack. It was not entirely easy, but it was far from impossible. Today, however, the various means of intelligence-gathering (of which satellite pictures are a very important, but not by any means the only one) allow the defender to know virtually with certainty the number of divisions in an enemy thrust, and hence to calculate reasonably accurately which will be the main one. Only if the two thrusts are mounted by forces of roughly equal size, or if the main thrust were to be mounted by the smaller one, could deception with regard to the direction of the

principal attack be reckoned no more difficult of achievement than it was in Hitler's time. Unless, that is, General Kir'yan's advice has been acted upon; unless, that is, the necessary R&D has been done and unless Brezhnev's secret weapon is revealed to be, not the achievement of a first-strike nuclear capability, but a tool for 'blinding' the various forms of Western intelligence-gathering. But that we shall come to later.

(4) The fourth point which favoured the Nazis in France in 1940 is that a distance of less than 250 miles separated them in their 'start' positions from the Channel. The Russians have an additional 250 miles (400 km) to go to reach the same objective. Admittedly, the roads are better than they were, and the tanks and guns go faster; and it may be that these latter factors cancel out the former. But it may be that they do not. All we can say for certain is that a Soviet strategist, planning an advance to the Channel (if that is what he is indeed planning), must reckon upon his troops being faced with a charge across 500 (800 km) miles minimum before they can reach their objective. Only if his objective is the Rhine and not the Channel are his distances commensurate with Guderian's distances. This should be borne in mind.

On the other hand, the Nazis were faced with a circumstance which should have been a great disadvantage to them. Britain and France were not defended by their regular forces only: they had been at war with Germany for 8 months when the Nazis struck in the West. It therefore should have been impossible to surprise them strategically at all – but it was not.

It is wrong to expect that the past will reveal the future. To the extent that history repeats itself, it does so only approximately. The differences that exist between the first time round and the second are always numerous, frequently very significant, and sometimes vital. Nevertheless, it is just as wrong to try to peer into the future without ever having looked at the past. We have just been looking at it. Our look there has told us that the Nazis were successful in Western Europe because (among many other reasons) they attained from the very outset the mastery of the air, and because they deceived the Allies concerning the date, and time and place, of their attack. In order to do the latter they needed to live in an age in which electronic reconnaissance had not yet been invented (which in fact they did), and to have 28 divisions to spare for the purpose of making a feint attack that should seem not too unrealistic. Today the Warsaw Pact commander lives in an age of electronic reconnaissance, and does not have many divisions to spare for trying to deceive NATO regarding the place of the main attack (not, that is, under the terms of our present scenario). So an attempt to achieve surprise with regard to *place* and the *direction of the main thrusts* must, under the terms of our present scenario, be reckoned extremely difficult, though not necessarily wholly impossible. An attack launched from a 'standing start' in the middle of the night without lights and in complete radio silence is one not inconceivable method of doing so.

But a basic means by which the Russians will today seek to attain their purpose is by achieving surprise in respect of date and time. Some methods of achieving surprise in this fashion have already been mentioned above: the period around Christmas, the day of a US presidential election, the hours around midnight – all these, we have agreed, are excellent for a Pact surprise offensive against the West. But even at Christmas, even on the day of a US presidential election, NATO's guard is not wholly and completely relaxed. It therefore becomes a matter of extreme importance for the Warsaw Pact, if it intends to attack NATO, to attack it when the latter's guard is relaxed to the maximum possible. There will not in that case be *total* strategic surprise; but then we have agreed already that total strategic surprise is never possible. There will, however, be a degree of surprise which may be sufficient, if all goes well, to attain victory in the 'initial period'. So how is the Pact to attain this essential minimum?

Its course of action can only be a negative one. It can do nothing by military means to relax its intended victim's guard still further: all it can do is to refrain from doing anything that would make it *less* relaxed. Of course, it is true that it remains possible to induce in NATO a lesser degree of wariness by the use of political and diplomatic means: the exploitation of detente, propaganda among the civilian populations of the member countries of NATO, certain kinds of arms control and disarmament proposals, all these can be used extremely effectively to make the NATO peoples and their governments relax. But such measures require for their fruition a time-scale that must be measured in terms of years rather than of months, and furthermore they are political measures. Hence they will act as the diplomatic precursor and the diplomatic background to the purely military measures to be taken by the Soviet General Staff. In this chapter we must take the background as given. We must assume that there is a certain level of tension in existence at the period in question (or, to put the thing conversely, a certain level of detente). This will have evoked in NATO a certain level of wariness which, at any time when detente is blooming, will not be very high. However low or high it may be, however, the Soviet military are quite unable to lessen it; though it is easy enough, by an ill-judged troop move or other military measure, to make it increase sharply. The problem, therefore, for the Soviet General Staff is *not to increase* the existing level of tension; and it is in this sense that, at the start of this lengthy paragraph, I spoke of its course of action as being a negative one.

Consequently, the more one looks at it, the more one becomes convinced that this tricky problem of securing surprise over NATO can only be resolved by the Soviet forces attacking from a 'standing start'. In other words, since any reinforcements in peacetime of the Pact forces in Germany and Czechoslovakia could only lead to a considerable increase in NATO's level of wariness, and since this increase is the cardinal thing which the Russians wish to avoid, it necessarily follows that their only course is to attack with what they have got. By this I mean 'to attack with the troops at present deployed in Germany, not reinforcing them in any way nor in any way redeploying them'. By this means they will secure for themselves the maximum degree of strategic surprise that is possible. Having thus managed to start their war against NATO when NATO's guard is relaxed to the maximum possible in view of the circumstances, it is the Pact's job to exploit this relaxation to the utmost by advancing as fast as they possibly can from the very beginning of the war. Admittedly by attacking from a 'standing start' they will be attacking with fewer numbers; but speed of advance can compensate for a certain reduction in numbers. In particular, speed of advance, if sustained and sufficiently speedy, can bring the attacker to his victim's jugular before the latter has recovered from his surprise. This is not possible, we all know, if the victim country is an enormous country; but Western Europe, as we also know, is far from being that.

So the Pact, we have concluded, will attack from a 'standing start'. It will also attack around midnight on, let us say, Christmas Eve. In this case it will be midwinter; and an attack started at midnight in midwinter will have to be sustained for approximately 8 hours in darkness before the arrival of daylight; by contrast, one started at 5 a.m. would have only 3 hours to run before the coming of the dawn. Each reader must decide for himself whether he thinks it would be in the Russians' interest to have a greater or lesser amount of darkness in the first few hours of the war: my own view is that a long period of darkness would be highly advantageous in the circumstances that we are imagining – that is, in the case of a dash for NATO's vitals before NATO is ready to defend itself. A Soviet advance in darkness, with radio silence and no lights, would be difficult for NATO to detect accurately, to assess its size and its main axes, and hence to counter effectively. By contrast, it would be the concern of the Russian forward detachments *not* to engage the NATO armies, but to get to certain *places* (to key road junctions, military head-quarters, communications centres); and this requires a know-ledge of the roads and an ability to move at night quickly. The latter the Russians have always proclaimed as a major quality of the Soviet armed forces, and many Western experts are inclined to accept their claim; while if the Russians have not already acquired a detailed knowledge of the relevant roads and waterways and bridges of West Germany, then the formidable Soviet intelligence network assigned to the Federal Republic has been wasting its time. For these reasons I am going to posit a Pact invasion beginning at 11 p.m. on the Christmas Eve of the year chosen by the Russians, whichever year that may be; and my calculations which follow are based upon that assumption. Those who believe that the Russians would start at about 5 a.m. need only advance by 6 hours the times I shall be extrapolating. Of course that will mean that some events that I shall describe as happening in the dark hours will by their reckoning be taking place in daylight; and this will affect their assessment of my scenario's probability. That is quite understood.

I am assuming, then, that the war will start at 11 p.m., as stated. If, for ease of argument, we concentrate our attention on Soviet 3rd Shock Army centred around Magdeburg, we can then say that the Soviet forward detachments will have reached the frontier between the two Germanies at some time around midnight. The main forces of 3rd Shock will get there approximately an hour later; and all will advance into West Germany as fast as they can go.

Of course they will have been faced with the problem of how to clear passages through their own minefields on the East German side of the border of sufficient size to allow whole divisions to traverse them. It is not an easy problem to solve, because Pact activities in the border areas, including the laying and lifting of mines, are naturally watched very closely by NATO observers. A naked lifting of Pact mines on the East German side of the internal frontier on a scale sufficient to allow the passage of over four divisions would therefore naturally arouse the suspicions of NATO, so somehow or other the necessary mines have got to be lifted secretly. I am not at all sure how this could be done; but for the sake of the argument I have got to assume that the Pact has succeeded in doing it. I am therefore positing that in the last few minutes of the Christmas Eve in question a way through the minefields has been thoroughly cleared, and the Soviet tank and motor rifle divisions can advance in complete safety.

I have argued elsewhere that on this occasion their will be no Soviet reconnaissance operating miles ahead of the forward detachments;[5] so it is the crossing of the frontier by the forward detachments that is going to alert NATO. The alarm bells, therefore, will ring in NATO at 1 minute past midnight on Christmas Day.

The reason why I do not believe that on this occasion there will be any Soviet reconnaissance is that reconnaissance units operate ahead of the forward detachments, and these in turn operate ahead of the main forces. The result of using reconnaissance units on this occasion, therefore, is that NATO would get an additional hour's warning. Of course, if it were absolutely necessary that fresh information should be gathered, no doubt the additional warning would be acceptable to the Russians; but there will have been no difficulty for Soviet agents in West Germany, before the attack begins, in inspecting, peacefully and at their leisure, the roads and bridges and waterways in the area that is to be traversed by 3rd Shock Army, and in reporting back to Moscow any changes in the condition of any of them that may have occurred in the last few hours. They can also report on any NATO troop movements, if such have occurred. Endowed with this wealth of latest information, confirming or supplementing the vast hard core of basic information which the Russians will have been gathering about West Germany in particular and NATO generally during the last quarter of a century, what more does a Soviet commander need? If to this be added the fact that the gathering of absolutely up-to-the-minute information gained by using reconnaissance units ahead of the forward detachments will have the consequence of reducing considerably the degree of surprise that can be expected to be sprung on NATO, what conceivable sense does it make to gather it? So it is my assumption that on this occasion there will be no reconnaissance units operating ahead of the forward detachments until after the frontier has been crossed. Once this has happened, no more surprise is possible, so the need for information reasserts its primacy, and the reconnaissance units forge ahead of the forward detachments. The fact remains, however, that the first forces to cross the frontier will be the forward detachments; and that these will cross at about midnight, and the Pact main forces at about 1 a.m.

Similar crossings of the frontier will be being made by other Soviet armies up in the north and down in the south at as nearly as possible exactly the same time.

A word about the nature of the forward detachments. These are a major feature of Soviet Army tactics, and they have an important role to play in any surprise attack.

That role is not in doubt. It is to advance ahead of their main forces as rapidly as possible, and in the process to destroy, by-pass or neutralize those enemy formations with which they come into contact. It is, above all, their mission to ensure that their own main forces are not put to the necessity of deploying for battle (and thus wasting valuable time) for the purpose merely of coping with enemy resistance of a purely secondary category. In the pursuance of this aim, the Soviet forward detachments will themselves engage and destroy persistent and worrying enemy defensive forces, whenever it appears that they can do this. Where it does not, where enemy resistance is too strong to be neutralized in this fashion, the Soviet forward detachments will mask the enemy, will themselves proceed upon their previously agreed way, and will leave the task of destroying the by-passed enemy forces to their own main forces or to those forces' second echelon.

But if the task set to the advance detachments can be reckoned to be fairly certain, their composition cannot. To begin with, obviously it depends greatly upon the size of their parent formation: an army will send out a bigger forward detachment than will a regiment or a division. On the other hand, by the rules governing normal Soviet deployment each of these formations will in turn send out its own forward detachment. Thus, an army (3rd Shock Army, for example) will send out one consisting of (if past experience is anything at all to go by) something of the order of one tank regiment, one motor-rifle battalion equipped with BMPs, one self-propelled artillery battalion, one anti-aircraft battalion and one company of engineers. Any one of that army's constituent divisions will send out one that is likely to consist of one company of tanks, one BMP battalion, one SP artillery battery, one AA battery and a platoon of engineers.

Our concern here is with those detachments that will hit the enemy first. If we look for guidance to the Manchurian Campaign of 1945, we shall there find that the forward detachments of Marshal Malinovsky's Trans-Baikal Front consisted of 61st Tank Division and 'all the separate [sic] tank brigades and regiments of the field armies and the Mechanised Cavalry Group', totalling about 1000 tanks.[6] Those of 36th Army, an all-arms army destined to attack prepared Japanese positions, consisted of a tank brigade, a rifle regiment, a SP battery, an anti-tank battery, a field artillery regiment, two mortar batteries, an anti-aircraft regiment and one company of Sappers.[7] It is really not very relevant to observe that the composition of these forward detachments, and also (and especially) their equipment, is obsolete by modern standards; and that therefore they are not worth citing. I disagree. The reason why, in my opinion, they are very well worth citing is that they attained speeds of advance which, at their fastest, averaged 120 km per day. Admittedly their equipment was obsolete by modern standards; but that of their enemy was equally old-fashioned. Admittedly their composition, in terms of numbers and arms of the Service, was not necessarily that which would obtain nowadays; but the same was true, *mutatis mutandis*, of their Japanese opponents. And still the fact remains that, under those conditions, the Soviet forward detachments in Manchuria covered up to 800 km in 10 days; and that the terrain they traversed was not particularly favourable to rapid motoring. It also remains a fact that, under these circumstances, their *average* rate of advance in 6th Guards

Tank Army was approximately 70 km per day. This includes the time taken to cross the Great Khinghan Mountains.[8]

The main forces of NATO in Germany are not based near the frontier. In other words, the garrisons of the frontier regions are really not very large. But if the USSR is to win in the 'initial period', these various garrisons have somehow got to be neutralized while the main Soviet armoured formations continue their advance westwards. This neutralization would most likely be done by the forward detachments, which might consequently have to be made much bigger than usual, in order to cope with this task as well as with that of acting as the spearhead of the Soviet advance. On the other hand it is possible that the job of neutralization would be entrusted to the main forces' first, or even second, echelon. Soviet military history provides quite a few examples of this having been done.

We can now return to the detailed calculations concerning 3rd Shock Army's advance. It appears probable that its main forces will have arrived in the vicinity of Brunswick at approximately 2 a.m. on Christmas Day. Consequently the situation in general will by that time be somewhat as follows:

(1) The Soviet advance westwards will have been detected by NATO at around midnight, the hour at which the Soviet forward detachments will have started to cross the frontier. At about the same time, Soviet airborne forces will be attacking key NATO installations located in the rear. These events will have resulted in the alarm being sounded throughout the whole of NATO (it will be remembered in this connection that we are also positing a simultaneous invasion of West German territory by the Soviet armies to the north and south of 3rd Shock).

(2) Because the crossing of the frontier will have occurred in the middle of the night, it is most unlikely that the NATO warnings will have been able to give with the desired precision the size of the Soviet invading forces or the direction of their principal thrusts. *A fortiori*, they are even more unlikely to be able to specify whether the thrusts of 3rd Shock Army form the principal thrusts of the whole of the Soviet offensive, or whether they are intended merely as holding or spoiling attacks.

(3) As a consequence of (1) the NATO forces nearest to the East

German frontier (and in these must be included the units of the West German *Grenzschützen*) will immediately start to engage the invaders in battle.

(4) Also as a result of (1), the NATO forces stationed further back in central West Germany will, upon receipt of the alert, at once start mustering their men and vehicles, prior to their movement eastwards towards the enemy. This business of mustering will start immediately upon receipt of the alert; but a certain amount of time must elapse between the moment when the Russians cross the frontier and that of the receipt of the alert by NATO units, and still more time before the NATO troops can be roused from their beds, collect their arms, draw their ammunition and get into their vehicles, move their vehicles out of their barracks, and be motoring towards the enemy. A Soviet ex-officer has been quoted as saying that a Soviet unit needs between 1½ and 6 hours for the accomplishment of these various tasks.[9] Let us therefore assume that an average NATO unit would need the mean of the Soviet times, which works out to 3.75 hours. Since a quarter of an hour is not going to make any difference to our present argument, we will make things easier by rounding up that average to a more easily manipulable 4 hours. We are assuming that this figure of 4 hours covers the time from the moment that the Soviet formations first cross the West German frontier to that when the NATO units emerge, fully armed, from their barracks.

According to our scenario, all this will be happening early on Christmas morning; so it is reasonable to assume that some of the NATO officers and men will have been to parties on the previous evening, and may very well still be at them when the alarm sounds. Others, again, will be on leave and a long way away from their units. It will therefore be a brigade or division of somewhat reduced battle-efficiency that will be motoring towards the enemy to repel his advance about 4 hours after that enemy has crossed the frontier; and that battle-efficiency must be reckoned to be reduced still further by the fact that NATO's reserves will not yet have mobilized. We are told repeatedly that NATO requires a minimum warning of 48 hours before its reserves can be called to the colours and actually join their units; and that NATO cannot be held to be fully efficient till this has happened.

The British Army exercise 'Crusader', which took place in September 1980, was designed to show that this could in fact be done. Furthermore it *was* done; though, according to 1 British Corps commander, Lieutenant General Sir Peter Leng, it was 'only just' done.[10] A cynic might say that, even then, it was done because it was not a surprise at all. The date of the commencement of the exercise had been known and publicized and mentioned in the Press a good many weeks before 'Crusader' happened; while the staff officers engaged in mounting the exercise had started work much earlier than that. Had it been really a surprise, a cynic would say, it might have taken not 48 hours but 48 days before 1 British Corps was fully complemented.

There is no pessimism in my house. At least for the purposes of this present chapter I will reject the cynics. I will assume that what happened on 'Crusader' will be repeated in a real energency, and that 1 British Corps will be fully mobilized within 48 hours of receipt of the alert.

Unfortunately, however, we are not at this moment speaking of 48 hours from the moment of receipt of the alert, but of 4 hours merely. By that time NATO units will, we have assumed, be leaving their barracks; but they will not have acquired their reservists nor those away on leave. Some of those present, as we have already mentioned, will just have come from parties; so the NATO units' battle-efficiency will not be 100 per cent. Upon this, I think, we can all of us agree.

We are by now talking of 4 a.m. on the morning of Christmas Day. It is 4 a.m., not 3 a.m.; because it was only at midnight, when the Soviet forward detachments crossed the internal frontier, that the NATO alert sounded. It is only at 4 a.m., therefore, that 1 British Corps will be just emerging from its barracks, by which time the Russians will have pushed on from Brunswick and will have got at least to Hanover and perhaps beyond.

Three comments need to be made at this point. It is received Western military opinion that thrusts made deep into enemy territory on a comparatively narrow front invite disaster. They are, it is said, far too vulnerable to attacks launched from the flank. Soviet doctrine, on the other hand, argues that if surprise has been achieved and command of the local air-space is not in enemy hands, this danger is minimal. Therefore the wise commander, having achieved surprise and a non-commanded air space, will thrust as deep and as rapidly as possible to tap the enemy's vitals. NATO's vitals are not to be found on the tenth degree of longitude, on which Hanover is situated, nor even on the ninth. They lie back deeper than that. So the Soviet commander, if he follows Soviet doctrine, will by-pass Brunswick and Hanover and make a dash for the Rhine. The air-space will not be effectively commanded by the NATO air forces for the simple reason that it is still the dead of night. Actual, effective command of the air is possible only in daylight; and in any case it would be a brave man who would asseverate that, when daylight comes, NATO's command of the local air will immediately be established.

The second comment is that current Soviet doctrine also demands, as we have seen in earlier chapters, that the advance of the aggressor's ground forces should be accompanied by strikes deep in the enemy's rear aimed at his nuclear installations, his command, control and communications centres and his supply depots. These strikes can be made by airborne forces, whether para-borne or heli-borne, by manned bombers and by missiles. Missiles give the least warning; so in the first hours of the operation it may be they which will be preferred. It is not by any means essential that their warheads should be nuclear: chemical and even conventional warheads could be usefully used for this purpose. After midnight, when the alert will in any case have sounded in NATO headquarters and there will be no further hope of extending surprise, airborne forces (and especially heli-borne forces) will surely be used. In addition, the Communist Fifth Column operating inside West Germany will come into action to carry out tasks of sabotage. Such sabotage will be aimed at making NATO's defensive measures hard to implement. A key bridge blown, a juggernaut lorry immobilized on a tricky stretch of road or a vital exit, these will not *defeat* the NATO effort, but they will impose delay; and the waste of time involved in any delay is what the Russians most want, and what NATO must most fear. The whole campaign, indeed, is a race for time – time for NATO to get to its preferred positions, time for the Russians to hit NATO before it has succeeded in doing so. This chapter examines the hypothesis that it is the USSR which wins.

The third comment is that, under these circumstances, one of two things seems almost bound to happen, neither of which is beneficial to the Western Alliance. Either the Soviet strategy will work in its entirety, in which case the NATO units will be caught almost literally napping, the units near the frontier being masked, and those to the rear not having had the time to sort themselves out properly and offer effective resistance. Consequently they will be liquidated; and in that case the Russians will have achieved their objective and the war will be over.

The other alternative is that NATO and the Pact forces fight an 'encounter battle' (or, if you prefer, a 'meeting engagement').[11] This concept is a favourite of the Russians. They write a lot about it;[12] they practise it regularly, naturally enough, because they favour mobile warfare of which the 'encounter battle' is a common ingredient. The concept of the 'encounter battle' is not, of course, unknown to NATO armies. They too write about it and practise it. It is not my purpose to seek to establish the relative merits of the two adversaries and practitioners of the 'encounter battle', and therefore which is likely to win if it came to actual fighting. I am concerned only to establish one incontrovertible fact; that the 'encounter battle' is not the ideal form of war for the defence.

It should perhaps be explained that an 'encounter battle' is one which occurs spontaneously when both sides are on the move. Neither side, in other words, is in an ideal position, whether for defence or attack. Consequently in an 'encounter battle' an element of tactical surprise is almost always present. Sometimes it is the aggressor who is surprised, sometimes the defender; not infrequently it is both. Victory in an 'encounter battle' therefore depends enormously upon quick and effective reaction by the local commander. Sensible decisions must be reached and transmitted speedily to his subordinates; and they in turn must implement them equally speedily.

In such a battle victory may go to the original aggressor or the original defender; but the point is that, if to the latter, this is very largely a matter of luck. That is, of course, over-stating it. The original defender may have deliberately reckoned on defeating his assailant in an 'encounter battle', have chosen that mode of fighting to bring him victory, and have trained his forces for the 'encounter battle' to the exclusion of everything else. Thereby his victory would be, not a matter of luck, but of military prescience.

Such a policy, however, would be eccentric, because it rejects virtually all the advantages which war bestows on the defence. These include the ability to choose and occupy in advance ground favourable to repelling the attack, a detailed knowledge of the ground in question, the ability to plan beforehand for fighting a battle on that stretch of ground, and so forth and so on. Only where the theatre of operations has no distinctive features of terrain – where it consists, for example, of a huge stretch of flat, unvariegated plain – does the defender stand on no more than an equal footing with his attacker. In such terrain, where one piece of ground is no more favourable to the defender than another piece (or where, to put it another way, all sectors are equally favourable to the attack and to the defence), an 'encounter battle' must be reckoned by the defender as being at least as valuable a form of war as any other. That, presumably, is why the Russians – born and reared on those vast, flat, empty steppes – have paid so much attention to it.

But the Soviet offensive westwards based on Magdeburg does not pass through such flat and empty plains. One up in the north, based on Fürstenberg and striking westwards parallel to the Baltic, would traverse something comparable; but one from Magdeburg would pass through country with definite topographical features. Such features, we have just established, favour the defence. Consequently NATO forces operating in such territory cannot wish to fight an 'encounter battle'. They must, on the contrary, wish to fight their battle in positions chosen and occupied beforehand, in terrain with which their troops will have been made familiar and on which they will have practised their tactics. To do anything else would be to surrender valuable advantages.

Therefore, if in the event the NATO troops are compelled to fight an 'encounter battle', they will be resisting the enemy in less than optimal circumstances; and what will have forced them to fight such a battle will have been the speed of the Russians' advance. The Russians, in other words, will have got much deeper into West German territory more quickly than NATO had expected; and NATO, instead of being ready for them, will have been simply caught on the hop. Catching your enemy on the hop is as good a way of defeating him as any; and a large-scale, successful 'encounter battle' may serve as well as any other method for winning the war for the Russians in its 'initial period'. In such a battle, fought under the conditions that have been described in earlier paragraphs, NATO would neither be fully mobilized nor properly deployed; and to catch your enemy in this situation is really the heart of the concept of winning your war in its 'opening phase'. And that is what this book is all about.

The above is no more than a very broad hypothesis. It does not seek to go into any detail. It portrays the main thrust of a Soviet offensive in Europe as being aimed at 1 British Corps' sector; but this is purely arbitrary. It would be neither a better nor a worse hypothesis if it showed the main thrust being aimed at the West German sector or the American sector or, for the matter of that, at the Dutch or the Danish or the Belgian sectors.

Wherever it went it would of course be only one of several thrusts; and wherever it went the same sort of military logic, the same sort of sequence of events could be expected to follow. For what we have here is a hypothesis aimed at exemplifying the thinking underlying General S. P. Ivanov's book *Nachal'nyi Period Voiny*. The chief point to remember is that it is based on the assumption that a Soviet offensive against NATO launched from a 'standing start' would stand a good chance of getting west of the ninth degree of longitude before NATO's units had got themselves assembled, drawn their arms and ammunition and were moving out from their barracks. Consequently, NATO's defensive battle would, according to this hypothesis, have to be fought west of the ninth degree of longitude; that is to say, west of Hanover. It is by no means obvious that this is favourable to NATO. It is, of course, irrelevant whether this crucial battle takes place up in the north of West Germany or in the centre or down in the south or in all these places together. From the Soviet point of view the only thing that matters is that it should be fought as deep into West German territory as possible, and not up near the frontier with East Germany. Only thus can the war be won in its 'initial period'. Furthermore the war can only be won in its 'initial period' if the battle is not only fought to the west of longitude 9°, but is practically a walkover. There must, that is to say, really be no crucial battle fought by NATO, because the Russians have got to fall upon NATO before NATO is ready to fight one. This is the second prerequisite for a Soviet success.

I must make it clear that I am not claiming to have proved the theorem that the Soviet forces are actually capable of winning a war against NATO in its 'initial period'. I have merely brought the theorem up for discussion. I have shown why the winning of a war like this must naturally be an attractive proposition for the

Russians (assuming, of course, that they decide on war at all); and, basing myself on Soviet writings on the subject, I have tried to show how they might well set about achieving this. I need hardly say that I have not been blessed with the sight of any actual Soviet plans for an offensive against NATO: I have merely taken their declared principles, fleshed out the military logic inherent in them, and presented the result as an outline plan as it might perhaps be conceived by Marshal Ogarkov. One can certainly find it adumbrated in General Ivanov's book.

Of course I fully realize that what I have written is open to objection and even to refutation. I would not be surprised, and would naturally be highly delighted, if a NATO officer could prove to me that what I have described as the 'Soviet plan' is impracticable. It very well may be. Inherent in it are a number of serious difficulties:

(1) twenty divisions is not a very large force;
(2) it is by no means easy, and perhaps may not even be possible, to clear a path through the minefields on the East German side of the frontier of sufficient size to allow of the passage of the required number of troops without being detected;
(3) the Soviet advance to the internal frontier, though done without lights and in radio silence, may not go unremarked by the NATO monitors, in which case NATO will have additional warning; and that additional warning may well be crucial;
(4) it may prove impossible in practice to maintain that average speed of 30 km per hour which is essential, if the Soviet forward detachments are to have penetrated as far as Hanover by 4 a.m. on the first day of the war. This is the time by which, it will be remembered, the NATO units are assumed to be leaving barracks, equipped with their arms and ammunition and spoiling for a fight. If by that time the Soviet forward detachments are significantly to the *east* of Hanover, it is a fair assumption that the USSR will *not* win its war in the 'opening phase', though that of course by no means signifies that it will not win the war at all.

If, on the other hand, the plan works and the Russians get to Hanover by approximately 4 a.m., they would be advancing west-ward into the heart of Germany at a time when it was still dark; at a time, therefore, when NATO itself was likely to be at least somewhat in the dark regarding the Russians' strength and their intentions. Such uncertainties must favour the Russians and make their success more probable. It is then up to the Soviet commanders to exploit the opportunities that under those circumstances must inevitably present themselves. In 1940 the Nazi generals exploited brilliantly the various opportunities that were offered to them: the fact that they did so was an important cause of their victory. The Soviet generals, as we have already seen, have a high regard for proper exploitation, but the generals of today have not as yet been able to find out whether on a real battlefield they can practise what they preach. If they can, if their troops actually succeed in profiting from their enemy's mistakes, and if moreover they can conduct a major 'encounter battle' as successfully 'for real' as they have done on exercise, the prospects for the Ivanov Plan cannot possibly be regarded as nugatory. But on this point, as indeed on all others in this chapter, each reader must make up his mind for himself. He will remember, of course, that the new concept of the operational manoeuvre group fits in beautifully with the Ivanov Plan.

NOTES AND REFERENCES

1. *The Military Balance 1980–81* (IISS, 1980) pp. 110–19.
2. The Soviet divisions in Poland, and the Polish divisions themselves, are located in various parts of Poland; and the distances between these peacetime locations and the West German frontier are therefore not identical. For the purposes of my present argument, my average of 250 miles (400 km) is good enough.
3. This whole argument is treated by Col. V. E. Savkin, *Osnovnie Printsipy Operativnogo Iskusstva i Taktiki* (Voenizdat, 1977) pp. 180–7.
4. The 14 divisions of French 2nd and 9th Armies deployed near the Ardennes, together with the 17 divisions of French 1st and 7th Armies deployed up near Belgium, the 13 divisions of the French reserve, the 9 divisions of the BEF, the 10 Dutch and the 20 Belgian divisions.
5. In *Royal United Services Institute for Defence Studies Journal*, December 1975.
6. Marshal M. V. Zakharov, *Finale*, (Progress Publishers, Moscow, 1972) p. 85.
7. *Istoriya Vtoroi Mirovoi Voiny; 1939–1945* (Voenizdat, 1974) vol. 11, p. 220.
8. S. P. Ivanov, *Nachal'nyi Period Voiny* (Voenizdat, 1974) p. 287.
9. *Österreichische Militärische Zeitschrift*, No. 6 (1979)
10. *The Times*, 30 September 1980.

11. The Russian for this is *ustrechnyi boi*. Both the English expressions mentioned in the text appear to be accepted synonyms for it.

12. See, for instance, D. F. Loza, *Marsh i Vstrechnyi Boi* (Voenizdat, 1968); Smirnov, 'Vstrechnie Srazheniya' (*Voenno-Istoricheskii Zhurnal*, 1943) and the entries under these two headings in *Sovietskaya Voennaya Entsiklopediya* vol. 2. (Voenizdat, 1976). See also *Krasnaya Zvezda* for 17 March 1976.

Epilogue
Key quotations from senior
Soviet officers

'Surprise is one of the most important principles of military art.... Experience shows that an aggressor, having achieved [strategic] surprise with his attack and exploiting the power of his previously deployed armed forces, has achieved tremendous results at the start of a war.'

Lieutenant General M. M. Kir'yan, 'Vnezapnost',
in *SVE*, vol. 2

'The decisive factor in securing for Germany [her astounding victories in the Second World War] was the first surprise blow, into which was put the whole weight of those ground and air forces which had been detailed for this operation and previously concentrated and deployed in the appropriate positions.... Simultaneously the enemy was hit over the whole depth of his operational deployment.... The [Nazi] tank formations usually raced ahead into the rear areas, in order to seize militarily important terrain before the Soviet reinforcements, coming up from the deep rear, could get there. This speedy advance by the Nazi tanks into the deep rear of the Soviet defence allowed the Germans to deal heavy blows at the Soviet reinforcements as they were coming up, to cross important water obstacles from the march, and to seize communications centres and other vital strategic installations.... Mastery of the air was essential.

General S. P. Ivanov, *Nachal'nyi Period Voiny*

'[Today] not even the wealthiest country can afford to keep the whole of its armed forces deployed in peacetime. The only

solution is to keep deployed in peacetime sufficient armed forces
to reach at least the nearest strategic objectives before successive
echelons are mobilised and sent into action. . . . it would seem
advisable to possess in peacetime armed forces of the right size
and type, so that the main aims of the war can be attained in the
initial period without additional mobilisation. . . . He who, right
from the start, can get his troops the deepest into enemy territory
will be best able to exploit the results of his own nuclear strikes
and to prevent the enemy from mobilising. This will be of great
importance in Europe because the distances are so small.'

Marshal V. D. Sokolovsky, *Voennaya Strategiya*,
3rd Russian edition

Index